DK EYEWITNESS TOP 10 TRAVEL GUIDES

ANDALUCIA
& COSTA DEL SOL

JEFFREY KENNEDY

Left **La Mezquita, Córdoba** Right **Ronda**

LONDON, NEW YORK,
MELBOURNE, MUNICH AND DELHI
www.dk.com

Produced by Sargasso Media Ltd,
London

Reproduced by Colourscan, Singapore
Printed and bound in China by Leo

First published in Great Britain in 2004
by Dorling Kindersley Limited
80 Strand, London WC2R 0RL
A Penguin Company

A CIP catalogue record is available from
the British Library.

ISBN 1-4053-1226-2
ISBN 978-1-4053-1226-4

Within each Top 10 list in this book, no
hierarchy of quality or popularity is
implied. All 10 are, in the editor's
opinion, of roughly equal merit.

Contents

Andalucía's Top 10

Andalucía's Highlights   6

Moorish Granada   8

Seville Cathedral
& La Giralda   14

Real Alcázar, Seville   16

Córdoba City   18

Cádiz   22

Ronda   24

Costa del Sol   26

Baeza & Úbeda   28

Parque Nacional
del Coto Doñana   30

Sierra Nevada   32

Moments in History   34

Aspects of Moorish
Heritage   36

The information in this DK Eyewitness Top 10 Travel Guide is checked regularly.
Every effort has been made to ensure that this book is as up-to-date as possible at the time of
going to press. Some details, however, such as telephone numbers, opening hours, prices,
gallery hanging arrangements and travel information are liable to change. The publishers cannot
accept responsibility for any consequences arising from the use of this book, nor for any
material on third party websites, and cannot guarantee that any website address in this book
will be a suitable source of travel information. We value the views and suggestions of our
readers very highly. Please write to: Publisher, DK Eyewitness Travel Guides,
Dorling Kindersley, 80 Strand, London, Great Britain WC2R 0RL.

Cover: Front – **Alamy Images**: Robert Fried bl; **DK Images**: Neil Lukas clb; **Getty Images**: The Image
Bank/David Barnes main image. Spine – **DK Images**: John Miller. Back – **DK Images**: Linda Whitwam tc, tl;
Peter Wilson tr.

Left **Alcalá La Real** Right **Costa del Sol**

Alcázares, Palacios & Castillos	38
Places of Worship	40
Villages	42
Nature Reserves	44
Paseos, Plazas, Parks & Gardens	46
Beaches	48
Outdoor Activities & Sports	50
Hikes & Drives	52
Museums & Galleries	54
Art & Culture	56
Aspects of Gypsy Culture	58
Religious Festivals	60
Children's Attractions	62
Andalucían Souvenirs	64
Bodegas & Wineries	66
Andalucían Dishes	68
Tapas Dishes	70

Around Town

Seville	74
Sevilla & Huelva	86
Málaga & Cádiz	94
Granada & Almería	108
Córdoba & Jaén	118

Streetsmart

Practical Information	126
Places to Stay	138
General Index	148

Left **View of La Mezquita, Córdoba** Right **Pueblo blanco, Cádiz Province**

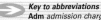

Key to abbreviations
Adm *admission charge* **Free** *no admission charge* **Dis. access** *disabled access*

ANDALUCÍA'S
TOP 10

Andalucía's Highlights
6–7

Moorish Granada
8–13

Seville Cathedral
& La Giralda
14–15

Real Alcázar, Seville
16–17

Córdoba City
18–21

Cádiz
22–23

Ronda
24–25

Costa del Sol
26–27

Baeza & Úbeda
28–29

Parque Nacional
del Coto Doñana
30–31

Sierra Nevada
32–33

Top Ten of Everything
34–71

TOP 10 Andalucía's Highlights

The diverse and politically semi-autonomous region of Andalucía has a population of some 7 million and embodies what is thought of as typically Spanish – an accurate portrait of the place and its people must include the bullfight, flamenco, gypsies, remote white villages, high sierras and mass tourism on endless stretches of beach. The memories you take with you after a visit here will be colourful, joyous, intense and deeply stirring.

Moorish Granada 1

Andalucía's 1,300-year-old Moorish heritage evokes pure Romanticism that is hard to equal. The delicate art and architecture is among the most splendid to be found on European soil (see pp8–13).

2 Seville Cathedral and La Giralda

These two chief wonders of Seville beautifully embody the juxtaposition of the Moors and the triumphalism of their Christian conquerors (see pp14–15).

3 Real Alcázar, Seville

A mix of styles is evident in this vast and luxurious pleasure palace, built almost entirely by Moorish artisans on behalf of their Christian overlords, including the lush gardens (see pp16–17).

Córdoba City & La Mezquita 4

This was once the most important city in Europe, a fact that is illustrated by the architectural masterpiece of La Mezquita, the Great Mosque (see pp18–21).

5 Cádiz

Said to be Europe's oldest city, Cádiz still retains an aura of age-old mystery. The golden-domed cathedral on the waterfront is a spectacular sight (see pp22–3).

6 Ronda

The largest of several white villages *(pueblos blancos)* scattered throughout the region, Ronda is built on a table of rock that is spectacularly split by the Tajo gorge. It is also reputed to be the birthplace of the modern style of bullfighting *(see pp24–5)*.

7 Costa del Sol

From the wealthiest of the yachting-set enclaves to all-inclusive package deals for young families, this famous expanse of sand and former fishing villages has something for everyone *(see pp26–7)*.

8 Baeza & Úbeda

Both of these exquisite towns in Jaén Province offer world-class Renaissance architecture set in perfectly preserved historic centres *(see pp28–9)*.

9 Parque Nacional del Coto Doñana

The vast delta of the Guadalquivir River constitutes one of the world's most important nature reserves, without which birdlife throughout Europe would be seriously compromised. The zone has a fascinating mix of terrains, but can be visited on guided tours only *(see pp30–31)*.

10 Sierra Nevada

Europe's second highest mountain range after the Alps offers the continent's southernmost ski resort, a wealth of wildlife for trekkers to wonder at, and dozens of remote villages along its southern slopes that preserve ancient cultural traditions and unique forms of vernacular architecture *(see pp32–3)*.

TOP 10 Moorish Granada: The Alhambra

The great complex of the Alhambra is the best-preserved medieval Arab palace in the world and, with nearly two million visitors annually, it is also the most popular monument in Spain. Built on the largely inaccessible Sabika Hill overlooking the city of Granada, its most distinctive phase began in the 11th century as the qa'lat al-Hamra (Red Fort) of the Ziridian rulers. From the 13th to almost the end of the 15th century the kings of the succeeding Nasrid dynasty embellished the site in a most spectacular fashion. The later Christian additions, although handsome in their own right, are generally thought to clash with the delicate, evocative architecture of the Moors.

View of the Alhambra

🍴 There are snacks and drinks available within the compound, but taking your own bottle of water is a good idea.

🎫 Since visitor numbers are restricted, avoid queues by booking tickets in advance, either through your hotel, by phone (902 22 44 60) or on the internet at www. alhambratickets.com

• Map S2
• Open Mar–Oct: 8:30am–8pm daily, 10–11:30pm Tue–Sat; Nov–Feb: 8:30am–6pm daily, 8–9:30pm Fri–Sat
• Adm €10.00
• Museo de la Alhambra: Open 9am–2:30pm Tue–Sat
• Adm €1.50 (Free to EU Members)

Top10 Features

1. Puerta de la Justicia
2. Puerta del Vino
3. Plaza de los Aljibes
4. Alcazaba
5. Palacio de Carlos V
6. Palacios Nazaríes
7. Palacio de Mexuar
8. Palacio de Comares
9. Palacio de los Leones
10. Partal

1 Puerta de la Justicia
Built in 1348, this magnificent horseshoe arch *(above)* makes use of Arab defensive techniques – a steep approach combined with four right-angled turns – to slow down invading armies.

2 Puerta del Vino
The "Wine Gate" – so called because it was used as a wine cellar in the 16th century – marks the main entrance arch to what was once the Medina (market).

3 Plaza de los Aljibes
From these ramparts *(below)* visitors can enjoy superb views of Granada. The giant cisterns *(aljibes)* underneath were built by the Christian conquerors.

4 Alcazaba
Although largely in ruins, this fortress is well worth a look. Don't miss climbing up onto the Torre de la Vela for views of the Sierra Nevada.

Each ticket is marked with a half-hour time slot of entrance, which cannot be changed.

5 Palacio de Carlos V

This Italian Renaissance palace is the masterpiece of Pedro Machuca, a student of Michelangelo. Housed here are the Museo de la Alhambra, with a fine collection of Nasrid art, and the Museo de Bellas Artes, with a range of interesting Christian works.

6 Palacios Nazaríes

The Nasrid palaces are built of simple brick, wood and stucco, in keeping with Islamic thought not to compete with the creations of Allah.

9 Palacio de los Leones

Dating from the late 1300s, this palace *(below)* was the Harem, the private zone reserved for the sultan and his family. The fountain of 12 lions – which may represent the 12 signs of the zodiac, the 12 hours of the clock, or the 12 tribes of Israel – has become emblematic of the whole Alhambra.

7 Palacio de Mexuar

The most poorly preserved of the three palaces, this area *(below)* was the most public space, dedicated to judicial and bureaucratic business. The original structure dates from 1365, but there are obvious Christian overlays, since it was converted to a chapel in the 16th century.

8 Palacio de Comares

Built in the mid-14th century, this area constituted the *Serallo*, where the sultan would receive dignitaries and deal with diplomatic issues. Inside is the Salón de Embajadores, the main throne room of the Alhambra. In front of the palace is the Patio de Arrayanes *(above)*, where serene fountains and pools, fragrant plantings, and elaborate wood and stucco work are all strictly geometric in design yet delicately refined, often featuring inscribed poems in praise of Allah.

10 Partal

As you leave the Alhambra, stroll through the gardens with their fountains and water-courses laid out in an area that used to have palaces of its own. All you can see of them now are five porticoed arches *(below)*. This area leads up to the Generalife, the summer palace. *(see pp10–11).*

Left **Jardines Altos** Right **Teatro**

Moorish Granada: Generalife

1 The Towers
Following the gardens of the Partal *(see p9)* as you walk towards the Generalife, you will encounter a number of restored Moorish towers built into the wall. The Torre de los Picos, Torre del Cadí, Torre de la Cautiva, Torre de las Infantas, Torre del Cabo de la Carrera and Torre del Agua are all worth a look for their fine detail, as well as for the views they command. The Torre de la Cautiva and the Torre de las Infantas are twin tower-palaces with richly decorated rooms.

Plan of Generalife

2 The Hill of the Sun
A footbridge flanked by two towers takes you over to the hill that rises above the Alhambra. A vast summer palace once stood here, amid 75 acres of gardens, which predated the Alhambra by a century, although little of it now remains.

3 The Name of the Garden
The word Generalife is generally considered to be a corruption of the Arab phrase *Djinat al-Arif*, which can be translated as "the Architect's Garden" (referring to Allah) or simply "the Best Garden" or "the High Garden". In an impressive engineering feat the Darro River was diverted 18 km (11 miles) to provide water for this lush sanctuary.

4 Teatro
The first thing you will encounter as you climb the hill is the amphitheatre, nestled into a tree-lined hollow. Recently expanded, dance performances and musical concerts are offered here as part of an annual festival of the arts.

5 Jardines Nuevos
The "New Gardens" are also called the Lower Gardens, and it is clear at a glance that they owe little to Moorish taste. Hedges and formal patterns echo the

Torre de los Picos

The Generalife is included in the ticket to the Alhambra, but is not open late night hours.

Jardines Nuevos

Italian style, but the sound of running water creates a soothing atmosphere in keeping with the Moorish ideal. In Islam, Paradise is defined as an oasis – a water garden full of fragrant blossoms.

6 Jardines Altos
As you reach the entrance to the upper gardens, you will first encounter the Patio de Polo, where visitors would leave their horses before ascending to the palace. On this level you will be welcomed by a series of fountains and formal plantings, interlaced with walkways and copses.

7 Patio de la Acequia
The "Court of the Long Pool" is the most famous water spectacle of the garden. Perfectly proportioned pools are set off by rows of water jets. At one end stands one of the complex's most harmonious buildings, the Sala Regia, with its decorated arcades and airy portico.

8 Patio de los Cipreses
The Court of the Cypresses is also known as the Patio of the Sultana, for this is where Zoraya, the wife of Boabdil *(see p35)*, is said to have secretly met her lover, the chief of the Abencerrajes clan. The sultan had the chief's men massacred upon discovery of the infidelity. A 700-year-old cypress tree commemorates the trysting place.

9 Escalera del Agua
These staircases above the palace, also known as the Camino de las Cascadas, have handrails that double as watercourses. They are best in spring, when the wisteria is in bloom.

10 Leaving the Gardens
As you exit the gardens you will pass along the Paseo de las Adelfas and the Paseo de los Cipreses, lined respectively with oleanders and cypresses. Back to the Hill of the Sun, take Cuesta del Rey Chico down to the Albaicín *(see pp12–13)*.

History of the Alhambra

This picturesque castle was the last bastion of al-Andalus, the Moorish hegemony that, at its height, included almost the entire Iberian Peninsula. By 1237 the Christians had reconquered all but this emirate, but the Moors managed to flourish here for some 250 years longer, only succumbing to the forces of King Fernando and Queen Isabel in 1492 *(see p34)*. The Generalife was the summer palace to which the Moorish leaders could escape the political life of the palace and the bustling city below and relax in the beautifully landscaped grounds. After centuries of neglect, and attempts by Napoleon's army to blow the palace up, the Moorish structures were preserved in the early 19th century, after the American writer Washington Irving inspired the world with his popular travel journal entitled *Tales of the Alhambra (see p57)*.

Left **Real Chancillería** Right **Baños Arabes**

Moorish Granada: Albaicín

1 Real Chancillería

The austerely impressive Royal Chancery dates from 1530, built shortly after the *reconquista* as part of the futile attempt to Christianize this Moorish quarter. The palace is attributed to architect Diego de Siloé. ◈ *Map Q2*

2 Iglesia de Santa Ana

At the end of Plaza Nueva stands this 16th-century brick church in Mudéjar style, built by Muslim artisans for Christian patrons. Inside the main chapel is a coffered ceiling in the Moorish tradition. The belltower was originally a minaret. ◈ *Map R2*

3 Baños Arabes

Dating from the 11th century, these are the best pre-served Moorish baths in Spain. They comprise several rooms that were used for changing, meeting, massage and bathing. ◈ *Carrera del Darro 31 • Map R2 • Open 10am– 2pm Tue–Sat • Free Entrance*

4 Casa de Castril

This ornate 16th-century mansion was originally owned by the secretary to King Fernando and Queen Isabel. Since 1879 it has served as the Archaeological and Ethnological Museum, displaying artifacts from Granada's past, from the Paleolithic era up until the

Casa de Castril

Map of Albaicín

Reconquest in 1492. A highlight is the 14th-century astrolabe, by which Moorish scientists could track the movements of the stars. ◈ *Carrera del Darro 43 • Map R2 • Open 3–8pm Tue, 9am–8pm Wed–Sat, 9am–2pm Sun • Adm (Free to EU Members)*

5 Iglesia de San Pedro y San Pablo

Across the road from the Casa de Castril, this church also dates from the 16th century and graces an attractive spot on the banks of the river. From here you can see the lovely towers of the Alhambra dominating the landscape. ◈ *Map R2*

6 Paseo de los Tristes

This tree-lined esplanade follows the course of the river upstream. It is broad enough to have once accommodated tournaments and processions, but now restaurants and bars dominate the scene. ◈ *Map S2*

The Albaicín is the Moorish quarter of Granada, dating from the 13th century and situated on the hill facing the Alhambra.

View from El Mirador de San Nicolás

Plaza Larga

7 From the Paseo de los Tristes follow Calle Panaderos to reach this busy market square, where you'll find mostly produce stalls as well as cheap eateries and bars. The square sports an Islamic gateway with a typically angled entrance as part of what remains of the upper fortifications. This is the Arco de las Pesas – if you pass through it you will come to the Albaicín's most popular square, Plaza San Nicolás. Ⓢ *Map R1*

El Mirador de San Nicolás

8 This magnificent terrace in front of the Iglesia de San Nicolás has such lovely views of the Alhambra and the Sierra Nevada that it has long been dubbed El Mirador ("The Lookout Point") de San Nicolás. The views are extraordinary at sunset, when the Alhambra glows softly ochre and the often snow-capped Sierra Nevada radiates pink in the distance. Ⓢ *Map R1*

Tearooms

9 As you wander around the labyrinth of whitewashed houses and sloping alleyways of the Albaicín quarter you will encounter many tearooms – a Moroccan tradition that is very much alive in this quarter. Possibly the best one, La Tetería

del Bañuelo *(see p116)*, consists of a series of rooms set amid delightful gardens. Here you can sip your minty brew, nibble honeyed sweets and contemplate the timeless panorama.

Moroccan Shops

10 Check out the hilly streets off Calle Elvira, especially Caldería Vieja and Caldería Nueva, for typically Moroccan shops. The scene is indistinguishable from what you would find in Morocco itself, with the colourful wares spilling out onto the pavements *(see p114)*.

Sacromonte Gypsy Caves

Leaving the Albaicín quarter to the north, follow the Camino del Sacromonte to reach the hill of the same name. The so-called "Holy Hill" is most noted for the presence of some 3,500 caves traditionally inhabited by gypsies (see p59). For more than six centuries, the zone has been notorious for wild goings-on, most especially *zambras*, impromptu gypsy fiestas of flamenco music and dance, and outsiders have always been welcome to witness their cultural celebrations. Today some 80 percent of the caves are still occupied and several of them continue to operate as venues for tourist spectacles.

Sacromonte

For information on flamenco events call Centro de Interpretación del Sacromonte (958 21 51 20, www.sacromontegranada.com)

13

Seville Cathedral & La Giralda

In 1248, after some 500 years of Islamic culture, Seville was reconquered by Christian forces, who paradoxically threatened the Moorish inhabitants with full-scale massacre if they damaged any of the city's magnificent edifices. Pragmatically, the conquerors simply rededicated the huge Almohad mosque to the Virgin and for about 150 years used it as their principal place of worship. In 1401, however, the momentous decision was taken to demolish the then mouldering building and erect a new cathedral of unprecedented proportions on its enormous rectangular base. In just over a century, the structure was complete, the renowned minaret now serving as the belltower.

Main entrance

🍽 For excellent *tapas*, you can't do better than Bar España *(see p85)*, a short walk from the cathedral.

✪ Note that the climb up La Giralda is fairly easygoing thanks to the 35 broad ramps, designed to accommodate a man on horseback. The unparalleled view makes it well worth the ascent.

• Plaza Virgen de los Reyes
• Map M4
• 954 21 49 71
• www.catedralsevilla.org
• Open 11am–5pm Mon–Sat, 2:30pm–6pm Sun (Jul & Aug: 9:30am–3:30pm)
• Services 8:30am, 9am, 10am, noon, 5pm Mon–Sat; 11am, noon, 1pm, 5pm, 6pm Sun
• Adm €6.00 (free Sun)

Top 10 Features

1. Exterior and Scale
2. Puerta del Perdón
3. Patio de los Naranjos
4. Biblioteca Colombina
5. Interior
6. Capilla Mayor
7. Sacristía de los Cálices
8. Sacristía Mayor
9. Sala Capitular
10. La Giralda

1 Exterior and Scale

In sheer cubic vastness, Seville Cathedral *(right)* is the largest Christian church in the world, and there's a certificate from the Guinness Book of Records on display here to prove it. It measures 126 m (415 ft) by 83 m (270 ft) and the nave rises to 43 m (140 ft). The best place to take it all in is from La Giralda.

2 Puerta del Perdón

The "Gate of Pardon" is set in a crenellated wall and is the main entrance to the only surviving section of the mosque. The arch and bronze-covered doors are a masterpiece of Almohad art, carved with 880 Koranic inscriptions. There are also sculpted Renaissance elements, most notably a bas-relief depicting the Expulsion of the Money-changers from the Temple.

3 Patio de los Naranjos

The Courtyard of Orange Trees *(below)* was the place where ritual ablutions were performed before entering the mosque for prayer.

For more places of worship See pp40–41

Biblioteca Colombina 4

The library of ancient manuscripts *(right)* is also an archive of Columbus's life *(see p34)* and his letters. It was founded by the explorer's son, himself an avid adventurer; he bequeathed more than 20,000 volumes of his travels to the city when he died in 1539.

Interior 5

Inside the cathedral the Gothic arches are so high that the building is said to have its own independent climate.

Capilla Mayor 6

The main altar's *tour de force* is its 15th-century *retablo*, which is the world's largest altar-piece *(below)*. Composed of gilded carved wood, it boasts some 45 Biblical scenes employing some 1,000 figures.

Sacristía de los Cálices 7

Part of the cathedral's treasury is housed here. The anteroom displays the Tenebrario, a 7.8-m (25-ft) Plateresque candelabrum used during Holy Week. Inside, the star turns are a painting by Goya of Seville's patron saints, Justa and Rufina, as well as canvases by Zurbarán, Jordaens and other Masters.

Sacristía Mayor 8

The Main Sacristy is dominated by a dome *(left)*, designed in the 16th century. The centre-piece of the sacristy is a 450-kg (990-lb), 3-m (10-ft) silver Baroque monstrance created by Juan de Arfe.

Plan of the Cathedral

Sala Capitular 9

The Chapter House contains Murillo's *Immaculate Conception* in the vault and boasts a lavish marble floor.

La Giralda 10

This grand tower *(above)* is the symbol of Seville, built between 1172 and 1195. It takes its name from the weathervane on top, called *El Giraldillo*.

Semana Santa Festivities

Seville's Holy Week celebrations leading up to Easter *(see p60)* are Andalucía's richest and most renowned. Here, 57 brotherhoods *(cofradías)* compete to bear aloft the most well-dressed Virgin in mourning and an image from the Passion of Christ. Floats are carried by *costaleros* (bearers), while the processions are lead by *nazarenos* – penitents donning conical hoods.

Real Alcázar, Seville

This extensive complex embodies a series of palatial rooms and spaces in various styles and from various ages. The front towers and walls constitute the oldest surviving section, dating from AD 913 and built by the Emir of Córdoba, Abd el-Rahman III, most likely on the ruins of Roman barracks. A succession of caliphs added their dazzling architectural statements over the ensuing centuries. Then came the Christian kings, particularly Pedro I the Cruel (or the Just) in the 14th century, and finally the rather perfunctory 16th-century apartments of Carlos V. Much of the structure underwent major modifications as recently as the 18th century, due to earthquake damage.

View of the Reales Alcázares

⏩ The Alcázar has a flow-control entry system whereby limited numbers of people are allowed in every half hour. To avoid long waits, visit at off-peak times.

• Patio de Banderas
• Map M4
• 954 50 23 23
• www.patronato-alcazarsevilla.es
• Open Apr–Sep: 9:30am–7pm Tue–Sat, 9:30am–5pm Sun; Oct–Mar: 9:30am–5pm Tue–Sat, 9:30am–1:30pm Sun
• Adm €5.00

Top 10 Features

1. Puerta del León
2. Sala de Justicia
3. Patio del Yeso
4. Patio de la Montería
5. Casa de la Contratación
6. Patio de las Doncellas
7. Salón de Embajadores
8. Patio de las Muñecas
9. Palacio Gótico
10. Gardens

Puerta del León
1 The entrance gate into the first courtyard *(above)* is flanked by original Almohad walls. Note the Gothic and Arabic inscriptions on the interior façade.

Sala de Justicia
2 Here and in adjacent halls and courts is some of the purest Mudéjar art to be found, commissioned by Alfonso XI of Castile around 1330 and executed by craftsmen from Granada. The star-shaped coffered ceiling and fine plasterwork are quite exquisite.

Patio del Yeso
3 The secluded Court of Plaster, greatly restored, is one of the few remnants of the 12th-century palace. The delicate stucco work features scalloped arches *(below)* and is set off by a shady garden with water channels.

For more alcázars in Andalucía See pp38–9

4 Patio de la Montería

The Hunting Courtyard has 14th-century Mudéjar decorative work – a perfect synthesis of differing cultural influences.

5 Casa de la Contratación

These halls are where Fernando and Isabel met with the explorers of the New World.

7 Salón de Embajadores

The most brilliant room in the entire Alcázar. Its crowning glory is the dazzling dome of carved, painted and gilded wood *(below)*, inscribed in Arabic as having been constructed by craftsmen from Toledo and completed in 1366.

Plan of the Reales Alcázares

9 Palacio Gótico

In a refurbished 13th-century Gothic structure built by Alfonso X the Wise, this palace *(above)* has a rather inharmonious Renaissance styling.

10 Gardens

Moorish touches are everywhere among these tranquil pathways and copses. Fountains, pools, lemon and orange groves, palms and hedgerows extend in all directions.

6 Patio de las Doncellas

The Court of the Maidens *(above)* commemorates the annual tribute of 100 virgins delivered to the Moorish rulers by the Christians. The *azulejos* (tiles) are fine examples of Granada craftsmanship.

8 Patio de las Muñecas

The intimate Court of the Dolls *(below)* was the living room of the palace and is named after two faces carved into the base of one of the arches.

Pedro I

Few Spanish kings have received such contradictory press over the centuries as Pedro I (1350–69). Called both "the Cruel" and "the Just", he killed his own brother in order to consolidate his position and flaunted his cohabitation with his mistress María de Padilla. The alcázar we see today is almost entirely the result of Pedro's rebuilding programme, primarily so that he and María would have a cosy place of retreat.

Mudéjar architecture is a blend of Moorish building styles and Christian themes and imagery.

🔟 Córdoba City

The main sight in Córdoba City is undoubtedly the Great Mosque, La Mezquita – one of the unsurpassed masterpieces of world architecture. But the entire city, in all its immaculately whitewashed splendour, is a major jewel in Andalucía's crown. In addition to the mosque and its incongruous but splendid cathedral within, other sights here include fine monuments and palaces from every age, art and history museums, one of Andalucía's greatest archaeological repositories, and a rather gruesome yet fascinating museum dedicated to the glories of the bullfight.

Palacio de los Marqueses de Viana

✪ Head for the Puente Romano at sunset for glowing views.

- Map D3
- Alcázar: Campo Santo de los Mártires; 957 42 01 51; Open daily (times vary); Adm €4.00 (free Fri)
- Palacio Episcopal: C/Torrijos 12; 957 49 60 85; Open Jun–Sep: 9am–3pm Mon–Sat; Oct–May: 9:30am–1:30pm, 4–6pm Mon–Fri, 9:30am–1:30pm Sat; Adm €1.50
- Museo de Bellas Artes: Plaza del Potro 1; 957 47 13 14; Open 2:30–8:30pm Tue, 9am–8:30pm Wed–Sat, 9am–2:30pm Sun; Adm €1.50
- Museo Arqueológico: Plaza Jerónimo Páez 7; 957 47 40 11; Open 2:30–8:30pm Tue, 9am–8:30pm Wed–Sat; Adm €1.50
- Palacio de los Marqueses de Viana: Plaza Don Gome 2; 957 49 67 41; Open Mon–Sat; Adm €6.00
- Museo Taurino: Plaza Judíos; 957 20 10 56; Closed from April 2005 for 1 year.

Top 10 Sights

1. La Mezquita
2. Judería
3. Alcázar de los Reyes Cristianos
4. Palacio Episcopal
5. Museo de Bellas Artes
6. Plaza del Potro
7. Museo Arqueológico
8. Palacio de los Marqueses de Viana
9. Museo Taurino
10. Puente Romano

1 La Mezquita
The world's third-largest mosque *(below)* remains a place of grandeur and mystical power *(see pp20–21).*

2 Judería
All around the Mezquita is the city's ancient Jewish quarter, dating back to the time of the Roman Empire. Its narrow alleyways are brilliantly whitewashed, hung with flowerpots, and graced with beautiful Moorish patios. This district also has Andalucía's only medieval synagogue, built in 1315.

3 Alcázar de los Reyes Cristianos
This fortified palace, built in 1328, was used by the Inquisition (1500s–1820) and as a prison (until the 1950s). But today it is tranquil, with gardens, water terraces and fountains *(above).*

4 Palacio Episcopal
To the side of the Mezquita, the former bishop's palace *(above)* was built over the original Moorish alcázar. Fine arts of the diocese are housed here.

Museo de Bellas Artes

A former 16th-century charity hospital is now the city's main art museum. It has a collection of works by local painters and sculptors, as well as paintings and drawings by Masters such as Goya, Ribera, Murillo, Zurbarán, and Valdés Leal.

Palacio de los Marqueses de Viana

This noble residence (14th- to 18th-century) includes preserved period rooms and furnishings *(above)*.

Map of Córdoba

Puente Romano

Crossing the Río Guadalquivir, this massive arched bridge *(above)* has Roman foundations, although it was rebuilt by the Moors. Halfway across is a statue of the Archangel Raphael, whom the people of the city still honour with flowers for saving it from the plague.

Plaza del Potro

This small but elegant square, adorned with a 16th-century fountain *(above)*, was once the livestock market.

Museo Arqueológico

Housed in a Renaissance mansion, this is one of the region's best archaeological museums. A highlight is the 10th-century Moorish bronze of a stag, found at Medina Azahara *(see p119)*.

Museo Taurino

If you want to see the hide of the bull Islero, who gored the renowned Manolete to death in 1947 – as well as a replica of the sarcophagus of the matador *(below)* – this museum is a must. Dedicated to the bullfight, it is filled with stuffed bulls' heads, posters, costumes and other memorabilia.

Multicultural Tradition

Córdoba's brilliance owes much to its rich multicultural history. Its most important edifices are emblematic of the cross-fertilization of Islamic, Christian and Jewish cultures, and at its height in the 10th century, Córdoba was the spiritual and scientific centre of the Western World, due to its policy of religious tolerance *(see p34)*. However, following the Christian *reconquista*, many non-Christian thinkers were banished and the city soon fell into decline.

10 La Mezquita, Córdoba

Although it has officially been a Christian site for almost nine centuries, La Mezquita's identity as a mosque is inescapable – notwithstanding the cathedral insensitively placed in its centre like a huge spider in its web. As with the Alhambra (see pp8–9), Emperor Carlos V can be blamed for this aesthetic indiscretion. Overriding the wishes of Córdoba's mayor, Carlos authorized the cathedral's construction in the 16th century, although he deeply regretted his decision upon beholding the completed travesty. Yet, despite time's every indignity, the world's third-largest mosque remains a place of grandeur, glory and ineffable mystical power.

View of La Mezquita

🍴 **El Caballo Rojo** (C/Cardenal Herrero 28 • 957 47 53 75 • €) is located just across from the Puerta del Perdón. It's a Córdovan favourite, and many of the recipes are Moorish influenced. Dine on the top-floor terrace for views of the mosque.

⏱ Note that the last visitors are permitted to enter 30 minutes before closing but try to allow at least an hour to do the site justice.

• Calle Torrijos, Córdoba
• Map D3
• 957 47 05 12
• Open Mar–Dec: 10am–early evening Mon–Sat, 9–10:15am, 2–6:30pm Sun (summer); 2–5:30pm Sun (winter)
• Adm €8.00

Top 10 Features

1. The Caliphal Style
2. Puerta del Perdón
3. Patio de los Naranjos
4. Torre del Alminar
5. Interior
6. Recycled Columns
7. Mihrab
8. Capilla de Villaviciosa & Capilla Real
9. Cathedral
10. Choir Stalls

1 The Caliphal Style
The mosque was begun by Caliph Abd el-Rahman I in AD 786. La Mezquita constitutes the beginning of the Caliphal architectural style, combining Roman, Gothic, Byzantine, Syrian and Persian elements.

2 Puerta del Perdón
Originally entrance to the mosque was gained via many doors, also designed to let in light. This door (above), the Gate of Forgiveness (1377), is in Mudéjar style and is now the only one open to the public.

3 Patio de los Naranjos
The delightful Courtyard of the Orange Trees (below) would have been used by worshippers to perform ritual ablutions before prayer.

4 Torre del Alminar
A minaret once stood where the belfry now is. Built in 957, it was enveloped in this Baroque belltower *(above)*.

5 Interior
The plan of the interior is that of a so-called "forest" mosque, with the rows and rows of variegated columns (856 remaining) and arches said to evoke date palms. Unlike Christian churches, based on earlier Roman basilicas with their focus on the central enthroned "judge", the Islamic aim is to induce an expansive, meditative state for prayer.

6 Recycled Columns
Great ingenuity was required to achieve the rhythmic uniformity inside, since most of the columns used in construction were recycled from Roman, Visigothic and other sources. They were a hotchpotch of varying sizes, so the longer ones had to be sunk into the floor. To reach the desired height, a second tier was added.

7 Mihrab
Dating from the 10th century, this is the jewel of the mosque *(left)*. An octagonal chamber set into the wall, it was to be the sacred focal point of prayer, directed towards Mecca. No amount of ornamentation was spared. Emperor Nicephorus III sent artisans from Constantinople to create some of the finest Byzantine mosaics in existence.

8 Capilla de Villaviciosa & Capilla Real
One of the happier Christian additions, the Villaviciosa Chapel *(above)* has exuberant arches in the Mudéjar style and dates from 1377. Next to it, the Royal Chapel sports appealing Mudéjar stucco work and *azulejo* (tile) decoration.

Plan of La Mezquita

9 Cathedral
In 1523 some 60 of the 1,013 columns were removed from the heart of the mosque and others walled up so as to construct the cathedral.

10 Choir Stalls
The Baroque choir stalls *(above)* date from 1758, and the exquisite carved mahogany depicts Biblical scenes.

A Spiritual Site

This magnificent edifice was not the first religious structure to be built on this spot. The Caliph bought the land from the Christians, who had built the Visigothic Cathedral of St Vincent here. In its last years, that building had been divided by a partition, so that it could serve the needs of Christian and Muslim communities. The Visigothic structure, in its turn, had been constructed on top of a Roman temple, and its columns are still visible in La Mezquita.

Climbing up to the top of the Torre del Alminar is a dizzying experience, but affords unmissable views over the town.

⁵⁰10 Cádiz

Glowing white in the intense southern light, Cádiz inspired the poet Lord Byron to praise its heavenly blue setting, gorgeous women and sensuous lifestyle. Nowadays it is one of Andalucía's under-visited treasures. According to ancient chronicles, it was founded by the Phoenicians as Gadir ("Fortress") in 1104 BC, giving it a good claim to being Europe's oldest city. Under the Romans it became Gades and was notable as the city where Julius Caesar held his first public office. Having been almost completely destroyed by an Anglo-Dutch raid in 1596, the old part of the present city is pure 18th-century and has remained virtually unchanged since then.

Barrio del Pópulo

🍽 El Faro *(see p107)* is the place to go for first-class seafood.

🎭 You must book up to a year ahead for accommodation during Carnaval.

• Map B5
• Torre Tavira: C/Marqués del Real Tesoro 10; 956 21 29 10; Open mid-Jun–mid-Sep: 10am–8pm daily; mid-Sep–mid-Jun 10am–6pm daily; Adm €3.50
• Hospital de Mujeres: C/Hospital de Mujeres; 956 22 36 47; Open 10am–1:30pm Mon–Sat; Adm €0.80
• Museo de las Cortes de Cádiz: C/Santa Inés 9; 956 22 17 88; Open 9am–1pm, 4–7pm Mon–Fri, 9am–1pm Sat–Sun; Free
• Museo de Cádiz: Plaza Mina; 956 21 22 81; Open 2:30–8pm Tue, 9am–8pm Wed–Sat, 9:30am–2:30pm Sun; Adm €1.50

Top 10 Sights

1. Barrio del Pópulo
2. Plaza San Juan de Dios
3. Catedral Nueva
4. Iglesia de Santa Cruz & Teatro Romano
5. Plaza de la Flores
6. Torre Tavira
7. Hospital de Mujeres
8. Museo de las Cortes de Cádiz
9. Oratorio de la Santa Cueva
10. Museo de Cádiz

Barrio del Pópulo

1 The Barrio del Pópulo is the medieval heart of the city, which still retains its three 13th-century gates. The main entrance of what's left of the 18th-century city wall, the Puerta de Tierra *(above)*, marks the boundary between the old city and modern-day Cádiz.

Plaza San Juan de Dios

2 On the edge of the Barrio del Pópulo is this palm-fringed plaza *(right)*, dating from the 16th century. Facing the port, it forms the hub of city life.

Catedral Nueva

3 The "New Cathedral" was begun in 1722. The best view is from the waterfront *(above)*, where the yellow dome is set off by the pastel house-fronts.

Iglesia de Santa Cruz & Teatro Romano

4 In the midst of the Barrio del Pópulo is this church dating from 1260 and the ruins of a Roman theatre.

Plaza de las Flores
5 This bustling market square *(above)* is also known as the Plaza de Topete – named after the tophet, a type of ancient Phoenician temple, that once stood here.

Map of Cádiz

Museo de Cádiz
10 Archaeological finds and Baroque paintings *(above)* are the museum's forte. Exhibits include a pair of 5th-century BC Phoenician marble sarcophagi, one male and one female, showing Greek and Egyptian influences; Roman shipwreck finds; and works by Zurbarán, Murillo and others.

Torre Tavira
6 The highest tower in the city *(below)* offers great views from its 46 m (150 ft) height.

Hospital de Mujeres
7 This Baroque former hospital's main attraction is the chapel's painting of the *Extasis de San Francisco* by El Greco.

Museo de las Cortes de Cádiz
8 Full of civic pride, this museum boasts a huge mural eulogizing Cádiz as the birthplace of liberalism. On 29 March 1812 Spain's first liberal constitution was conceived here, a document that played a major role in shaping modern European politics.

Oratorio de la Santa Cueva
9 This elliptical Neo-Classical chapel has an upper church with an elegant dome supported by Ionic columns. Three frescoes by Goya depict miraculous moments from the life of Christ.

Los Carnavales

The vibrant Carnaval celebrations in this port town are the most exhilarating in all of Spain *(see p60)*. In fact, so dear is this annual blow-out to *gaditanos* (as the locals call themselves), that it was the only such event in the country that Franco's forces failed to suppress during the decades of dictatorship. The festival's various traditions date back to the 15th century, when the town had a significant Genoese enclave, though some claim there is also a strong Cuban influence.

The Torre Tavira sports Spain's first camera obscura, which projects live images of the city onto a large screen.

TOP 10 Ronda

This is the most famous of the pueblos blancos (white towns) – a scattering of evocative hamlets that reveal their Moorish roots between Málaga, Algeciras and Seville (see p96). Ronda is in the southwest corner of this zone and the only town in the wildly mountainous region of the Serranía de Ronda. Located just half an hour's drive from the Costa del Sol, Ronda hosts up to 75,000 tourists per day, yet has managed to retain its timelessness and charm, despite the inevitable modernization of recent decades. Its natural setting is so spectacular that the views alone make it a must-see experience.

Puente Nuevo

- Map D5
- Casa del Rey Moro: C/Santo Domingo 9; 952 18 72 00; Open (gardens only) 10am–8pm daily (until 7pm Nov–Feb); Adm €4.00
- Palacio del Marqués de Salvatierra: C/ Marqués de Salvatierra; Closed to the public
- Baños Árabes: Barrio de Padre Jesús; 656 95 09 37; Open 10am–6pm Mon–Fri, 10am–3pm Sat & Sun; Adm €2.00
- Museo del Bandolero: C/Armiñán 65; 952 87 77 85; Open 10:30am–1pm daily; Adm €3.00
- Iglesia de Santa María la Mayor: Plaza Duquesa de Parcent; 952 87 22 46; Open 10am–8pm daily (until 6pm Nov–Mar); Adm €2.00
- Palacio de Mondragón: Plaza de Mondragón; 952 87 84 50; Open Mar–Oct 10am–7pm Mon–Fri, 10am–3pm Sat & Sun; Adm €2.00

Top 10 Sights

1. El Tajo & Puente Nuevo
2. Casa del Rey Moro
3. Palacio del Marqués de Salvatierra
4. Puente Viejo & Puente de San Miguel
5. Baños Árabes
6. Minarete del San Sebastián
7. Museo del Bandolero
8. Iglesia de Santa María la Mayor
9. Palacio de Mondragón
10. Plaza de Toros

1 El Tajo & Puente Nuevo

Ronda perches upon a sheer outcrop that is split by a precipitous cleft, El Tajo, 100 m (330 ft) deep *(right)*. The spectacular 18th-century Puente Nuevo bridge links the old city, La Ciudad, with the commercial district.

2 Casa del Rey Moro

A visit to the gardens of this 18th-century mansion *(below)*, built on the foundations of a Moorish palace, will provide wonderful views.

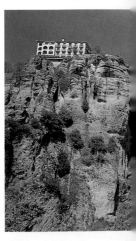

3 Palacio del Marqués de Salvatierra

Another 18th-century mansion sports an ornate façade with a carved stone portal. The upper section is adorned with four squat figures *(left)* that may represent South American Indians.

4 Puente Viejo & Puente de San Miguel

The Puente Viejo (Old Bridge) dates from 1616 and is thought to be a rebuilding of a Roman span, though some say its pedigree is Moorish, like the Puente de San Miguel. Both cross the gorge at the upstream end of the Río Guadalevín.

The best views of the town and its stunning setting are from the road from Algeciras or the one from San Pedro de Alcántara.

5 Baños Árabes

These wonderfully preserved Moorish baths date from the 1200s or early 1300s. The multiple barrel vaulting pierced with star-shaped lunettes is typical of such structures, but the beautifully designed octagonal brick columns supporting horseshoe arches are highly original.

8 Iglesia de Santa María la Mayor

Much of this church incorporates a 13th-century mosque, notably the base of the Mudéjar belfry *(above)*.

Map of Ronda

10 Plaza de Toros

Inaugurated in 1785, Ronda's bullring was constructed in limestone in an elegant double-tiered sweep; it is the widest in the world and one of the oldest in Spain. Since Ronda is the birthplace of the sport, this is the spiritual home of the tradition. It also houses a museum about the bullfight.

The Origins of Bullfighting

The establishment here of the Real Maestranza de Caballería (Royal Academy of Knights) in 1572 set the stage for the birth of bullfighting as we know it. The Maestranza's role was equestrian training of Spain's aristocracy and students would challenge wild bulls on horseback. Legend relates that when one rider fell from his horse and was attacked by a bull, a bystander distracted the animal by waving his hat. The man's grandson Pedro Romero (1754–1839) perfected the Ronda School of bullfighting. Ronda stages only a few fights a year, but they are the most prestigious.

6 Minarete de San Sebastián

This graceful 14th-century tower *(above)* is all that remains of a Nasrid mosque.

7 Museo del Bandolero

For some 1,000 years, the Sierras were the haunt of bands of rebels and outlaws. The museum chronicles the history of such notorious brigands.

9 Palacio de Mondragón

One of Ronda's most beautiful palaces *(below)* dates from 1314. Some of the original polychrome mosaic work and a magnificent Mudéjar ceiling can still be seen, but the rest was altered by the Christian overlords. Part of the palace is now the city's archaeological museum.

In early September, Las Corridas Goyescas are held in Ronda, in which matadors fight in costumes based on Goya's etchings.

⭐ Costa del Sol

The former fishing villages of the "Sun Coast" welcome millions of international visitors each year – not counting the estimated 300,000 expats who call the coast home. The winning formula is 320 sunny days a year, warm, clean waters and beaches, and good-value, though somewhat brash, entertainment options. Heavy on neon and tower blocks, most of what's here has little to do with local culture, but what is exuberantly Andalucían is the verve with which visitors enjoy themselves in the sun. Nights, too, are given over to typically Spanish merriment that continues until dawn.

Málaga Old Town

🔅 Note that most sights and many shops close for the siesta from about 1pm to 5pm.

• *Estepona: Map D5; Tourist Office: Avda San Lorenzo 1; 952 80 09 13*
• *Marbella: Map D5; Tourist Office: Plaza de los Naranjos 1; 952 82 35 50*
• *Mijas: Map D5; Tourist Office: Plaza Virgen de la Peña; 952 48 59 00*
• *Fuengirola: Map D5; Tourist Office: Avda Jesús Santos Rein 6; 952 46 74 57*
• *Benalmádena: Map D5; Tourist Office: Avda Antonio Machado 10; 952 44 24 94*
• *Torremolinos: Map E5; Tourist Office; Plaza de las Comunidades Autónomas; 952 37 19 09*
• *Málaga: Map E5; Tourist Office: Pasaje de Chinitas 4; 952 21 34 45*
• *Vélez-Málaga: Map E5*
• *Nerja: Map E5; Tourist Office: C/Puerta del Mar 2; 952 52 15 31*

Top 10 Towns

1. Estepona
2. Marbella
3. Mijas
4. Fuengirola
5. Benalmádena
6. Torremolinos
7. Málaga
8. Torre del Mar
9. Vélez-Málaga
10. Nerja

1 Estepona
The first major resort on this coast is an excellent quieter choice, with 19 km (12 miles) of beach *(right)*. In the *casco antiguo* (old town), Plaza Las Flores *(below)* retains considerable charm.

2 Marbella
The 15th-century Plaza de los Naranjos is the heart of the old town of Marbella, Spain's most expensive resort. Nearby Puerto Banús is the town's glittering marina *(right)*, where you can admire the fabulous yachts and breathe the same air as the super-rich.

3 Mijas
Come here for the views of the coast, as well as the maze of old Moorish streets filled with charming shops in the numerous tiny squares.

4 Fuengirola
This large resort is the most family-orientated, with a good beach and a recently remodelled seafront promenade. There is a restored 10th-century Moorish castle overlooking the town.

 Estepona still has a large fishing fleet, with a fish auction every dawn when the boats come in with their catch.

5 Benalmádena

This resort comes in three parts: the old town inland; the beach and port area *(above)*; and Arroyo de la Miel, a lively suburb.

Map of Costa del Sol

9 Vélez-Málaga

The old quarter of this market town *(below)* has beautiful Mudéjar features. An annual flamenco guitar competition is held here every July.

10 Nerja

No high-rises here; Nerja is all white-washed good taste, surmounting attractive, verdant cliffs with quiet sandy beach coves below.

6 Torremolinos

Torre de los Molinos (Tower of the Windmills) refers to a Moorish watchtower that was at one time surrounded by 19 flourmills. The ancient Torre Vigia is still here, but surrounding it now is a big, brash and trashily modern resort that is the quintessence of inexpensive fun *(below)*.

7 Málaga

Málaga is mostly a transit point for the average visitor and thus remains very Spanish in character. Andalucía's second largest city has an interesting historic district dominated by a vast 8th-century fortress and the ruins of the 14th-century Castillo de Gibralfaro *(see p96)*.

8 Torre del Mar

This resort is favoured by Spanish families, so is less tawdry than others to the west. The tree-lined seafront promenade is part of a recent attempt to prettify facilities.

Franco's Costa Dream

It was General Franco, Spain's dictator until 1975, who had the idea of transforming this impoverished zone of fishing villages into the "Florida of Europe". He implemented his plan in the 1960s with money loaned by the US, in return for the right to build nuclear bases on Spanish soil. The jet-set glamour and cheap package deals were a runaway success, so much so that by the 1970s the area was an aesthetic and environmental disaster – with added corruption and organized crime. Since the 1980s, steps have been taken to clean up all these issues.

Baeza and Úbeda

These two Jaén Province towns, only 9 km (5.5 miles) apart, are like matching jewel boxes overflowing with Renaissance architectural treasure, and so were awarded the title of UNESCO Word Heritage Sites in 2003. Of the two, quiet Baeza has managed to stay almost completely out of the modern age, while Úbeda has a thriving new zone and even some light industry. Nevertheless, its stunning historic district is, if anything, even more spectacular than Baeza's.

Plaza Santa María, Baeza

🍴 In Baeza, the Restaurante Andrés de Vandelvira *(see p123)* is situated in the restored Convent of San Francisco, making it a very special treat. In Úbeda, enjoy a drink in the courtyard of the fabulous Parador Condestable Dávalos *(see p140)*.

✪ The Úbeda potters are all located along Calle Valencia; look for the workshops of the premier ceramists, the Tito family.

• Baeza: Map F2; Tourist Information Office: Casa del Pópulo, Plaza del Pópulo; 953 74 04 44; Open 8:30am–2:30pm, 4–6pm (5–7pm summer) Mon–Fri, 10am–2pm Sat, 10am–1pm Sun.
• Úbeda: Map F2; Tourist Information Office: Palacio del Marqués de Contadero, C/Baja del Marqués 4; 953 75 08 97; Open 8am–3pm, 4–7pm (5–8pm summer) Mon–Fri; 10am–2pm Sat & Sun.

Top 10 Sights

1. Puerta de Jaén, Baeza
2. Plaza del Pópulo, Baeza
3. Plaza Santa María & Catedral, Baeza
4. Palacio de Jabalquinto, Baeza
5. Paseo de la Constitución, Baeza
6. Plaza de Vázquez de Molina, Úbeda
7. Plaza del Primero de Mayo, Úbeda
8. The Pottery Quarter, Úbeda
9. Plaza San Pedro, Úbeda
10. Plaza San Lorenzo, Úbeda

1 Puerta de Jaén, Baeza
This section of the ancient wall, the Jaén Gate *(above)*, supports an additional arch with coats-of-arms set above.

Plaza del Pópulo, Baeza 2
The town's most charming area, the Plaza del Pópulo, is surrounded by Renaissance edifices. It is also called the Square of the Lions, after its fountain, which sports four stone lions and a female figure *(right)*.

3 Plaza Santa María & Catedral, Baeza
This square is fronted by several glorious 16th-century structures, including the cathedral. One of the many masterpieces by Renaissance architect Andrés de Vandelvira, it was originally a Gothic church, built over a mosque in the 13th century.

Palacio de Jabalquinto, 4 Baeza

One of the most unusually decorated palaces in town is the 15th-century Palacio de Jabalquinto *(right)*. Its façade is sprinkled with coats of arms and stone studs in Isabelline Plateresque style.

9 Plaza San Pedro, Úbeda

Visit the patio of the Real Monasterio de Santa Clara, the town's oldest church, where the sisters will sell you their distinctly Arabic *dulces* (sweetcakes). The Palacio de la Rambla is another graceful Vandelvira creation and is now home to a small luxury hotel *(see p141)*.

10 Plaza San Lorenzo, Úbeda

The Casa de las Torres has a Plateresque façade *(above)*, flanked by two vast square towers and with gargoyles on the cornice. The Church of San Lorenzo is unique in that its façade is on the parapet of the old wall.

5 Paseo de la Constitución, Baeza

Here the 16th-century Alhóndiga (Corn Exchange) has an elegant façade with three-tiered arches, while the Torre de los Aliatares is an ancient remnant of the old wall.

6 Plaza de Vázquez de Molina, Úbeda

In this square *(above)* the Capilla del Salvador, built by Vandelvira, marks a high point in the Spanish Renaissance.

7 Plaza del Primero de Mayo, Úbeda

The variety of riches here includes the Iglesia de San Pablo *(above)*, displaying an array of styles, the 15th-century Casa Mudéjar, now an archaeological museum, and the 16th-century Ayuntamiento Viejo, with its superb arcades.

8 The Pottery Quarter, Úbeda

Passing through the Puerta del Losal, a splendid 13th-century Mudéjar gate, takes you into the town's age-old pottery quarter. Ceramic artists renowned all over Spain and beyond ply their ancient trade here.

Architecture of the Spanish Renaissance

Spanish Renaissance architecture divides into three periods: Plateresque, Classical High Renaissance and Herreran. The first refers to the carved detailing on silverwork (*platero* means silversmith), a carry-over from the late Gothic style popular under Queen Isabel (Isabelline Plateresque). The High Renaissance style is noted for its symmetry and its Greco-Roman imagery. Herrerean works are very sobre, practically devoid of decoration.

Typical Úbeda pottery is glossy forest green decorated with piercings reminiscent of Moorish patterns See p122

Parque Nacional del Coto Doñana

The largest nature reserve in Europe and southern Spain's only national park was established in 1969. It covers more than 247,000 acres, including its surrounding buffer zones, and its wide variety of ecosystems, rare fauna and abundance of bird life make it so vital to the environmental stability of Western Europe that it enjoys the status of a UNESCO Biosphere Reserve. To the untrained eye, it yields up its natural wonders gradually, but a visit to the coastal area of western Andalucía is not complete without taking it in.

Birdlife on the wetlands

🍴 The main visitor centre has an acceptable snack bar.

🔎 Bring binoculars, mosquito repellent, sunscreen and comfortable walking shoes – and watch out for quicksand.

If you join in the Romería del Rocio, you will also need your own sleeping bag, water and food.

• Map B4
• www.parquenacional donana.com; Reservations 959 443 808
• Open 8am–9pm daily (summer), 8am–7pm daily (winter); Tours 8:30am & 5pm (summer) 8:30am & 3pm (winter)
• Adm €23.00
• Centro de Visitantes El Acebuche: Ctra A483, 3 km (2 miles) from Matalascañas; 959 44 87 11
• Centro de Información La Rocina; 959 44 23 40; Open 9am–1pm, 4–9pm daily (until 7pm in winter)
• El Rocío Turismo: Avda de la Canaliega; 959 44

Top 10 Features

1. Setting and History
2. Habitats
3. Flora
4. Fauna
5. Visitor Centres
6. Guided Tours
7. Bird Shelter
8. Huts
9. El Palacio de Acebrón
10. El Rocío's Romería

1 Setting and History

Located at the estuary of the Guadalquivir River, the area probably owes its present pristine condition to the fact that it was set aside as a hunting preserve for the nobility in the 16th century.

2 Habitats

The park comprises three distinct types of ecosystem: dunes, *coto* (pine and cork forests and scrubland) and *marisma* (wetlands). The wetlands *(below)* can be broken down into marshes, salt marshes, lagoons and seasonally flooded areas.

3 Flora

Umbrella pines and cork-oaks flourish here and both types of tree provide crucial nesting sites for many birds. Wildflowers in the dunes and scrubland areas include the bright pink spiny-leafed thrift, besom heath, yellow gorse and the bubil lily. Marshland vegetation is made up of bullrushes, other types of reeds and white-flowered buttercups.

Access to the park is strictly controlled, but there are a limited number of marked footpaths along its borders.

4 Fauna
The endangered pardel lynx *(below)* is the emblem of the park. As many as 25 pairs of the very rare Iberian eagle also survive here. Other birds include the rare purple gallinule and the flamingo, but at least 300,000 birds make their home in the park.

5 Visitor Centres
Several Visitor Centres offer exhibitions as well as planned trails which lead to bird-watching opportunites *(below)* and rest areas.

6 Guided Tours
Tours in all-terrain vehicles *(above)* depart from the Visitor Centres. Two visits per day have varying itineraries, depending on the time of year. The marshes dry up in the summer months, which limits birdwatching, but increases the chance of seeing rare mammals.

7 Bird Shelter
The Centro de Visitantes El Acebuche, the main visitor centre, is set on a lagoon. At the eastern end there is an aviary where rescued and recuperating birds get intensive care. It's an opportunity for visitors to view them – including some unusual species – fairly close-up.

8 Huts
Dating from the 18th century, these traditional huts *(above)* are found in the *pinares* (pine forests). Sometimes clustered into small villages, the uninhabited structures are pinewood frames covered with local thatch.

9 El Palacio de Acebrón
This Neo-Classical style hunting lodge, built in 1961, has a permanent exhibition on the history and ethnography of the region. There are good views from the upper floors and the site is a starting point for a 12-km (8-mile) trail through the nearby woodlands.

10 El Rocío's Romería
This town *(see p87)* is the focal point of one of Spain's largest festivals, the Romería del Rocío. The four-day pilgrimage leading up to Whitsun has dispensation to wind its way through the park *(below)*. Thousands of people come to honour Nuestra Señora del Rocío, a medieval statue with miraculous powers.

Ecological Issues
Despite vigilant efforts to protect the park, in 1998 a Río Tinto mining toxic waste storage burst, dumping pollutants into the Guadiamar River, one of the wetlands' main tributaries. Thankfully, the poisonous wave of acids and heavy metals was stopped just short of the park, but damage was done to its border areas. Although the ramifications are now under control, the clean-up continues.

Booking guided tours in advance is essential, as each 4-hour trip is limited to about 20 participants.

🔟 The Sierra Nevada

The Sierra Nevada ("Snowy Mountains") include Spain's tallest peaks and are Europe's second-highest mountain range after the Alps. Until the 20th century, their only regular visitors were the so-called neveros ("icemen"), who brought back blocks of ice to sell in nearby Granada, and for many years the only part they played in a tour of the region was as the glistening backdrop to the Alhambra Palace. But in recent decades they have become more and more popular in their own right – for trekking, skiing and exploring the remarkable collection of villages on their southern slopes, Las Alpujarras.

Sierra Nevada mountains

🍴 Lovers of *jamón serrano* (mountain ham) must not fail to try the snow-cured version from the town of Trevélez *(see p65)*.

☀ Extra sun protection is vital here, particularly for skiers. Hikers and trekkers should have good walking shoes, something to wear against the wind, water, some food and binoculars.

If you're driving in Las Alpujarras, be aware that petrol stations are a rarity. Coming from the west, Órgiva is a good place to fill up.

• Map F4
• Parque Nacional de la Sierra Nevada: Ctra Antigua de Sierra Nevada, km 7; 958 02 63 00
• Sierra Nevada Club (skiing): Plaza de Andalucía, Solynieve; 958 24 91 11 (bookings), 958 480 011 (info); www. sierranevadaski.com

Top 10 Features

1. Setting
2. Flora & Fauna
3. Hiking
4. Skiing
5. Puerto del Suspiro del Moro
6. Las Alpujarras
7. Valle de Lecrín
8. Lanjarón
9. Órgiva
10. Barranco de Poqueira

1 Setting
This mountain chain and its national park are home to Spain's highest peak, Mulhacén (3,482 m/11,425 ft) at the western end and fertile valleys to the south.

2 Flora & Fauna
Snow-capped most of the year, these heights are nevertheless rich in wildflowers. Some 60 varieties are unique here, including a giant honeysuckle. The ibex is the most common species of fauna, but there are also butterflies, and birds such as the golden eagle.

Snow-capped Sierra Nevada

3 Hiking
There is a paved road over the top of the range but the uppermost reaches have been closed to cars since the national park was established in 1999. In summer it's a hiker's paradise – the second highest peak Veleta (3470 m/ 11,385 ft) is a relatively easy 5-hour roundtrip.

4 Skiing
The main ski resort, Solynieve, is Europe's highest and most southerly, in operation from December to April or even May. The pistes and facilities *(left)* are good enough to have hosted the world Alpine skiing championships in 1996.

Puerto del Suspiro del Moro

5 Heading south from Granada on the N323, you'll come to the spot known as the "Pass of the Moor's Sigh". Here, bereft Moorish ruler Boabdil *(see p35)*, expelled by the Christians, is said to have looked back on his beloved city for the last time.

Valle de Lecrín

7 This bucolic valley is filled with olive, almond and citrus groves – the almond blossom is stunning in late winter.

Órgiva

9 Made the regional capital in 1839, this town *(left)* remains the area's largest. It's at its best on Thursday mornings, when everyone comes alive for market day, and you can find traditional local products such as hand-woven rugs.

Barranco de Poqueira

10 This vast and gorgeous ravine *(above)* is home to a stunning collection of tiny villages. Much loved by visitors seeking tranquillity, the remote site even boasts its own Tibetan Monastery, founded in 1982. The ravine is an excellent place for easy day walks, and each town offers traditional local crafts.

Las Alpujarras

6 On the southern side of the Sierra Nevada is this dramatic zone, home to a stunning series of white villages *(above)*. The architecture here is pure Moorish, almost identical to that found in the Rif Mountains of Morocco. Houses are flat-roofed, untiled, clustered together and joined by neighbourly bridges.

Lanjarón

8 Famous since Roman times for its curative mineral springs, the town *(below)* is now a modern *balneario* (spa) and marks the beginning of the Alpujarras proper. Below the long main street you'll find a ruined Moorish castle, from which the views across the gorge are breathtaking.

Brenan's South from Granada

In the 1920s British writer Gerald Brenan, a member of the Bloomsbury set, came to live in the village of Yegen in the eastern Alpujarras. A plaque in the town marks the house he lived in. He recorded his experiences in his book *South from Granada*, a wonderful evocation of the place and its people, whose way of life still prevails largely unchanged. The 2002 Spanish film *Al Sur de Granada*, based on the book, is a true and delightful dramatization of his story.

Left **Moorish fort** Right **Discovery of America**

🔟 Moments in History

1 Bronze Age Developments
The Iberian (Tartessian) civilization got its strongest start around 2500 BC when bronze began to be smelted and worked in Andalucía. Some early tribes built the oldest megalithic tombs *(dolmens)* in western Europe.

2 Phoenician and Greek Colonies
Attracted by the area's mineral wealth, the Phoenicians founded a trading post at what is now Cádiz in 1100 BC, while the Greeks established a toehold near Málaga in 636 BC. The two maintained a mercantile rivalry until Carthage, a former Phoenician colony, dominated the region.

3 Roman Spain
The first Roman town in Spain, Itálica *(see p89)*, was established in 206 BC; Rome finally wrested the entire region from the Carthaginians in 201 BC. Due to abundant local produce, Andalucía became one of the empire's wealthiest outposts.

Andalucían Roman ruins

4 Arab Domination
Some 700 years later, when the Roman Empire began to come apart, tribes from northern Europe laid claim to the peninsula. The Vandals and then the Visigoths ruled for some three centuries. Politically unstable, a question of rightful succession in AD 710 led to the enlistment of Muslim armies from North Africa. The Moors saw their chance and within 10 years had taken over.

5 Moorish Sophistication
The Moors were custodians of the best features of Roman civilization: religious tolerance, scientific and philosophical thought, and engineering and cultural refinements *(see pp34–5)*. In the 10th century, under the Caliphate of Abd ar-Rahman III, Córdoba became the largest and wealthiest city in Europe.

6 Reconquista
The dissolution of the Caliphate in 1031 marked the beginning of the end for Moorish Spain. Some 30 *taifas* (principalities), jostling for political hegemony, proved no contest for the Christians. The eight-month siege and *reconquista* of Granada in 1492 was the most poignant loss.

7 Discovery of America
That same year the New World was discovered for Spain by Christopher Columbus. The result was a wealth of gold and silver from the new empire.

8 Imperial Collapse

Colonial losses that began in 1713 following the War of Spanish Succession reached their *dénouement* with Spain's defeat in the Spanish-American War of 1898. In Andalucía this long decline meant grinding poverty and mass emigration.

9 Civil War and Franco

The Spanish Civil War (1936–9) was ignited by a military coup led by General Francisco Franco, who was against Spain's continuance as a Republic. On 18 July 1936 the war began when they took Cádiz, Seville and Granada. Then followed the grim years (1939–75) of Franco's repressive dictatorship.

10 Seville Expo '92

The world fair in 1992 celebrated the quincentenary of Columbus's discovery of the New World. It brought a sprucing up of Seville and 42.5 million visitors to Andalucía, but it left bankruptcy in its wake. The scale of the economic disaster was political; charges of corruption led to a loosening of the Socialist Party's hold on power, in favour of today's right-wing government.

Pabellón de Andalucía, Seville Expo '92

Top 10 Historic Andalucían Figures

1 Melkarth
The Phoenician's name for Hercules, whom legend claims to have founded Andalucía.

2 Trajan
One of the greatest Roman emperors (AD 98–117) was a native of Itálica.

3 Hadrian
Trajan's successor (117–38) was a great builder, emphasizing Rome's Classical Greek roots.

4 Abd el-Rahman III
The Syrian leader (912–61) established the autonomous Caliphate of al-Andalus.

5 Boabdil
The final Moorish ruler (r.1482–92) lost Granada to the Catholic Monarchs.

6 Isabel and Fernando
Isabel of Castilla and Fernando of Aragón (1479–1516) were dubbed "The Catholic Monarchs".

7 Christopher Columbus
The Genoese sea captain (1451–1506) set sail from Huelva Province and, on 12 October 1492, landed on one of the Bahamian islands.

8 Emperor Carlos V
His reign (1516–56) left Spain nearly bankrupt, but with cultural legacies such as his palace in Granada *(see p9)*.

9 Felipe V
Felipe V (1700–46) had his court in Seville until a claim to the throne by Archduke Charles of Austria led to the War of Spanish Succession.

10 Felipe González
A native of Seville, this left-wing leader (1982–96) brought rapid change to Spain and to Andalucía, which was given relative autonomy.

Left **Horseshoe arches, Moorish architecture** Right **Moorish ceramic azulejo tile**

Aspects of Moorish Heritage

1 Art and Architecture

Moorish art and architecture is full of signs and symbols and often incorporates calligraphy into its designs, quoting the Koran or poetry. The point was to inspire the viewer to reflect upon the unity of all things under Allah, whose power and perfection could never be equalled by the achievements of man.

2 Religious Tolerance

Although non-Muslims had to pay a special tax and wear distinctive clothing, Moorish policies towards Jews and Catholics were generally easygoing. There was greater repression after the fundamentalist Almohads came into power in the 12th century, but on the whole the faiths were well integrated for centuries.

3 Music

The Moors can be credited with the development of the guitar, which they adapted from the four-stringed lute. The Middle Eastern musical forms they imported were also to have an effect later on flamenco *(see pp58–9)*.

4 Gardens

Moorish gardens make prominent use of water – so important to people from a perpetually arid land. It was sprayed, channelled, made to gurgle and fall, to please the ear and eye. Jasmine, honeysuckle and roses are just a few of the flowers the Moors brought to the region.

5 Agriculture

Inheriting many of their techniques from the Romans, the Moors were masters of agricultural engineering. Their system consisted of three main elements: the aqueduct, the waterwheel and the irrigation channel. Thereby, they were able to cultivate vast areas, often building ingenious terracing on slopes. They also introduced many crops, including bitter oranges, lemons, almonds, rice, cotton, pomegranates, aubergines (eggplants), artichokes, asparagus and mulberry trees (to feed silk-worms).

6 Philosophy

Great minds of Andalucía, such as the Moor Averroës and the Jew Maimonides, were considered among the most advanced thinkers of their age. The former almost single-handedly preserved the writings of Aristotle, while the latter's writings sought to reconcile Biblical faith and reason.

Moorish garden, Generalife

7 Science
Moorish scientists excelled in the fields of metallurgy, zoology, botany, medicine and mathematics. Moorish inventors also developed revolutionary devices such as the astrolabe and the quadrant, essential for navigation. Arabic numerals were introduced, as well as algebra (from *al-jebr*, meaning "reuniting broken parts") and the algorithm.

8 Food
The simple fare that had existed prior to the Moorish incursion – centred around olives, wheat and grapes – gave way to a bounty of flavours. Almonds, saffron, nutmeg, pepper and other spices became commonplace in the region.

Almonds

9 Language
Modern Spanish is full of everyday terms that come from Moorish heritage – the word for "left" *(izquierda)* is almost pure Arabic and any word beginning with the prefix *al-* (the) comes from Arabic too.

10 Crafts
The hand-tooled leather of Córdoba, silver and gold filigree jewellery, pottery, silk and embroidered goods, and inlaid creations all owe their existence to the Moors' 800-year hegemony.

Top 10 Moorish Sites

1 Moorish Granada
The spectacular Alhambra palace is the gem of Spain's Moorish heritage, while the adjacent Generalife offers sumptuous gardens *(see pp8–11)*.

2 Real Alcázar, Seville
The front towers and gateway of Seville's royal palace retain their Moorish origins *(see pp14–15)*.

3 La Mezquita, Córdoba
This vast mosque marked the beginning of the Arab-Hispanic style known as Caliphal *(see pp20–21)*.

4 Baños Arabes, Ronda
These Moorish baths feature horseshoe arches, typical of Arabic architecture *(see pp24–5)*.

5 Medina Azahara, Córdoba
Sadly now in ruins, this one-time splendid palace epitomized the city's glory in the 10th century *(see p119)*.

6 Almonaster La Real
The village's mosque is one of Andalucía's finest, with great views from the minaret *(see p90)*.

7 Alcazaba, Almería
One of the largest surviving fortresses in the region *(see p111)*.

8 Alcazaba, Málaga
Remains of the original Moorish walls and tower can still be seen *(see p96)*.

9 Las Alpujarras
The villages on the slopes of the Sierra Nevada retain distinctive Moorish architecture *(see pp32–3)*.

10 Vejer de la Frontera
The most Moorish of the *pueblos blancos (see p42)*.

Left **Fortaleza de la Mota, Alcalá la Real** Right **Castillo de Vélez Blanco**

Alcázares, Palacios and Castillos

1 Real Alcázar, Seville

This sumptuous palace and extensive gardens constitute a world of royal luxury. The architectural styles are a blend of mainly Moorish traditions – note the lavish use of the horseshoe arch, glazed tilework and wood ceilings *(see pp16–17)*.

2 La Casa de Pilatos, Seville

Few palaces are more opulent than this 15th–16th-century mansion. A mix of Mudéjar (Christian-Islamic), Flamboyant Gothic and Renaissance styles, it is also adorned with Classical sculptures, including a 5th-century BC Greek Athena and important Roman works. A noble residence to this day, it is filled with family portraits and antiques from the last 500 years *(see p75)*.

Roman relief, Casa de Pilatos

3 Ayuntamiento, Seville

Seville's town hall dates from the 16th century, with later modifications added in the 19th century. The original sections are in Plateresque style, begun by architect Diego de Riaño in 1526 – note the mix of motifs used on the main façade (on Plaza de San Francisco). Inside, a collection of art features paintings by Zurbarán and Velázquez *(see p76)*.

4 Palacio del Marqués de la Gomera, Osuna

This 18th-century palace is a striking example of the Spanish Baroque style. The cornice is composed of waves and volutes, lending it a sense of movement. The family escutcheon crowns the carved stone doorway, which also has elaborate pillars. The palace has now been converted into a hotel and restaurant. ◈ *C/ San Pedro 20, 954 81 22 23 • Map D4*

5 Fortaleza de la Mota, Alcalá la Real

This Moorish castle, crowning the hill above the town, is the chief attraction here. Created by Granada's rulers in the 14th century, it incorporates 12th-century structures and earlier elements, since the strategically situated town dates from pre-historic times. After the Christian reconquest in 1341 *(see p32)*, additions to the fortress continued until the 16th century. The castle keep houses an archaeological museum *(see p122)*.

6 Castillo de Santa Catalina, Jaén City

Restored by the Christians, this 13th-century castle towers above the town and affords spectacular views. ◈ Map F3 • Open 10am–2pm, 5–9pm Tue–Sun (summer); 10am–2pm, 3:30–7:30pm Tue–Sun (winter) • 953 12 07 33 • Adm

Castillo de Lacalahorra

7 Castillo de Burgalimar, Baños de la Encina

This Moorish castle is one of the best preserved in Andalucía. Its horseshoe-arched main gate bears an inscription dating its construction to AD 967. Some 14 square towers provide vistas far and wide. ◈ Map F2 • Visit by appt, 953 61 44 34 • Free

8 Palacio de Jabalquinto, Baeza

This splendid 15th-century palace is a study in originality. The façade's columns defy categorization, while the gallery evokes the Renaissance style, as does the double-tiered patio. The latter also sports a monumental Baroque staircase (see p29).

9 Castillo de Lacalahorra

One of the few castles newly built after the Christian reconquest, this was also one of the first in Spain to be built according to Italian Renaissance tenets. Despite its forbidding situation and exterior, its inner courtyard is exquisite, with staircases, pillars and arches carved from Carrara marble. ◈ Map F4 • Open 10am–1pm, 4–6pm Wed • 958 67 70 98 • Free

10 Castillo de Vélez Blanco

In Italian Renaissance style, this structure has the grace of a fairytale castle. Unfortunately, it was gutted in the early 1900s, but a reconstruction of one of the patios gives you some idea of its original splendour. ◈ Map H3 • Open 11am–2pm, 4–6pm Sat & Sun; Mon, Thu & Fri by appt, 607 41 50 55 • Adm €1.00

Next to the Castillo de Santa Catalina is a parador, built in imitation of its style, where you can stop for a drink (see p142).

Left **Arches, La Mezquita** Right **Retablo Mayor, Seville Cathedral**

Places of Worship

1 Seville Cathedral
Seville's most striking architectural masterpiece is its vast cathedral. Inside are soaring columns, precious artworks and the world's largest altarpiece *(see pp14–15)*.

2 La Mezquita, Córdoba
This spectacular mosque may have been savagely reconsecrated but visitors can still see its Byzantine mosaics and other exquisite marvels *(see pp20–21)*.

3 Mosque, Almonaster la Real
Virtually unchanged for 1,000 years, this is one of the few surviving rural mosques in Andalucía and has the oldest *mihrab* (Mecca-facing prayer niche) in Spain *(see p90)*. ◈ Map B3 • Open 10am–7:30pm daily; Ayuntamiento 959 14 30 03 • Free

4 Oratorio de San Felipe Neri, Cádiz
As the commemorative plaques adorning the façade reveal, this fine Baroque church is one of the most significant buildings in Spain – and not simply due to its unusual elliptical floorplan. On 29 March 1812 a group of Spanish patriots defied a Napoleonic blockade and met here to compose the country's first constitution. The document's liberal ideas have inspired fledgling democracies ever since. ◈ Plaza San Felipe Neri • Map B5 • Open 10am–1pm Mon–Sat; 956 21 16 12 • Adm

5 La Colegiata de Santa María de la Asunción, Osuna
From its hilltop, this massive Spanish Renaissance church dominates the town. Its austere façade is relieved by a fine Plateresque portal, the Puerta del Sol. Inside, treasures include five masterpieces by José de Ribera, a Crucifixion sculpture by Juan de Mesa, beautiful Renaissance ornamentation and a wonderfully high-spirited Baroque altarpiece *(see p88)*.

6 Iglesia de San Mateo, Lucena
It's intriguing to find one of the masterpieces of Andalucían Rococo design in this industrial town – especially because Lucena was famous for having been a virtually independent Jewish enclave during Moorish rule. The gem of this 15th-century church is its 18th-century octagonal sacristy and the complex decoration of the chapel and its dome. ◈ Map E3 • Open during services • Free

Plaques, Oratorio de San Felipe Neri

If visiting places of worship during services, be as courteously unobtrusive as possible and avoid wearing skimpy clothing.

7 Capilla Real and Catedral, Granada

Although not without aesthetic merit, these two structures are more about Christian triumph and royal ego than they are about spirituality. At the Royal Chapel's sarcophagi, note how Queen Isabel's head presses more deeply into her marble pillow than that of King Fernando – said to indicate greater intelligence. In the cathedral is the equestrian statue of El Matamoros ("The Killer of Moors") by Alonso de Mena *(see p109)*.

8 Monasterio de San Jerónimo, Granada

This Renaissance magnum opus is largely the creation of Diego de Siloé, one of the great masters of the age. The façade's upper window is flanked by sinuous mythological animals and medallions. Inside, the altar is complex and monumental, consisting of row upon row of high reliefs framed by columns.
Ⓢ *C/Rector López Argueta 9 • Map F4 • Open Apr–Oct: 10am–1:30pm, 4–7:30pm daily; Nov–Mar: 10am–1:30pm, 3–6:30pm daily; 958 27 93 37 • Adm*

Catedral, Granada

Catedral de Jaén

9 Catedral de Jaén

The cathedral was primarily the work of famed Renaissance architect Andrés de Vandelvira, although the west façade was designed later, decorated with Baroque sculptures by Pedro Roldán. Every Friday between 11:30am and 12:45pm, one of Spain's holiest relics, the Reliquia del Santo Rostro de Cristo, is brought out for the faithful to kiss. It is believed to be the cloth that St Veronica used to wipe Christ's face on the road to Calvary. An impression of the holy face is said to have been miraculously left upon it *(see p121)*.

10 Capilla del Salvador, Úbeda

Designed by Siloé and Vandelvira, this masterpiece of Andalucían Renaissance was commissioned as a family pantheon and is still privately owned. The sacristy is the highlight, employing caryatids and atlantes as columns and pilasters. It was once embellished by a Michelangelo sculpture, a sad casualty of the Spanish Civil War *(see p29)*.

Left **La Iruela, outside Cazorla** Right **Zahara de la Sierra**

Villages

1 Almonaster La Real
From a distance, this lovely *pueblo blanco* in Huelva Province looks like a sprinkling of snow amid the green of the surrounding forests. The citadel features one of the oldest mosques in the region, dating from the 10th century *(see p90)*.

2 Alájar
Another pretty Huelva Province village, where the stone houses seem ageless. There are some nice Baroque churches too. More intriguing, however, is the mystical importance of the place, as seen in the hallowed caves and hermitage on the cliff above the town *(see p90)*.

3 El Rocío
Deserted most of the year except for the handful of residents – who still customarily get around on horseback – this

Church, El Rocío

town fills up to overflowing with as many as one million pilgrims during the annual Romería *(see p31)*. It's worth a visit at any time, however, to take in its wonderful Wild West-style architecture, as well as to book a tour of the nearby Coto de Doñana nature reserve *(see p87)*.

4 Vejer de la Frontera
This inland village in Cádiz Province probably retains its quintessential Moorishness more than any other town in Andalucía. It stands gleaming white on a hill with a view of the coast, and its warren of maze-like alleys and byways is virtually indistinguishable from any North African town. Before the Spanish Civil War, women here wore a traditional veiled garment like the Muslim *heshab*, called the *cobijado*; now they are only worn during August festival *(see p99)*.

5 Arcos de la Frontera
The historic part of this town is from the Cuesta de Belén to the Puerta de Matrera – a zone that has been a recognized national monument since 1962. Consequently, it is beautifully preserved. Central to the area is the Plaza del Cabildo, with ancient walls in evidence and set about with orange trees. Unfortunately the castle below the square is not open to the public, but the terrace of the parador opposite is a fine place for a drink with a view *(see p98)*.

Gothic-Mudéjar church, Arcos de la Frontera

by the famed architect Andrés de Vandelvira, who was born here. He also designed several mansions for local nobility. ⊗ *Map F2*

6 Zahara de la Sierra

The town's name means "flower" in Arabic and this quiet little hamlet lives up to its implications. Scented with orange groves, it's a delight to see on the approach and offers equally fine views once there. The ruined castle, however, stands witness to tougher times. In the 15th century it was attacked continually, sought by both Muslims and Christians for its position guarding the northern access route to the Serranía de Ronda. ⊗ *Map C4*

7 Sabiote

This hamlet is a hidden gem. It boasts a Roman pedigree, its medieval walls are largely intact, and it has one of the most impressive castles in the region – Moorish in origin but restored

8 Iznatoraf

This mountain eyrie of a place opens out onto 360-degree panoramas of the Cazorla highland. The best view is from the mirador above the cliff at the village's northern edge. ⊗ *Map F2*

9 Cazorla

Simple whitewashed cubes cluster around a citadel here, while birds of prey overhead remind you that this is the southwestern entrance to the Sierra de Cazorla *(see p44)*. The town's position made it a prize for Moors and Christians, hence the castle in town and the ruined La Iruela, 1 km (0.5 miles) away. ⊗ *Map G3*

10 Castril

At the foot of an imposing stone outcropping and surrounded by the Parque Natural de la Sierra de Castril, this enchanting town dates back to Roman times. The parish church dominates the upper reaches, while down below there surges a mountain torrent. ⊗ *Map G3*

Left **Parque Nacional del Coto Doñana** Right **Sierra de Aracena**

🔟 Nature Reserves

1 Parque Nacional del Coto de Doñana

These important floodplains are a UNESCO Biospheric Reserve and have been a national park since 1969. The ecosystems include sand dunes, pine and cork forests, marshes, scrubland and riverbank. More than six million birds stop here on their annual migrations and fauna includes the last of the Iberian lynx population *(see pp30–31)*.

2 Sierra Nevada

Spain's highest mountains and Europe's southernmost ski resort can be found in this national park. It's a wonderful area for hiking, horse-riding and mountain biking *(see pp32–3)*.

3 Sierra de Aracena y Picos de Aroche Park

This part of the Sierra Morena in Huelva Province is very rural in character; traditions cling tighter here, notably the culinary techniques that give rise to its world-famous ham, *jamón ibérico*.

Again, these forested hills lend themselves to exploration on foot or horseback *(see p90)*.

4 Sierra Norte

Sevilla Province's northern reaches are wild and beautiful. In fact, hiking is a better option than driving in many cases, due to rough, pot-holed roads. The area is a great choice for outdoor enthusiasts of any sort – anglers, hunters and climbers are in their element here. ◈ *Map C3*

5 Parque Natural de la Sierra de Cardeña y Montoro

This beautiful park is home to prolific forests of holm oak, cork and pine. For the most part gently rolling, it gives way to more dramatic topography in the west. There are plenty of marked hiking trails, and it's a good place for spotting local fauna. ◈ *Map E2*

6 Sierra de Cazorla

In eastern Jaén Province, this vast and enormously diverse park is home to some 1,300 known species of flora, including 20 that are unique to the zone. Steep cliffs, deep gorges and an intricate pattern of rivers, lakes and streams typify the terrain. The landscape offers plenty of walking opportunities along marked trails. ◈ *Map G2*

Sierra Nevada

Cabo de Gata-Níjar

7 Cabo de Gata-Níjar

In Almería Province a stretch of pristine coastline has been set aside as a nature reserve, with towering rocks setting off beaches and coves. The semi-desert massif was designated a UNESCO Biosphere Reserve in 1997. The zone is excellent for scuba-diving *(see p49)*. ◈ *Map H4*

8 Sierra de Grazalema

Some 132,200 acres of verdant wilderness were designated a UNESCO Biosphere Reserve in 1984. Access is strictly controlled and is only possible on foot. ◈ *Map C5*

9 El Torcal

Málaga Province's most dramatic natural sight is this limestone massif, carved by the weather over countless millennia into bizarre forms. The visitors' centre explains how the wonders came to be *(see p99)*.

10 Parque Natural de los Montes de Málaga

Most of this park was planted to cloak Málaga's once barren heights so as to prevent the seasonal flooding the city experienced for several centuries. Just 30-minutes' drive from town, it's a fine place for hiking and biking, with colour-coded trails taking you through a land of gorges, forests and valleys. ◈ *Map E5*

Top 10 Flora and Fauna

1 Trees
These include black and umbrella pine, holm oak, hazel, olive, citrus, cypress, juniper, ash and the rare Spanish fir.

2 Shrubs
Along the coast you'll see agave, brought here from America in the 18th century. Also prickly pear, bullrush, club rush, oleander and arbutus.

3 Wildflowers
Look for the Cazorla violet, bubil lily, Nevada daffodil and white celandine.

4 Raptors
Birds of prey include the Spanish imperial eagle and the peregrine falcon.

5 Songbirds
Warblers include the red-legged partridge, collared pratincole and hoopoe.

6 Marsh birds
Watery areas abound in cranes, flamingo, gull-billed terns, purple gallinules, stilts, glossy ibis and redshanks.

7 Mammals
Wild creatures include wolves, lynxes, boar, genets, civets, mongoose, monk seal, dolphins, whales and the Barbary macaques of Gibraltar.

8 Reptiles and Amphibians
This group includes the Montpellier snake, the Spanish lizard and the natterjack toad.

9 Fish
Local catch includes black perch, eel, gambusia, tuna, monkfish, sardines, anchovies and cephalopods.

10 Insects and Arachnids
Most of Europe's butterflies are found here, along with mosquitoes, scorpions and tarantulas.

Andalucía's Top 10

There is a 1.5-km (1-mile) trail around El Torcal called the Ruta Verde, or you can book a 2-hour guided tour.

Left **Parque de María Luisa** Right **Parque Genovés**

Paseos, Plazas, Parks and Gardens

1 Parque de María Luisa, Seville

Seville's glorious main park was a gift to the city from a Bourbon duchess in 1893. A few decades later it was redesigned and embellished for the 1929 Ibero-American Exhibition. Numerous lavish structures have been left behind, including the stunning Plaza de España and several other fine buildings, now used mostly as cultural centres. The grounds are largely the creation of Jean-Claude Nicolas Forestier, the French landscape gardener who also designed the Bois de Boulogne in Paris *(see p79)*.

2 Paseo Marqués de Contadero, Seville

This central promenade is one of Seville's loveliest. Stretching along the riverfront, within sight of most of the major monuments, its tree-lined walkways make a pleasant break from the crowded city streets. The *paseo* is also pedestrianized so you don't have to worry about traffic *(see p79)*.

Paseo de Marqués de Contadero

3 Parque Zoológico, Jerez

Jerez's small zoo, set in botanical gardens, is also an active centre for the rehabilitation of regional endangered species or any injured animals. The star turns are a pair of white tigers. This is also the only chance you may get to see the elusive and extremely rare Iberian lynx, of which only an estimated 1,000 remain in the wild. ◎ *C/Taxdirt • Map B5 • Open Oct–May: 10am–6pm Tue–Sun; Jun–Sep: 10am–8pm daily; 956 18 23 97 • Adm*

4 Parque Genovés, Cádiz

Lying along the west side of Cádiz, this swathe of landscaped greenery facing the seafront has paths for strolling along, some civic sculpture and interesting flora, including an ancient dragon tree originally from the Canary Islands. This is one leg of a two-part park, the other half curving around along the northern seafront. ◎ *Map B5*

5 Plaza San Juan de Dios, Cádiz

This is one of Cádiz's busiest hubs of commercial and social life. Lined with cafés, bars and palm trees, its chief adornment is the monumental Neo-Classical façade of the Ayuntamiento (town hall), along with several handsome towers. The square opens out onto the port, ensuring a constant stream of pedestrians and opportunities for people-watching. ◎ *Map B5*

6 Jardín Botánico La Concepción, Málaga

Just north of Málaga City lies this impressive botanical garden, the work of a 19th-century English woman, Amalia Livermore, and her Spanish husband, Jorge Loring Oyarzábal. The garden is composed of a collection of palms and exotic plants from around the world. The grounds are also embellished with charming touches here and there, such as a domed gazebo decorated with tiles and columns. ✆ *Carretera N-331, km 166, Málaga • Map E5 • Open 10am–4pm Tue–Sun (until 6:30pm Apr–May & 7:30pm Jun–Sep); 952 25 21 48 • Adm*

7 Plaza de la Corredera, Córdoba

Córdoba gave this 17th-century arcaded square a long overdue sprucing up for the tourist onslaught of 1992 *(see p33)*, even putting in an underground car park. But it still retains some of its customary functions, including an open-air market on Saturday morning, in addition to the regular covered market in the building with the clock-tower. The arches provide shade for a number of cafés and *tapas* bars, where you can sit and admire the brick façades with their wrought-iron balconies. ✆ *Map D3*

Plaza de la Corredera

8 Alcázar de los Reyes Cristianos, Córdoba

Another of the major delights of Córdoba are the grounds of this palace *(see p18)*. The gardens are lavishly done in Moorish style, indulging in a profusion of colour – wisteria, bougainvillea, calla lilies and geraniums, to name only a few – gorgeously setting off the sun-bleached stone walls and ancient carvings. ✆ *Campo Santo de los Mártires • Map D3 • Open Tue–Sun • Adm €4.00 (free Fri)*

Plaza Nueva

9 Plaza Nueva, Granada

Located at the base of both the Alhambra hill and the Albaicín *(see pp8–13)*, and providing views along the banks of the river that runs beneath the city, this is a great place to while away the time. There are street performers, an endless stream of people and plenty of cafés with tables on terraces. ✆ *Map Q2*

10 Paseo de la Constitución, Baeza

Baeza's hub for strollers and café-goers is all along this oblong central promenade. Fountains grace its tree-lined length, and there are bars with open-air seating in the shade. Interesting buildings facing the square include La Alhóndiga, the old corn exchange, with its triple-tiered arches *(see p29)*.

Left **Cabo de Gata** Right **Marbella**

🔟 Beaches

1 Ayamonte
Andalucía's westernmost town is located at the mouth of Río Guadiana, and just to the east are the beach resorts Isla Canela and Isla Cristina. Isla Canela has a long, broad beach and a laidback array of bars and bungalows, while Isla Cristina boasts a fine sandy stretch and an attractive harbour. ◈ Map A4

Mazagón

2 Mazagón
Huelva Province's Costa de la Luz has several appealingly remote beaches, and Mazagón is one of them. Located 23 km (14 miles) southeast of Huelva City, this low-key resort is surrounded by pines and has lovely dune beaches. Deserted in winter, it comes alive in summer, mostly with Spanish families, but there's plenty of empty expanse to find solitude. ◈ Map B4

3 Chipiona
Cádiz Province has some very special beach resorts that lack the high tourism of further along the coast, and Chipiona is

one of the nicest. The beaches are excellent and, as an added plus, the town has retained its age-old traditions. It's still a thriving fishing port, for example, as well as a renowned producer of the local sweet muscatel wine. In addition, historic attractions include the longest jetty in the Guadalquivir estuary, known as Turris Caepionis to the Romans and these days as Torre Scipio *(see p99)*.

4 Tarifa
Cádiz Province's – and Europe's – southernmost point is one of the best spots in the world for devotees of the West Wind. The fact is that the wind practically never ceases blowing here, which makes it a top beach for windsurfers and the like, but something of a misery for sun-bathers. Still, it is possible to find protected niches that protect you from the wind, and the nightlife and sense of fun here are second to none *(see p99)*.

Windsurfers, Tarifa

5 Marbella

The Costa del Sol's smartest town naturally has several fine beaches to recommend. To the east there are Cabo Pino, a nudist beach, and Las Dunas, sand dunes beside a modern marina. To the west you'll find a string of party beaches, good for barbecues and dancing, including Victor's Beach and Don Carlos, perhaps Marbella's best *(see p26)*.

6 Torremolinos

Given the fact that they are in the number one Costa del Sol nightlife magnet, Torremolinos's beaches come as a pleasant surprise. Because of the steep streets, most of the action gets left up above as you make your way down to the sand *(see p27)*.

7 Torre del Mar

Very much off the beaten Costa del Sol track, this area – frequented mostly by local Spanish families – has quite a bit going for it if you want a more low-key time *(see p27)*.

8 Nerja

This little town is a perennial favourite for those who want an alternative to the brash Costa del Sol. It's a welcoming spot, with a wonderful position on top of an imposing cliff and palm-fringed beaches down below *(see p27)*.

Nerja

9 Almuñécar

The main resort on the Costa Tropical of Granada Province is a more relaxed alternative to the intensity of the Costa del Sol. The two central beaches are the Playa San Cristóbal and the Playa Puerto del Mar, separated by a headland. Good diving and windsurfing spots can be found along here *(see p110)*.

10 Cabo de Gata

Almería Province offers some of the finest unspoilt beaches in the region, centred on this natural park. The main resort town is San José, and from here you can walk to a number of perfect finds, including the Cala de la Media Luna and the Playa de Mónsul *(see p45)*.

Left **Costa del Sol marina** Right **Mountain horse-riding**

🔟 Outdoor Activities and Sports

1 Diving
Off Gibraltar you can check out the many sunken ships, while the wilds around Cabo de Gata offer the most profuse underwater life. The Costa de la Luz also has some good spots, including watersport heaven, Tarifa. ⓢ *Centro de Buceo Isub: C/Babor, San José; Map H5; 950 38 00 04; www.isubsanjose.com • Tarifa Diving: C/Alcalde Juan Nuñez 8, Tarifa; Map C6; 956 68 19 25*

2 Windsurfing and Surfing
Thanks to the constant winds, Tarifa is one of the world magnets for windsurfing, while good possibilities also can be found along the Costa Tropical. For board surfing, the Costa de la Luz provides sufficiently high waves. Mediterranean waves are only good for body-surfing. ⓢ *Club Mistral: Hurricane Hotel, Ctra N340 km 78, Tarifa; Map C6; 956 68 49 19 • Windsurf La Herradura: Paseo Marítimo 34, La Herradura; Map F5; 958 64 01 43*

Windsurfer, Costa Tropical

3 Horse-riding
Andalucía is renowned for breeding some of the finest horses in the world, so one would expect to find a range of riding options. There are trails and schools in every province. ⓢ *Camino Verde, Cortijo El Sabuco 18416, Busquistar; Map F4; 958 76 62 35 • Rancho Los Lobos: Estación de Jimena, nr Jimena de la Frontera; Map C5; 956 64 04 29*

4 Hiking
Andalucía is blessed with sierras in which to hike, from verdant, to desert-like, to rocky *(see pp44–5)*. If mountaineering appeals, head for the Sierra Nevada. Maps and lists of refuges are available from the Federación Española de Deportes de Montaña (FEDME). ⓢ *FEDME • 958 29 13 40 • www.fedme.es*

5 Spelunking
The region is home to some of the world's most interesting caves, many of them commercially developed. For information and organized jaunts, contact Safari Shop. ⓢ *Safari Shop: Avda Naciones Unidas Centro Commercial Cristamar B61, Puerto Banús, Marbella • Map D5 • 952 90 50 82;*

6 Skiing
The resort near Granada, Solynieve, is the only possibility in Andalucía. Although a little too sleek compared to its Alpine cousins, it offers a variety of runs and, best of all, skiing fairly late in the season *(see p33)*.

The entire coast is great for general swimming, with many blue-flag (safe) waters on the Costa del Sol.

7 Boating and Fishing

With so many marinas along the coast, sailing is big here. For deep-sea fishing, you need to obtain a five-year licence; for freshwater fishing, you'll need a two-week licence. Contact the Spanish Fishing Federation for details. ◎ *Spanish Fishing Federation: Navas de Tolosa 3, Madrid • 915 32 83 52*

Costa del Sol golf course

8 Golf

So copious are the golf courses that the Costa del Sol has often been dubbed the "Costa del Golf". Courses include everything from world master-pieces, designed by top golfers, to putting greens *(see p103)*.

9 Fútbol

Football (soccer) is a national obsession, stirring up the deepest of passions. In season, you'll encounter it in every bar, blaring out from the TV.

10 Bullfighting

In the Spanish view, this is not really a sport, but an art form, and to many Andalucíans, it embodies the soul of the region. The fight season runs from April to October and tickets are available from bullrings.

Top 10 Aspects of Bullfighting

1 History
The bullfight may have roots in primordial religions involving bull sacrifice.

2 Scheduling
There are about 500 bullfights each year in Spain, usually as part of a festival.

3 The Fight
Usually three groups fight two bulls each. Each of the six confrontations is a drama in several acts, called *tercios*.

4 Cast of Characters
The fight *(corrida)* begins with a procession of all the bullfighters.

5 Picadores
In the first *tercio* the matador taunts the bull with a red cape. The picadors goad the bull on horseback with steel-pointed lances to weaken the animal's powerful drive.

6 Banderilleros
Next the *banderilleros* enter on foot, sticking pairs of spikes in his back, to provoke the bull further into a frenzy.

7 Matador
In the final *tercio* the matador makes passes with the *muleta* cape, bringing the fight to its climax.

8 The Kill
This ideally amounts to a quick thrust of the sword, straight to the heart.

9 Post Mortem
Matadors are idolized in Spain, and the crowd jeers when his job is done and the bull's corpse is dragged away.

10 Celebration
At the end of the fight, a band plays, roses are tossed, hankies are waved, and the matador may be carried out on his men's shoulders.

Left **Guadalquivir Valley** Right **Southern Tahá**

🔟 Hikes and Drives

1 Hike from Alájar to Linares de la Sierra

The Sierra de Aracena is defined by soaring cliffs, wooded valleys and whitewashed villages. A good hike along the marked trails is the 6-km (4-mile) route from Alájar to Linares, via the hamlet of Los Madroñeros. It begins at the main square in Alájar and follows the old road, with only one steep section. ✆ Map B3

2 Río Borosa Hike

From the visitors' centre at the village of Torre del Vinagre, near Cazorla, this hike takes you along the narrow rock walls of the Cerrada de Elías gorge above the Río Borosa, criss-crossed by wooden bridges. ✆ Map G3

3 Hike around the Villages of the Southern Tahá

This hike begins in Pitres and descends south, to arrive first at Mecinilla, then along a ravine to Mecina-Fondales. From here, you take the short or long route to Ferreirola, climb up to Atalbéitar and then back to Pitres. ✆ Map F4

4 Hike from Rute to Iznájar

Leave Rute on the A331 south, veer left at the fork and then take the trail on the right about 500 m (550 yd) further on. This leads down to the reservoir; turn right and continue to a rocky promontory. Enjoy the views, then go up the hill and cross the bridge to the scenic village of Iznájar. ✆ Map E4

5 Serranía de Ronda Hike

An easy, picturesque hike connects the village of Benaoján Estación with Jimera de Líbar Estación. Begin at the Molino del Santo hotel, walk down the hill and left along the railway and then over at the second crossing. Across the river is the path; when it divides, take the left fork and continue on to Via Pecuaria and into the town. ✆ Map D5

Drive from Nerja to Almería

6 Drive from Nerja to Almería

A route along some of the region's most panoramic coastline. Nerja is built up on cliffs *(see p27)*, and as you approach Almería City the views are dramatic *(see p111)*. ✆ Map E5 • Rte N340

7 Drive from Ronda to Jerez

The attraction of this drive is the *pueblos blancos (see p96)* along the way, in particular Grazalema, Zahara and Arcos de la Frontera. You can also include the Roman ruins at Ronda la Vieja, and a sidetrip to Olvera. ✆ Map C5 • Rte N342

 Marked hiking trails are called senderos *in Spanish.*

8 Drive from Tarifa to Cádiz

This wild sweep of the Costa de la Luz (see p98) is the best of the Atlantic shore. Expect immense cliffs, mammoth sand dunes and a scattering of rather subdued resorts. The villages of Bolonia, with its ancient Roman sites, and Vejer de la Frontera, which is steeped in Moorish heritage, both make excellent sidetrips. ❧ Map C6 • Rte N340

9 Drive from Guadalquivir Valley through Córdoba Province

Starting to the east of Córdoba, in the attractive hill town of Montoro, this drive follows the river downstream. West of Córdoba, visit the once-fabulous Medina Azahara (see p119), enjoy the view from the castle walls at Almodóvar del Río, and end at Palma del Río. ❧ Map D3

10 Drive in Las Alpujarras, Sierra Nevada

This zone comprises scores of villages and hamlets, many perched on the slopes of the Sierra Nevada. Begin at Lanjarón, then head for the market town of Órgiva. Continuing eastward, the landscape becomes more arid; eventually you'll come to Yegen, made famous by Gerald Brenan's autobiographical South from Granada. ❧ Map F4

Sierra Nevada road

Top 10 Town and City Walks

1 Seville
Once you've done the main city-centre sights, head across the Puente de Isabel II and into the old gypsy quarter of Triana (see pp74–7).

2 Granada
Lose yourself in the maze of hilly streets in the Albaicín district (see pp12–13).

3 Córdoba
Have a free-form wander around the ancient Jewish quarter and then make for the Puente Romano for sunset views (see pp18–21).

4 Cádiz
Start at the northeast corner of Plaza de España and circumambulate the city, taking in the seascapes and gardens (see pp22–3).

5 Jerez
Stroll through the Barrio de Santiago, the town's gypsy quarter (see p98).

6 Ronda
Cross the Puente Nuevo, turn left and follow the town clockwise, being sure to pass the main church (see pp24–5).

7 Baeza
From Plaza del Pópulo most of the main sights are found in a counterclockwise direction (see pp28–9).

8 Úbeda
Take a westerly walk to the monumental Hospital de Santiago and the Plaza de Toros (see pp28–9).

9 Málaga
Málaga's historic sights are on the north side of the Paseo del Parque (see p96).

10 Antequera
This ancient town's main attractions are located at the foot of the Alcazaba (see p96).

Some of these hikes can be steep but none of them requires anything more than general fitness. Carry water with you.

53

Left **La Maestranza façade** Right **Archivo de las Indias**

🔟 Museums and Galleries

1 Museo de Bellas Artes, Seville

Housed in an exquisite former convent, this art museum is second only to Madrid's famed Prado. Paintings include early works by Velázquez, important works by Zurbarán, Ribera, El Greco, Murillo, Valdés Leal and Vásquez *(see p75)*.

2 Archivo de Indias, La Lonja, Seville

This museum is a vast archive given over to the discovery and conquest of the New World; four centuries of Spanish empire are painstakingly catalogued. The museum is housed in an 18th-century edifice that was built as the merchants' exchange *(see p78)*. It has been closed for five years but is expected to open in the summer of 2005.

Museo de Bellas Artes

3 Museo de la Maestranza, Seville

One of the corridors of what is perhaps Spain's most famous bullring is devoted to a Museo Taurino (Museum of the Bullfight). In addition to stacks of posters and other memorabilia, you can see the *trajes de luces* (suits of lights) – brightly coloured silk outfits embroidered with gold sequins – worn by many a celebrated toreador, along with portraits of some of the greats. There are also the inevitable stuffed remains of various noble animals *(see p78)*.

4 Museo de Cádiz

A Neo-Classical mansion houses Cádiz's main museum, a rich juxtaposition of archaeological treasures and fine art. In Europe's oldest city there are naturally artifacts from ancient cultures, including jewellery, pottery and small bronzes, but most notably a pair of 5th-century BC marble sarcophagi. Among the art are works by Zurbarán, Rubens, Murillo and Cano. An ethnological collection features artisanal pieces that highlight aspects of the city's culture *(see p23)*.

5 Museo del Bandolero, Ronda

This offbeat museum celebrates the story and legend of the Serranía's famous bandits and highwaymen. They were mostly active in the 19th century and managed to capture the imagination of many writers of the period, who portrayed them as romantic figures living a devil-may-care life in communion with nature. As the exhibits here will attest, they were anything but "diamonds in the rough" *(see p25)*.

Museo del Bandolero

that do, however, are the life-size 1st-century AD Roman bronze representing a naked young man, possibly Ganymede, cupbearer to the gods, and a life-like carving of St Francis of Assisi, executed in wood by Pedro de Mena, a 17th-century Andalucían master *(see p96)*.

6 Museo Arqueológico, Córdoba

A small 16th-century Renaissance mansion is home to this excellent collection, essential for understanding the city's importance in Roman times. In fact, the mansion was built over a Roman structure and there is an ancient patio to prove it. A sculpture of the Persian god Mithras, from a mithraeum found at Cabra, is particularly fine. Other parts of the collection focus on Iberian finds and Moorish artifacts *(see p19)*.

7 Museo Municipal, Antequera

This museum is located in a striking 18th-century ducal palace, which means that many of the exhibits simply cannot compete with the context. Two

Museo Arqueológico, Córdoba

8 Museo Picasso, Málaga

Newly opened, after years of planning and several setbacks, this is the world's third largest museum dedicated to the modern master. It was endowed by his daughter-in-law, Christine Ruiz-Picasso, and her son Bernard with some 187 paintings, including some major canvases, that give an idea of the breadth and depth of his career *(see p96)*.

9 Museo Arqueológico Cueva de Siete Palacios, Almuñécar

This space was built into the side of the hill in the 1st century. The small collection includes artifacts from Phoenician, Roman and Moorish periods *(see p110)*.

10 Museo Provincial y de Bellas Artes, Jaén

The archaeological lower floor has an interesting assortment of finds, but the 5th-century BC Iberian stone sculptures are truly extraordinary. Found near the town of Porcuna, in the western part of the province, they show clear influences from Greek works. Upstairs, the fine arts museum has some fine medieval wood sculpture and a Picasso drawing *(see p121)*.

Left **Palacio de San Telmo façade by Figueroa** Right **Alonso Cano portrait**

🔟 Art and Culture

1 Andrés de Vandelvira
Andrés de Vandelvira (1509–75) was the quintessential architect of the Spanish Renaissance in Andalucía. His work spanned the three major phases of the style's predominance, from ornamental Plateresque, to Italianate Classical, to austere Herreran. He can be given virtually sole credit for the architectural treasures in the town of Úbeda and many important edifices in Baeza *(see pp28–9)*.

2 Francisco de Zurbarán
The great painter (1598–1664) spent most of his life in and around Seville, where his art adorns churches and museums. His works are noted for their mystical qualities, dramatized by striking *chiaroscuro* (light and shade) effects – hallmarks, as well, of his contemporaries Caravaggio and José de Ribera.

St Luke before Christ, Zurbarán

3 Velázquez
Born in Seville, Diego Rodríguez de Silva y Velázquez (1599–1660) left for Madrid in 1623 to become court painter to the king. His was the most remarkable talent of the golden age of Spanish painting, taking naturalism and technique to new heights. The works that remain in his home town were mostly religious commissions, although his real genius lay in portraiture.

4 Alonso Cano
Most of the works by Cano (1601–67) can be seen in Granada, largely because after he was accused of killing his wife the city vowed to protect him if he would work exclusively for them. Sadly, such a predicament limited the opportunities for this gifted painter, sculptor and architect to fully blossom.

5 Bartolomé Esteban Murillo
Murillo (1618–82) was the most successful of the Baroque painters from Seville. He received countless commissions to produce devotional works, notably the many *Immaculate Conceptions* seen in Andalucía.

6 Pedro Roldán
Roldán (1624–99) was one of the chief proponents of the Spanish aspiration to combine painting, sculpture and architecture into unified works of art, such as the altarpiece in Seville's Hospital de la Caridad *(see p78)*.

7 Leonardo de Figueroa

Figueroa (1650–1730) was a highly accomplished Baroque architect. His commissions in Seville included the Hospital de los Venerables *(see p76)*, the Palacio de San Telmo and the Museo de Bellas Artes *(see p73)*.

8 Manuel de Falla

Andalucían de Falla (1876–1946) was Spain's finest classical composer. One of his major works, *The Three-Cornered Hat*, has its roots deep in flamenco.

9 Pablo Picasso

Picasso (1881–1973) was born in Málaga, although he settled in France in 1909. His native land, with images of the bullfight and later of the horrors of the Franco era, turned up in his work throughout his career.

10 Federico García Lorca

The Granada-born writer (1898–1936) was also an artist, musician, theatre director and more. Homosexual and Socialist too, he was murdered by Franco's Nationalists at the start of the Spanish Civil War. His work shows his love for Andalucían culture.

Portrait of Federico García Lorca

Top 10 Writers on Andalucía

1 Lord Byron

The English Romantic poet's fascination with Andalucía is chronicled in his mock-epic poem *Don Juan* (1819).

2 Chateaubriand

The French writer's 1826 novel *The Last of the Abencerrages* was a bestseller.

3 Washington Irving

The American writer lived in Granada for some time and produced the hit *Tales from the Alhambra* (1832).

4 Théophile Gautier

The French writer's *Journey to Spain* (1841) gives a descriptive clarity to the region.

5 Calderón

This Málaga-born writer's *Andalucían Scenes* (1847) featured the first ever description of a gypsy festival.

6 Opera

Operas set in Andalucía include *The Marriage of Figaro* (1786, Mozart), *The Barber of Seville* (1816, Rossini) and *Carmen* (1875, Bizet).

7 Manuel Machado

The works of Machado (1874–1947), such as *Cante Jondo*, evoke a poetic passion for Andalucía.

8 Dalí and Buñuel

This Surrealist pair created the shocking avant garde film *Un Chien d'Andalou* in 1928.

9 Ernest Hemingway

The American writer was a newspaper correspondent in Spain during the Civil War. *For Whom the Bell Tolls* is based on his Andalucían experiences.

10 Salman Rushdie

The Indian author's *The Moor's Last Sigh* (1995) was inspired by the exile of Granada's last Moorish king.

Left **Flamenco musicians** Centre **Guitar-maker** Right **Cave dwelling**

🔟 Aspects of Gypsy Culture

1 Origins
Gypsies *(Roma)* arrived in Eastern Europe in the 14th century and in Andalucía in the 15th century. Linguistic research shows that their language, Romany, was related to ancient dialects from northern India. Why they left India is unclear, but was possibly due to war with invading Muslims.

2 History
Although gypsies have remained outsiders throughout their history, they found a more congenial civilization in Andalucía than anywhere else. The culture was decidedly Middle Eastern and not dissimilar to that of their native land. With the Christian reconquest, however, "pagan" gypsies were forced into hiding or into further wanderings.

3 Song
Fortunately for Andalucían culture, many gypsies stayed, and eventually developed a unique strain of music, flamenco, drawing on Arabic, Jewish and Byzantine sources, as well as their own Indian traditions.

Similar to the American Blues, it is the raucous, rhythmic music of the dispossessed and marginalized, full of pathos and catharsis. The word flamenco is probably a corruption of the Arabic *felag mengu* (fugitive peasant), an epithet that 19th-century Andalucían gypsies used with one another.

4 Dance
Similarities between Middle Eastern and North African dance forms and flamenco are obvious. But using the feet to create rapid and complex staccato rhythms, combined with the expressive arm and hand gestures, clearly resembles traditional kathak dancing from northern India, confirming its true roots.

5 Guitar
The six-stringed flamenco guitar can be traced back to the medieval lute. Compared to the classical guitar, it is lighter, shallower and less resonant, so that it can be played extremely fast, and also features a thick plate below the soundhole for tapping out rhythms.

Gypsy singers

6 Flamenco Legends
A few of the names who advanced the art include: singers El Fillo and La Niña de los Peines; guitarist Paco de Lucía; and dancers La Macarrona and Carmen Amaya.

7 Sevillanas
This strident dance, with clapping rhythms, has been infused with the flamenco spirit. It is danced with enthusiasm at festivals throughout the region.

8 Horses
Andalucían gypsies have a reputation for their ability to train their steeds. To watch a gypsy horseman putting an animal through its paces is to witness an amazing display of communication between man and beast.

Gypsy horseman

9 Cave-dwellings
In remote hills and mountains gypsies escaped Christian persecution by turning caves into homes. Although flooding and other natural mishaps have decimated these communities in recent decades, many gypsies return to their former dwellings to perform lively and authentic flamenco shows for visitors.

10 Performances
Historically, flamenco is an improvized performance that arises spontaneously from a gathering, but the rule these days tends towards scheduled spectacles. Still, if the mood is right, these events still generate a great deal of emotion.

Top 10 Flamenco Venues

1 La Taberna Flamenca, Jerez
Flamboyant shows. ◈ *Callejón Angostillo de Santiago • Map B5 • 12–4pm, 8pm–midnight*

2 La Bulería, Jerez
This club is named after a flamenco festival held in September. ◈ *C/Mariñiguez 15; 956 33 34 68 • Map B5*

3 Sanlúcar de Barrameda
This town holds the Feria de Flamenco in July. ◈ *Map B5*

4 Juan Villar, Cádiz
A good *peña* for genuine flamenco. ◈ *Paseo Fernando Quiñones, Puerta la Caleta • Map B5 • Open Tue–Sun; 956 22 52 90*

5 El Arenal, Seville
First-class performances. ◈ *C/Rodo 7 • Map L4*

6 Casa de la Memoria de al-Andalus, Seville
Another museum, with performances (see p83).

7 Tablao Flamenco Cardenal, Córdoba
Authentic shows. ◈ *C/Torrijos 10 • Map D3 • Open Mon–Sat, 957 40 33 20*

8 Venta El Gallo, Granada
Come to this cave for professional performances. ◈ *Barranco de los Negros 5; 958 22 05 91 • Map F5*

9 La Peña Platería, Granada
One of Spain's oldest *peñas*. ◈ *Placeta de Toqueros 7; 958 22 77 12 • Map F5*

10 Peña El Taranto, Almería
Named after the province's contribution to the genre, the *taranto* dance. ◈ *C/Tenor Iri Barne 20; 950 23 50 57 • Map G4*

Granada's La Peña Platería is a private flamenco club but is sometimes open to the public. Telephone 958 21 06 50 for details.

Left **Carnaval, Cádiz** Right **Feria de Abril, Seville**

Religious Festivals

Fiesta de los Reyes Magos
Traditionally, this evening commemorates the arrival of the Three Kings at the infant Jesus's manger crib. Parades across the region feature the trio, lavishly dressed, progressing through towns in small carriages drawn by tractors or horses. The next day, Epiphany, is the day that children receive gifts. ⚜ *5 Jan*

Carnaval
Most Andalucían towns celebrate this Catholic festival, the most spectacular extravaganza being in Cádiz. Costumes and masked balls and lots of carousing are the order of the day and night during these chaotic revels. The implicit anarchy invites every sort of political lampoon, which is why Franco tried to abolish these events – unsuccessfully *(see p23)*. ⚜ *Feb*

Semana Santa
Holy Week is observed in every town and village in the region, with dramatic and spectacular processions,

Semana Santa procession

especially in Seville. Effigies of Christ and the Virgin are carried through the streets on huge floats, sometimes accompanied by music. The people, dressed in traditional outfits, either maintain penitential silence or express their commiseration with the suffering Lord and His mournful Mother *(see p15)*. ⚜ *Easter week*

Corpus Christi
This festival celebrates the miracle of Transubstantiation, when the host becomes the body of Christ and the wine His blood. Granada's celebration is the most famous, with parades and partying, followed by bullfights and flamenco. ⚜ *Dates vary*

Romerías
Taking part in one of these local festivals is an experience no visitor will forget – almost every community has its own *romería*. Usually, the programme involves a colourful pilgrimage to a shrine outside of town, followed by days of merrymaking. The name may recall ancient pilgrimages, when devotees walked to Rome *(see p31)*. ⚜ *May–Oct*

Fiesta de las Cruces
The Festival of the Crosses celebrates the discovery of the True Cross in the 4th century by St Helena. Modes of veneration vary widely in the region, but may include competitions for producing the most gorgeous flower-decked cross. ⚜ *3 May*

Romería celebrations

7 San Juan

This feast is important in many parts of Andalucía. In celebration of John the Baptist, midsummer fireworks and bonfires seem to be the rule in most communities. ◎ *23 & 24 Jun*

8 Virgen del Carmen

The patron of sailors is all-important in coastal communities. Statues of the Virgin are put onboard a decorated fishing boat and floated out to sea and back again, amid flowers, fireworks, music and cheering. Thus the waters are blessed for the coming year. ◎ *15 & 16 Jul*

9 Ascension of the Virgin

At the height of the summer heat, the day of the Virgin's ascension into heaven is celebrated. In colourful marquees there is much socializing, drinking and dancing. The day marks the beginning of the Feria de Málaga, a week-long festival. ◎ *15 Aug*

10 Fiesta de San Miguel

This mix of bullfights, exhibitions and dancing is particularly noteworthy in Seville, Úbeda and the Albaicín quarter of Granada. In Torremolinos it closes the summer season in festive style. ◎ *Last week Sep–first week Oct*

Top 10 Ferías and other Festivals

1 Flamenco Festivals

These take place during the summer months all around the region.

2 Moros y Cristianos

Festivals centre on re-enactments of Christian take-overs of various towns throughout the year.

3 Feria de Abril

Held in Seville two weeks after Easter, this is the largest fair in Spain *(see p76)*.

4 Feria del Caballo

This fair in Jerez de la Frontera centres on Andalucían horses. ◎ *May*

5 Music & Dance Festivals

The most famous of these takes place in Granada from late June to early July.

6 Wine Festivals

Celebrations of the fruit of the vine occur from April to September, when *La Vendimia* (grape harvest) takes place.

7 Sherry Festivals

The "Sherry Triangle" *(see p98)* celebrates their fortified wines at various times, notably in Jerez. ◎ *Sep–Oct*

8 Feria de Jamón

Late summer and autumn sees the traditional *matanza* (slaughter) of pigs and several celebrations of ham, notably in Trevélez. ◎ *15 Aug*

9 Fiesta de la Aceituna

The olive is celebrated in the Jaén province town of Martos. ◎ *1st week Dec*

10 Fiesta de los Verdiales

In Málaga Province at Puerta de la Torre, this is a day for practical jokers and a chance to wear funny hats. It dates back to Moorish times. ◎ *28 Dec*

Left **SeaLife** Right **Mini Hollywood**

🔟 Children's Attractions

1 Muelle de las Carabelas, La Rábida, Huelva Province
Down by the waterfront, the "Pier of the Caravels" is a great treat for kids. They'll love the chance to climb aboard full-size replicas of Columbus's ships *Niña*, *Pinta* and *Santa María* and imagine themselves setting sail to discover the New World. There's also a recreation of a 15th-century European village *(see p89)*. 🔊 *Paraje de La Rábida • Map A4 • Open 10am–2pm, 5–9pm Tue–Fri, 11am–8pm Sat–Sun (summer); 10am–7pm Tue–Sun (winter) • 959 53 05 97 • Adm*

2 Parque Zoológico, Jerez
Primarily, this is a care station for the rehabilitation of injured animals, in particular indigenous endangered species. As a result, it can give children a close-up encounter with the wonderful Iberian lynx, which is extremely rare in the wild. There are also white tigers, red pandas and ibis *(see p46)*.

3 Isla Mágica, Seville
This amusement park occupies part of what was Expo '92. One of its themes is to recreate the exploits of the explorers who set out from Seville on voyages of discovery in the 16th century – rides have names such as Jaguar, Anaconda and Orinoco. 🔊 *Pabellón España, Isla de Cartuja • Map J1 • Open Apr–Jun: 11am–7pm Mon–Fri, 11am–10pm Sat–Sun; Jul–Aug: 11am–11pm daily (to midnight on Sat); Sep–Oct: 11am–9pm Sat–Sun • 902 16 17 16 • Adm*

4 Carromato de Max, Mijas
Claiming to be a compendium of the world's smallest curiosities, this is certainly an oddball collection. There's a fine copy of Da Vinci's *The Last Supper*, executed on a grain of rice, fleas in full suits of clothing and a bust of Churchill's head sculpted from a stick of chalk. 🔊 *Avda del Compás • Map D5 • Open 10am–10pm daily (summer); 10am–7pm daily (winter) • 952 48 58 20 • Adm*

5 Tívoli World, Benalmádena
Attractions at this theme park include a flamenco extravaganza and a Wild West show, but it's really all about rides. None of them will particularly appeal to adrenaline addicts, but what it lacks in speed it makes up for in old-fashioned fun. 🔊 *Avda de Tívoli • Map D5 • Open Oct–Apr: 12–8pm Fri–Sun; May–Jun: 4pm–1am; July–early Sep: 6pm–2am (to 1am late Sep) • 952 57 70 16 • www.tivolicostadelsol.com • Adm*

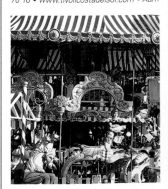

Tivoli World

6 SeaLife, Benalmádena

Viewing rescued sharks, seahorses, seals, turtles and other sea creatures is a wonderful experience for kids. They will also love the Lost City of Atlantis, the Mediterranean Tunnel and the Touchpool. ◈ *Puerto Deportivo de Benalmádena • Map D5 • Open Oct–Mar: 10am–6pm daily, Apr–Sep: 10am–midnight daily • 952 56 01 50 • Adm*

7 Cuevas de Nerja

Only discovered in 1959, these caves go back some five million years. The chambers will stimulate children's imagination – with a little help from fanciful names and evocative lighting. The central column in Cataclysm Hall is the tallest in the world, the product of waterdrops falling over countless aeons. ◈ *Ctra Maro • Map E5 • Open 10am–2pm, 4–6:30pm daily (until 8pm Jul–Aug) • 952 52 95 20 • Adm*

8 Aquatropic, Almuñécar

Hours of fun with rides called Kamikaze, Waterfall Lake, Wavebreaker, Ring Rapids, Blackhole Rapids, Soft Runs and a special Children's Lake for the littlest ones. ◈ *Playa de Velilla • Map F5 • Open Jun, Sep: 11am–6pm daily; Jul–Aug: 11am–7pm daily • 958 63 20 81 • Adm*

Cuevas de Nerja

9 Mini Hollywood, Almería

The Wild West rides again at this old "spaghetti western" movie set. At show time the kids can see Jesse James reach his ignominious end *(see p111)*.

10 Parque Acuático Aquavera, Vera

This place will save the day when what your children need most is to cool off. Five pools of various sizes, loads of undulating slides and tubes, as well as shaded areas. ◈ *Ctra Vera/Garrucha-Villaricos • Map H4 • Open mid-May–Jun: 10am–6pm daily, Jul & Aug: 10:30am–7:30pm, Sep: 10am–6pm daily • 902 36 12 94 • Adm*

Left **Taracea craftsman from Granada** Right **Ceramic dishes**

Andalucían Souvenirs

1 Granada Pottery
Andalucía's most famous pottery celebrates the symbol of Granada, the pomegranate, and is glazed in turquoise and cobalt blue over white.

2 Granada Taracea
Granada's Moorish-inspired marquetry uses bone, mother-of-pearl, amber and marble in the finest inlays, although humbler objects employ coloured wood chips. You'll find chessboards, tables and boxes of all sizes.

3 Moroccan Crafts
The Albaicín area of Granada *(see pp12–13)* has become a mini-Morocco. Here you can buy leather slippers, embroidered robes, silver tea services and decorative ceramics.

4 Flamenco and Traditional Accessories
If you plan on attending a *romería (see p60)* or any other local festival – or you just feel like taking home a bit of local

Traditional Spanish fans

colour – consider investing in some traditional flamenco paraphernalia. Embroidered silk shawls, ornate tortoiseshell combs and hand-painted silk and ivory fans are the top of the line, but there are plenty of more affordable versions. Synthetic shawls, these days often imported from China, wood or even plastic combs and paper and wood fans are all just as vivid.

5 Silver and Gold Filigree
Two cities, Córdoba and Granada, are known for their delicate filigree work in precious metals. Since ancient times, when Andalucían mines were a primary source of silver and gold for the Mediterranean, craftsmen have created brooches, earrings and necklaces. Designs often reflect the Moorish taste for complex geometrics, but can also depict insects, birds or lizards, set with precious stones.

6 Woodwork
Furniture manufacture of high-quality mahogany items takes place in Cádiz Province, while Ronda is known for its rustic styles and Granada Province is reputed for Mudéjar *(Capiliera)* and Renaissance *(Baza)* styles. Also of note, of course, are Andalucían guitars, with excellent examples created in Algodonales (Cádiz Province) and Marmolejo (Jaén Province), as well as in the main centres of Granada, Córdoba and Seville.

 When shopping in markets for traditional crafts, the ancient art of haggling is acceptable, even expected.

7 Iron and Metalwork

Wrought-iron and other metal pieces that might tempt you include tin lamps from Úbeda, grilles from Arcos de la Frontera and Torredonjimeno, cowbells from Cortegana and locks from Estepona and Cártama.

8 Leather

Leather goods of all sorts abound. Principal towns of production include Jerez de la Frontera, Almodóvar del Río, Almonte and Ubrique for bags, belts, gloves and jackets. For handmade shoes try Montoro; for handmade boots, Valverde del Camino, both in Huelva Province. Most traditional are *cordovans* – embossed and handdecorated leather pieces from Córdoba.

Leather bag

9 Ceramics

Ceramics come in almost as many styles and forms as there are towns – items as diverse as traditional *azulejos* (glazed tiles), *botijos* (double-spouted pitchers) and Hispano-Moorish lustreware. Most tend towards the Islamic style but many carry on the European tradition of depicting scenes from daily life or myths.

10 Weavings

The various weaving arts are well represented in Andalucía. Wickerwork and basketry are notable in Almería, Níjar, Jerez, Lanjarón and Jaén. *Jarapas* (handwoven rugs and blankets) are famous in Almería Province, as well as in Arcos de la Frontera and Grazalema in Cádiz Province, Las Alpujarras and Jaén Province.

Top 10 Local Produce

1 Fish and Seafood

Mediterranean and Atlantic bounty offers a vast array of fish and shellfish.

2 Olives

Introduced in ancient times, the olive and its oil are vital to Andalucían cuisine. Try olives stuffed with anchovies, or cured with spices and herbs.

3 Grapes

Also dating from ancient times, cultivation of the vine remains a vital part of life.

4 Garlic and Spices

Ajo (garlic) plays a large part in Andalucian cooking, while spices introduced by the Moors include cumin, cinnamon, coriander and saffron.

5 Ham

The most noteworthy hams are from Jabugo and Trevélez.

6 Almonds and Fruits

Almonds are used mainly in honey-based desserts. Fresh fruits include *chirimoyas* (custard apples), figs, pomegranates and persimmons.

7 Meats

The taste for *cordero* (lamb) and *cabra* (goat) can be traced back to the Moorish/Jewish period. *Rabo de toro* (oxtail) is a popular dish.

8 Game

In mountainous areas, rabbit, hare, wild boar, quail, pigeon, pheasant, partridge and venison appear on menus.

9 Vegetables

Artichokes and asparagus were introduced by the Moors; potatoes and tomatoes came from the New World. Wild mushrooms also grow here.

10 Cheese

Goat's and sometimes sheep's milk are used to make most local cheeses.

Left **Bodegas Gomara** Right **Moorish cellar, Pedro Domecq**

🔟 Bodegas and Wineries

1 Pedro Domecq
One of the most legendary of the names associated with sherry, with a flawless discernment for this world-class tipple. The company was founded in 1730, and a tour of the famous Moorish-style cellar "de la Ina" is *de rigueur* when in Jerez *(see p98)*. ◈ *C/San Ildefonso 3, Jerez • Map B5 • 956 15 15 00 • Tours 10am, 11am, noon, 1pm Mon–Fri, noon Sat • Adm*

2 González-Byass
Although most of the main sherry producers are now largely owned by British multinationals, this *bodega* is an encouraging example of one that was bought back by the family, disillusioned with the way things were going. Founded in 1835, their operation has two historic cellars, as well as the original tasting room. ◈ *C/ Manuel María González 12, Jerez • Map B5 • 956 35 70 00 • Tours 11:30am, 12:30pm, 1:30pm, 2pm, 3:30pm, 4:30pm daily • Adm*

González-Byass cellar

3 Sandeman
The distinctive silhouetted figure, The Don, dating from 1928, is one of the first trademark images ever created. In a Portuguese black cape and a wide-brimmed Spanish hat, he is recognized worldwide. The House of Sandeman was founded in London in 1790; the tour here includes tastings. ◈ *C/Pizarro 10, Jerez • Map B5 • 956 15 17 00 • Tours 10:30am–2:30pm Mon–Fri • Adm*

4 Osborne Bodega
Visitors cannot fail to notice the black cutouts of the noble bull adorning many Andalucían roadside hills. It is the symbol of this venerable sherry and brandy producer and is a protected part of regional heritage. ◈ *El Puerto de Santa María • Map B5 • 956 86 91 00 • Tours 10:30am Mon–Fri (call to book) • Adm*

5 Bodegas Alvear, Montilla
What distinguishes the wines here is two-fold. Giant terracotta containers *(tinajas)* are sunk into the ground to keep the contents at a constant temperature, while the hot local climate ripens the grapes for a stronger wine *(see p120)*.

6 Bodegas Robles, Montilla
This organic wine producer employs an old system called *solera*, in which young wines on top are blended with older ones below, until they mature. ◈ *Ctra. Córdoba-Málaga km. 447 • Map D3 • 957 65 00 63 • Open Mon–Fri.*

Bodega *is the Spanish term for a wine cellar.*

7 Bodega El Pimpi, Málaga

Not only can you get the best of Andalucía's vintages here, but there's also a good selection of Spain's finest, such as Ribera del Duero. Delicious *tapas*, too. ⊗ *C/Granada 68; 952 22 89 90 • Map R5 • Open daily*

8 Bodegas Gomara

This *bodega* produces the traditional Málaga wines as well as its own *fino* that is dry and pale. They sell the wines in souvenir bottles that may take the form of a matador, a guitar or castanets. ⊗ *C/Lima 6, Málaga • Map E5 • 952 34 20 75*

Andalucían vintner

9 Bodegas Andrade

This *bodega* was one of the first to realize the potential of the Zalema grape varietal for creating young wines. ⊗ *Avda Coronación, 35, Bollullos Par del Condado, Huelva • Map A4 • 959 41 01 06*

10 Agroalimentaria Virgen del Rocío

This producer has taken use of the Zalema grape a step or two further. A series of large underground fermenting vats form a subterranean cellar, where they make Andalucía's only sparkling wine, Raigal. ⊗ *Almonte, Huelva • Map B4 • Visit by appt • 959 40 61 03*

Top 10 Sherries and Wines

1 Fino
Clear, crisp and dry, with an aroma of almonds, *fino* is served chilled as an aperitif.

2 Manzanilla
The *fino* sherry made in Sanlúcar de Barrameda. It is dry, pale and slightly salty.

3 Oloroso
The layer of flor yeast is thin, or absent, as a *fino* ages, allowing partial oxidation. *Oloroso* is a rich amber, with an aroma of hazelnuts.

4 Amontillado
Midway between a *fino* and an *oloroso*. The layer of flor yeast is allowed to die off, so it gets darker in colour.

5 Palo Cortado
This has an aroma reminiscent of an *amontillado*, while its colour is closer to *oloroso*.

6 Cream Sherry
This international favourite results when you take an *oloroso* and sweeten it by mixing in a measure of Pedro Ximenez wine.

7 Pedro Ximénez
This naturally sweet wine, when aged with care, is elegant and velvety.

8 Brandy de Jerez
This brandy is made by ageing wine spirits in casks that have previously been used to age sherry. It is sweeter and more caramelized than French brandy.

9 Málaga
Málaga's famous sweet wines are made from the Moscatel and Pedro Ximénez grape varieties.

10 Raigal
This recent addition, the region's only sparkling wine, is refreshing on the palate.

Left **Tortilla española** Right **Fish soup**

Andalucían Dishes

1 Gazpacho

This signature Andalucían dish is a cold soup made of fresh tomatoes, green peppers, cucumber, garlic, olive oil, wine vinegar or lemon, breadcrumbs and salt. There are dozens of local variations of this nourishing refresher, which may involve almonds, grapes, melon, red peppers, and boiled egg or chopped ham garnishes.

Gazpacho

2 Tortilla Española and Patatas Bravas

Both of these dishes are ubiquitous not just in Andalucía but all over Spain. The first is a dense potato omelette with onions, fried into a savoury cake. It is served cold by the slice and is so filling it can make a full meal. The second consists of fried potato wedges served with a spicy sauce.

3 Fish Soups

The array of *sopas de mariscos* or *pescado* (shellfish or fish soups) seems to be limited only to the cooks' imagination. Málaga favourites include *sopa viña*, a sherry-spiked version, and *cachoreñas*, with orange flavouring. Cádiz is known for its *guisos marineros* (seafood stews), made with the best fish of the region.

4 Calamares

All along the coast, you will encounter whole baby *calamares* (squids) served grilled – the essence of simplicity and delicious as long as they are fresh. A common alternative is to cut them into rings and batter-fry them – again, if they are fresh, they will taste sweet and tender. A complete *fritura de pescado* or *fritura mixta* (mixed fish fry) might add anchovies, prawns, chunks of cod or whatever is good that day.

Calamares

5 Rape

Monkfish *(rape)*, also called anglerfish, is one of the top choices for quality maritime eating in Andalucía. Only the tail of this very unprepossessing looking fish is eaten, and it has a succulent quality similar to lobster tail or scallops. It is preferably served grilled, but can also be stewed in a rich sauce, most likely to be tomato-based.

6 Arroza a la Marinera

This is the Andalucían version of *paella*, an appellation that also appears on some menus. Saffron-flavoured rice is served with an assortment of fish and shellfish, which can

Vegetarians, and especially vegans, will face very narrow choices – mostly salads – in Andalucían restaurants.

Arroza a la Marinera

include prawns, clams and squid. Unlike the Valencia variety, it does not generally include sausage or chicken. The dish is also known as *arroz con mariscos*.

7 Salads
Andalucían *ensaladas* (salads) are substantial and often come with asparagus, hard-boiled eggs, tuna, artichoke, olives and onions, in addition to lettuce and tomato. You can ask that any of these ingredients be left off your order if you prefer.

8 Valle de los Pedroches
This soft sheep's cheese from Córdoba Province is typical of the regional type: strong in taste. The cheese is preserved in olive oil and enhanced with herbs.

9 Dessert Tarts
The variety of cakes and sweet biscuits you will see typically involve Moorish ingredients such as anise, sesame, almonds and cinnamon. Most are also sweetened with honey rather than sugar. Two common types are *alfajores*, with honey and almonds, and *piononos*, which are soaked in liqueur.

10 Tocino de Cielo
This rich custard pudding or flan ("heavenly bacon") is made by nuns in Jerez de la Frontera and elsewhere in Cádiz Province.

Top 10 Drinks

1 Sherry
The region's most famous wine comes from Cádiz Province *(see p67)*.

2 Brandy
Brandy is distilled in Cádiz Province, Córdoba Province and Huelva Province.

3 Wine
Málaga's sweet wines come from Moscatel and Pedro Ximenez grapes, while fruity Condado wines are produced from Zalema grapes.

4 Beer
Cruz Campo is a local, Pilsner-type *cerveza* (beer) that is among Spain's best.

5 Liqueur
Aniseed-based liqueurs come primarily from Montilla in Córdoba Province. Other liqueurs include *aguardiente* from Huelva Province and *cazalla* from Sevilla Province.

6 Sangría
This classic red wine punch is world famous. The lighter *Tinto de Verano* is very popular in Andalucia.

7 Coffee
Opt for *café solo (espresso)* or *cortado* (with milk). *Café con leche* (with lots of milk) is drunk for breakfast.

8 Mint Tea
Moroccan-style *teterías* serving mint tea are popping up more and more *(see p116)*.

9 Soft Drinks
Refrescos include *granizados* (iced fruit crush), *batidos* (milkshakes) and *horchata* (a milky drink made from a type of tuber).

10 Mineral Water
Bottled water, *sin gas* (still) or *con gas* (fizzy), is available, the best being from Lanjarón in Granada Province.

If you want a glass of draft beer, rather than bottled beer, ask for una caña.

Left **Anchoas** Right **Aceitunas**

Tapas Dishes

1 Aceitunas

There are innumerable types of olives, from small to large, green to black, salty to sweet, or whole to stuffed. The name of the dish can be confusing – although the Spanish name for the tree is the *olivo*, which comes from Latin, the word for the fruit comes from the Arabic *az-zait*, which means "juice of the olive".

2 Chorizo al Vino

Chorizos are spicy, paprika-red garlic sausages that can be served grilled, sautéed with wine *(al vino)*, or stewed with other ingredients. They are generally made of pork. *Morcilla* (blood sausage or black pudding) is a classic country delicacy.

3 Jamón Serrano

A complementary slice of ham laid over the top of a *copa* (glass) is said to be how the custom of *tapa* (which literally means "lid") got started. The finest regional type available is mountain-cured ham, but there

Jamón Serrano

is also *jamón York* (regular ham), as well as other cured pork products, including a local *tocino* (bacon) and *fiambres* (cold cuts). These are often served with cheese and bread as a perfect complement.

4 Ensaladilla

"Russian salad" is sometimes an option for vegetarians – but not for vegans, as it usually consists of diced vegetables mixed in a thick mayonnaise. Watch out, however, as there are versions with cubes of ham mixed in as well. And make sure that this, and all mayonnaise-based dishes, are freshly prepared.

5 Mariscos

Berberechos (cockles), *almejas* (clams), *mejillones* (mussels), *pulpo* (octopus), *sepia* (cuttlefish) and *zamburiñas* (baby clams) are favourite seafood options everywhere in Spain. Roasted *caracoles* (snails), prepared with garlic, can be a rich but delicious treat.

6 Champiñones al Ajillo

Mushrooms sautéed with garlic are a standard item on *tapas* menus. Other popular vegetable dishes include *judias* (green beans), particularly good stewed with tomatoes and garlic, and *escalibadas* (aubergines/eggplants) served in a salad that also features *pimientos* (green peppers).

Tapas are usually eaten standing up at the bar and sometimes come free with a drink.

7 Anchoas (Boquerones)

Anchovies and sardines are often served lightly fried in batter, but can just as likely be offered marinated and preserved in oil, or with a tomato sauce. You generally eat them minus the head but with all the bones.

8 Croquetas

Croquettes are made with chicken or fish and mashed potatoes, formed into balls and deep-fried. A variation on this theme are *soldaditos* (fritters), which can be made of vegetables, chicken or fish.

9 Albóndigas

"Meatballs" can be made from meat or fish and will most likely be stewed in a tomato sauce, together with garlic and spices. An alternative method of preparing chunks of meat, seafood or fish is by skewering them and grilling them as kebabs, either plain or spicy Moroccan-style.

Albóndigas

10 Alioli

This is mayonnaise laced with a powerful dose of garlic and is served as a dish in its own right, for dipping bread into or as a condiment. Another popular relish is *pipirrana*, a compote made of tomato, onion and pepper.

Top 10 Tapas Preparation Styles

1 Pickled

Mixed in with olives, you'll often find miniature gherkins, and possibly pearl onions, bits of garlic and hot peppers.

2 Marinated

Anchovies, sardines and seafood all come marinated. You'll see them sitting out on bars, possibly under glass, steeped in olive oil.

3 Cured

The hams of Andalucía are lightly salted – mountain-cured are the best.

4 With Mayonnaise

Any dish can be an excuse to slather on the *alioli*. Two dishes that often have mayonnaise are *patatas alioli* and *ensaladilla*.

5 On Bread

Many *tapas* don't really come to life until applied to bread. Some are served already perched on a slice.

6 Egg-Based

Eggs are essential in *tortilla (see p68)* or come hard-boiled as a garnish.

7 Fried

Almost anything you can think of will turn up *frito* (batter-fried or sautéed), from fish to mushrooms.

8 Grilled or Roasted

If you want to ingest a little less oil, *a la plancha* (grilled) and *asado* (roasted) are the options to choose.

9 Stewed

Estofado variations include fish, meat, potato and vegetables, often in tomato sauce.

10 A la Marinera

This technique, commonly used for fish and seafood, is similar to poaching and involves wine, garlic and parsley.

Fino *is the most traditional drink to accompany* tapas, *although beer is also common.*

AROUND ANDALUCÍA

Seville
74–85

Sevilla & Huelva
Provinces
86–93

Málaga & Cádiz
Provinces
94–107

Granada & Almería
Provinces
108–117

Córdoba & Jaén
Provinces
118–123

ANDALUCÍA'S TOP 10

Left **Courtyard, Museo de Bellas Artes** Right **Tiled sign, Fábrica Real de Tabacos**

Seville

NDALUCÍA'S CAPITAL IS AN ARISTOCRATIC YET RELAXED CITY, *with a fabulous and ancient cultural heritage that dates back beyond recorded history. Its fate has always been tied to its river, the Río Guadalquivir ("the great river" in Arabic), and the trade it offered the city. Today much of the riverfront is made up of an attractive tree-lined promenade. To take in all of the historic centre of Seville would require at least a week, as there is so much to see in the way of art and architecture as well as distinctive neighbourhoods each with their own charm. But its highlights, including the spectacular cathedral, Moorish and Renaissance palaces and fine museums, are all within walking distance of each other and could be handled in a weekend, giving you just a taste of one of Spain's most beautiful cities.*

Seville Cathedral

Sights

1 Seville Cathedral & La Giralda

2 Real Alcázar

3 Casa de Pilatos

4 Museo de Bellas Artes

5 Fábrica Real de Tabacos

6 Ayuntamiento

7 Plaza de España

8 Museo Arqueológico

9 Torre del Oro & Torre de Plata

10 Cartuja de Santa María de las Cuevas

1 Seville Cathedral & La Giralda

Legend has it that when the *sevillanos* decided to build their cathedral in the 15th century, they proclaimed their intention to erect an edifice so huge that later generations would call them mad. They achieved their aim with the largest church (by volume, not floorplan) in Christendom *(see pp14–15)*.

2 Real Alcázar

This exotic palace was primarily the brainchild of Pedro I, who had it built as a lavish love-nest for himself and his mistress, María de Padilla *(see pp16–17)*.

3 Casa de Pilatos

Erroneously said to be based on the house of Pontius Pilate in Jerusalem, this 15th-century gem is the most sumptuous of Seville's urban mansions. It is a delightful blend of Mudéjar (Christian-Islamic), Gothic and Renaissance styles, punctuated with Classical statuary. Look for the head of the Greek boy, Antinous, who died as a teenager and was deified by his grief-stricken lover, Emperor Hadrian, in the 2nd century *(see p38)*. ✆ Plaza de Pilatos 1 • Map N3 • Open 9am–7pm daily (until 6pm Oct–Feb); 954 22 52 98 • Adm

Courtyard, Casa de Pilatos

Domed ceiling, Museo de Bellas Artes

4 Museo de Bellas Artes

Among Spain's finest art repositories, it is second only to the Prado in Madrid for its range of great Spanish paintings. Housed in a former 17th-century convent, the collection focuses on the Seville School, led by Zurbarán, Cano, Murillo and Valdés Leal, including Murillo's touching *Virgen de la Servilleta*. Don't miss El Greco's poignant portrait of his son and the polychrome terracotta of St Jerome by Florentine sculptor Pietro Torregiano, a colleague of Michelangelo's *(see p54)*. ✆ Plaza del Museo 9 • Map K2 • Open 3–8pm Tue, 9am–8pm Wed–Sat, 9am–2pm Sun • Adm €1.50 (free for EU Nationals)

5 Fábrica Real de Tabacos

Now a part of Seville University, this handsome 18th-century edifice is the second-largest building in Spain, after El Escorial in Madrid. Famous for its fun-loving female workers, who at one time rolled three-quarters of Europe's cigars, the old factory has been immortalized by *Carmen*, the world's most popular opera. The doomed heroine, a hot-blooded gypsy *cigarrera*, remains, for many, the incarnation of Spanish passion. ✆ C/San Fernando 4 • Map M5 • Open 8am–8:30pm Mon–Fri • Free

6 Ayuntamiento

This building has been the town hall since the 16th century. Inside, the rooms are decorated with historic paraphernalia of the city and the monarchy, in a blend of Gothic and Renaissance styles. Outside, the façades reflect the evolution of taste, from the original Renaissance Plateresque work with its finely carved stone-work, to the 19th-century attempt to copy the style, seen from Plaza de San Francisco *(see p38)*. ✆ *Plaza Nueva 1 • Map L3 • 954 59 01 45 • Open for pre-booked guided tours only, mid-Sep–Jul: 5:30 & 6pm Tue–Thu, noon Sat • Free*

7 Plaza de España

This semicircular plaza was designed as the centrepiece for the Ibero-American Exposition of 1929. Almost completely covered with gorgeous glazed tiles, its surfaces depict historic moments and heraldic symbols of the 40 regions of Spain. A boating canal follows the arc of the structure, crossed by colour-ful footbridges. The site was used as a set in the film *Star Wars: Attack of the Clones*, for its other-worldly feel. ✆ *Map N6*

Feria de Abril

The six-day Spring Fair, about two weeks after Easter, is a riot of colour and high spirits. Andalucían horses strut on parade, ridden by *caballeros* in traditional leather chaps, waistcoats and wide-brimmed *sombreros cordobeses*, often with dazzling, flower-like women perched behind. Fairy lights and fireworks brighten the way, the air is alive with music, the town is overflowing with marvellously decorated *casetas* (party marquees – most of them by invitation only), and drinking and dancing continues until dawn.

Museo Arqueológico

8 Museo Arqueológico

This Renaissance-style pavilion was also one of the fab-ulous structures created for the 1929 Exposition and now houses Andalucía's principal archaeologi-cal museum. The assemblage of artifacts ranges from Paleolithic finds, exhibited in the basement, to splendours of Roman and Moorish art, displayed on the upper floors. Outstanding are the Carambolo treasures of Tartessian gold, and the Roman sculpture collection is Spain's most prestigious. ✆ *Parque María Luisa • Open 3–8pm Tue, 9am–8pm Wed–Sat, 9am–2pm Sun; 954 23 24 01 • Adm*

9 Torre del Oro & Torre de Plata

Tradition states that the imposing 13th-century Moorish dodeca-hedral (12-sided) watchtower, the Torre del Oro (Tower of Gold), is named after the golden tiles that once adorned it. Others say its name derives from its use as a warehouse for the gold coming in from the New World during Seville's heyday. It now houses a small maritime museum. Nearby stands the Torre de Plata (Tower of Silver), a more modest octagonal tower, which most likely gets its name as a complement to its neighbour. Both towers originally formed part of the city's defences.

🔹 *Torre del Oro: Paseo de Colón; Map L4; Open Sep–Jul: 10am–2pm Tue–Fri, 11am–2pm Sat–Sun; Adm (except Tue)* • *Torre de Plata: C/Santander; 954 22 24 19; Map L4; Closed to the public*

10 Cartuja de Santa María de las Cuevas

This 15th-century monastery has had its ups and downs over the centuries. During Spain's Golden Age it was the favoured retreat of Christopher Columbus, whose remains were interred here for several decades. The monks went on to decorate their vast enclave with commissions from some of Seville's greatest artists – most of the works are now in the Museo de Bellas Artes *(see p75)*. In 1841 it became a ceramics factory. Finally restored as part of Expo '92, the complex is today home to a contemporary art museum. 🔹 *Isla de Cartuja* • *Map J1* • *Centro Andaluz de Arte Contemporáneo: Open 10am–9pm Tue–Sat (until 8pm Nov–May), 10am–3pm Sun; www.caac.es; Adm (except Tue)*

Torre del Oro

A Half-Day Walk Around the Barrio de Santa Cruz

Start at the exit to the **Real Alcázar** *(see pp16–17)*, which is on Patio de las Banderas. Turn right to find the Arco de la Judería, a covered alleyway that leads to the Callejón del Agua, running along the old Jewish Quarter's southern wall. As you proceed, you will be able to peep into some of the famously lush patios of these perfectly whitewashed houses. The writer Washington Irving once stayed at No. 2. After the wall ends, you'll see the **Jardines de Murillo** on your right *(see p79)*, where you can enjoy a tranquil stroll.

Then turn back to find **Plaza Santa Cruz** *(see p79)*, where the church that gave the neighbourhood its name once stood, until it was burned down by the French in 1810. A 17th-century wrought-iron cross stands here now. Cross a couple of streets west to find the **Hospital de los Venerables** *(see p78)*, and take in its delightful central courtyard and important art gallery. From here, go east to Calle Santa Teresa 8, the former home of the great artist Bartolomé Murillo *(see p56)*, who died here in 1682 after a fall while painting frescoes in Cádiz.

Finally, work your way back towards the **Cathedral** *(see pp14–15)* along Calle Mesín del Moro and then to Calle Mateos Gago. At No. 1 you'll find the **Cervecería Giralda** *(see p84)*, excellent for a drink and some *tapas* for either lunch or dinner.

Around Andalucía – Seville

Left **La Maestranza bullring** Right **Detail, Hospital de los Venerables**

🔟 Best of the Rest

1 La Lonja
Established in 1785, this is a storehouse for documents relating to the Spanish colonization of the New World *(see p54)*. ◈ Avda de la Constitución 3 • Map M4 • Open 8am–3pm Mon–Fri to researchers • Free

2 Hospital de los Venerables
Founded in the 17th century as a home for the elderly, the structure is now a cultural centre. The church features a *trompe-l'oeil* ceiling by Juan de Valdés Leal. ◈ Plaza de Doña Elvira 8 • Map M4 • Open 10am–2pm, 4–8pm daily • Adm

3 Museo de Artes y Costumbres Populares
Exhibits here include displays on flamenco and bullfighting. ◈ Plaza de América 3 • Open 3–8pm Tue, 9am–8pm Wed–Sat, 9am–2pm Sun • 954 23 25 76 • Adm

4 Hospital de la Caridad
This charity hospital was founded by reformed rake Miguel de Mañara, the inspiration for the mythical lady-killer, Don Juan. ◈ C/Temprado 3 • Map L4 • Open 9am–1:30pm, 3:30–7:30pm Mon–Sat, 9am–1pm Sun • 954 22 32 32 • Adm

5 La Maestranza
The "Cathedral of Bullfighting" becomes the focal point when the sporting season opens in April. ◈ Paseo de Colón 12 • Map L3

6 Barrio de Triana
This quarter, once home to Seville's gypsies, was known for producing flamenco artists and bullfighters. It still creates fine ceramics *(see p82)*. ◈ Map K4

7 Casa de la Condesa de Lebrija
A 15th-century mansion, embellished with mosaics from Itálica *(see p89)*. ◈ C/Cuna 8 • Map M2 • Open 10:30am–1:30pm, 5–8pm Mon–Fri, 10am–2pm Sat (10:30am–1:30pm, 4:30–7:30pm in winter) • 954 22 78 02 • Adm

8 Iglesia de San Luis
This is the most sumptuous Rococo-style church in Seville. ◈ C/San Luis • Map N1 • Open 9am–2pm Wed–Thu; 9am–2pm, 5–8pm Fri–Sat • Free

9 La Macarena
This district is home to Seville's adored religious icon, the Virgen de la Macarena. During Semana Santa *(see p60)* she is paraded on a silver float. ◈ Map N1

🔟 Convento de Santa Paula
The portal of this 15th-century convent is graced with decorations by Italian master Nicola Pisano. ◈ C/Santa Paula 11 • Map N1 • Open 10:30am–1pm, 4:30–6:30pm Tue–Sun • 954 536 330 • Adm

On the way out of the Convento de Santa Paula you can acquire some of the nuns' famous marmalades and other delights.

Left **Parque María Luísa** Right **Columbus monument, Jardines de Murillo**

🔟 Parks, Paseos and Plazas

1 Real Alcázar
These gardens are a blend of Moorish and Italian Renaissance styles *(see pp16–17)*.

2 Parque de María Luísa
This huge park dominates the southern end of the city. Its present design was laid out for the 1929 Exposition. Keep an eye out for peacocks perched in the trees. ◎ *Map M6*

3 Plaza de San Francisco and Plaza Nueva
These squares represent the heart of the city. Plaza de San Francisco (also called Plaza Mayor) is Seville's oldest and the focal point of public spectacles. Plaza Nueva is a pleasant park with a monument to King Fernando the Saint. ◎ *Map L3 & M3*

4 Jardines de Murillo
These formal gardens used to be the orchards and vegetable plots for the Alcázar. Donated to the city in 1911, they are named after Seville painter Bartolomé Murillo *(see p56)*. A monument to Columbus features the bronze prows of the *Santa María*, the caravel that bore him to the New World in 1492. ◎ *Map N4*

5 Plaza de Santa Cruz
This square was opened up when Napoleon's soldiers destroyed the church that once stood here. The square is now adorned with an ornate iron cross, La Cruz de la Cerrajería. ◎ *Map N4*

6 Calle Sierpes
This pedestrianized promenade is the principal shopping street of old Seville. Here's the place to window-shop for all the traditional flamenco and *feria* gear, and certainly the place to be seen during the early evening *paseo*. ◎ *Map L2*

7 Alameda de Hércules
Set off by pairs of columns at either end – the southern set are ancient Roman and are surmounted by 16th-century sculptures of Hercules and Julius Caesar – this once fashionable promenade is now a rather dusty affair, but is very popular for its nightlife. ◎ *Map M1*

8 Plaza de la Alfalfa
Once the location of the hay market, but now home to a Sunday morning pet market. Birds, puppies, exotic fish, lizards, mice and even silkworms have been known to turn up here. Also good for bars and restaurants. ◎ *Map M2*

9 Paseo Alcalde Marqués de Contadero
With the Torre del Oro at one end *(see p77)*, this tree-lined riverfront promenade makes for a pleasant stroll. ◎ *Map L4*

10 Jardines de San Telmo
The park of this Churrigueresque palace is one of the city's largest. The palace, built in 1682, is the headquarters of the regional government. ◎ *Map M5*

Following pages: **Parque María Luisa**

Left **El Mercadillo** Right **El Corte Inglés** sign

🔟 Shops and Markets

1 El Corte Inglés
Although you're unlikely to find any bargains here, the range of merchandise is impressive. Spain's main department store chain carries not only clothes and accessories, but also perfume, housewares, decorative items, CDs and sporting goods. There's also a food hall and supermarket, which stock gourmet foods. ✪ *Plaza del Duque de la Victoria 10 • Map L2*

2 Mango
For the latest in younger women's fashion trends, this is the place to come. ✪ *C/Velazquez 7–9 • Map L2*

3 Zara
Here you'll find hip, affordable clothing for the entire family. In summer, the linen blends and light cottons are just right for the Andalucían climate. Scents and sunglasses too.
✪ *Plaza del Duque de la Victoria • Map L2*

4 Angeles Méndez
This is a good spot to load up on all the flouncy dresses, mantillas, shawls and so forth that you will need to participate in the various festivals that abound in the region *(see pp60–61)*.
✪ *C/Alcaicería de la Loza 24 • Map M2*

5 Compás Sur
For music lovers there are CDs, DVDs and books covering a variety of genres from Fúsion to Flamenco. ✪ *C/Cuesta del Rosario 7-E; 954 21 56 62 • Map M2*

6 Sargadelos
Household items with an artful twist are the speciality here. Complete dinner and tea or coffee services are traditional but at the same time inventive.
✪ *C/Albareda 17; 954 21 67 08 • Map L3*

7 El Mercadillo
Just off the Alameda de Hércules *(see p79)*, El Jueves flea market, held every Thursday, consists mostly of old junk, books and posters. Still, it's fun to look for the occasional treasure. But beware of pickpockets. ✪ *C/de la Feria • Map M1*

8 Crafts Market
This is the place to find handmade jewellery, leather goods and cheap clothes. Thursday to Saturday. ✪ *Plaza del Duque de la Victoria • Map L2*

9 Old Train Station Shopping Centre
The old Córdoba train station has been restored to its former beauty and is now home to a shopping centre and entertainment complex. ✪ *Antigua Estación de Córdoba, Plaza de Armas • Map K2*

10 Cerámica Santa Ana
The place to buy the famous Triana pottery. In operation since 1870, this shop sells everything from replicas of 16th-century tiles to ashtrays. Similar workshops can be found on Calle Covadonga. ✪ *C/San Jorge 31, Barrio de Triana; 954 33 81 76 • Map K4*

Left **Teatro de la Maestranza** Right **Teatro Lope de Vega**

Flamenco and Theatre Venues

1 Teatro de la Maestranza
Seville's main theatre was constructed on a former munitions works, as part of Expo '92. It serves primarily as the city's opera house, putting on productions of all the standards, particularly those set in Seville, including *Carmen*, *Don Juan*, *The Marriage of Figaro* and *The Barber of Seville*. ⊗ *Paseo de Colón 22; 954 22 65 73 • Map L4*

2 Teatro Lope de Vega
Named after the "Spanish Shakespeare", who wrote more than 1,500 plays, this neo-Baroque theatre was built in 1929 as a casino and theatre for the Ibero-American Exposition. Modern and classical works, both musical and dramatic, are performed here. ⊗ *Avda de María Luísa; 954 59 08 67 • Map M5 • Closed Jul–Aug*

3 Teatro Alameda
Popular performances of all genres take to the stage of this modest theatre, with a strong emphasis on flamenco. It's also a good venue for contemporary Andalucían theatrical works. ⊗ *C/Crédito 13; 954 90 01 64*

4 Teatro Central
In season, this theatre highlights the *Flamenco Viene del Sur* series, concurrently with all sorts of theatre, dance and classical music. It's a starkly modern facility right on the river. ⊗ *C/José de Gálvez, Isla de Cartuja; 955 03 72 00 • Map J1 • Closed Jul–Sep*

5 El Palenque
Another modern venue, the main focus here is contemporary song and dance acts. ⊗ *C/Blas Pascal, Isla de Cartuja; 954 46 71 70 • Map J1*

6 El Arenal
The least tacky of the flamenco shows aimed at tourists, although without the soul-stirring authenticity of the real thing. If you come for the first show, the second is free. *(See p59).*

7 La Carbonería
A relaxed and authentic bar. Flamenco shows tend to happen on Monday and Thursday nights. ⊗ *C/Levíes 18; 954 21 44 60 • Map N3*

8 Los Gallos
Despite its popularity with tourists, the atmosphere here is genuine. First-rate flamenco performers. ⊗ *Plaza de Santa Cruz 11; 954 21 69 81 • Map N4 • Shows 9pm & 11:30pm daily*

9 Casa de la Memoria de al-Andalus
This cultural centre is dedicated to Jewish influence. Top flamenco artists and renditions of Sephardic music. ⊗ *C/Ximénes de Enciso 28; 954 56 06 70 • Map N3 • Shows 9pm daily*

10 El Patio Sevillano
Another venue that caters to the throngs of tourists who want a rousing flamenco show. ⊗ *Paseo de Cristobal Colón 11A; 954 21 41 20 • Map L4 • Shows 7:30pm & 10pm daily*

Left **Cervecería Giralda** Right **Tiled decoration, Patio San Eloy**

Cafés & Tapas Bars

1 Cervecería Giralda
This elegant establishment is built inside an ancient Moorish *hammam* (baths). It's a pleasant stop, with an excellent view of La Giralda *(see pp14–15)*. ✆ *C/ Mateos Gago 1; 954 22 74 35 • Map M3*

2 Barbacoa Coloniales
On a pleasant square, between the Iglesia San Salvador and the Convento de Santa Paula, lies this old-fashioned bar. The walls are decorated with faded photos of Seville in an earlier era. ✆ *Plaza del Cristo de Burgos 19; 954 21 41 91 • Map M2*

3 Patio San Eloy
Large and noisy, this place captures the genuine feel of old Seville, everyone drinking and snacking with animation. ✆ *C/San Eloy 9; 954 22 11 48 • Map L2*

4 Gran Tino
This enjoyable square's best-known bar offers outside seating and an interesting range of refreshments. It's particularly appealing on Sunday mornings, when there's a colourful pet market here. ✆ *Plaza de la Alfalfa 2; 954 21 08 83 • Map M2*

5 Bar San Lorenzo
Virtually the same since it opened in 1893; expect a littered floor, old wood, lots of regulars and some choice comestibles. An Alameda district institution. ✆ *Plaza de San Lorenzo 7; 954 38 15 58 • Map L1 • No credit cards*

6 La Ilustre Víctima
The name, "The Illustrious Victim", refers, of course, to the bull. Murals on the walls and a laidback ambience make it a favourite hangout for writers who frequent the Alameda district. ✆ *C/Correduría 35; 954 38 94 90 • Map M1*

7 La Alicantina
Great outdoor seating on the terrace and some delectable seafood delicacies to savour as you watch the hubbub on this busy square. ✆ *Plaza del Salvador 2–3; 954 22 61 22 • Map M3*

8 Plata
La Macarena district's modern choice for breakfast. It's right next to the equally modern basilica, where the revered La Macarena *(see p78)* holds court. ✆ *C/Resolana 2; 954 37 10 30 • Bus No. 34*

9 El Tejar
This tile-covered café is a fine vantage point in the Barrio de Triana *(see p78)* from which to watch the world go by. In the evenings, the owners sometimes mount flamenco shows, and often display the works of local artists. ✆ *C/San Jacinto 68; 954 34 44 87 • Map J4*

10 Bar Bistec
The "Steak Bar" is another characteristic Triana venue, traditional and full of local colour. It stays open late, as does almost everything in Andalucía. ✆ *C/Pelay Correa 34; 954 27 47 59 • Map K4*

Note that many Spanish bars and restaurants do not open until about 9pm for their evening trade.

Price Categories

For a three-course meal for one with half a bottle of wine (or equivalent meal), taxes and extra charges.

€	under €20
€€	€20–€30
€€€	€30–€40
€€€€	€40–€50
€€€€€	over €50

Above **El Rinconcillo**

TOP 10 More Places to Eat

1 Bar España
Not far from the cathedral and in a picture-perfect setting next to the Jardines de Murillo, this *tapas* bar is part of the very up-market Basque restaurant that it adjoins – Egaña Oriza.
◈ *C/San Fernando 41 • Map M5*

2 Casa Morales
Reputedly the second-oldest bar in town (1850), and it doesn't seem to have changed much. Drinks are still poured from old casks. Simple *tapas*. ◈ *C/García de Vinuesa 11 • Map L3*

3 La Sacristía
Generous *tapas* and a good selection of wines and sherries.
◈ *C/Mateos Gago 18 • Map M3*

4 La Albahaca
Set in a converted mansion, decorated with *azulejo* tiles. The seasonal menu may feature fish, wild mushrooms or almonds. ◈ *Plaza Santa Cruz 12 • Map N4 • 954 22 07 14 • €€€*

5 Hostería del Laurel
Old enough to have been mentioned in the 19th-century play *Don Juan*, this Santa Cruz favourite has hams hanging from the ceiling. The *tapas* are as memorable as the ambience. ◈ *Plaza de Doña Elvira 5 • Map M4*

6 Casa Plácido
Convenient for all the major sights, this venerable bar has more hams dangling, barrels of sherry, old posters and traditional *tapas*. ◈ *C/Mesón del Moro 5 & C/Ximenes de Enciso 11 • Map M3*

7 Taberna del Alabardero
This restaurant has earned itself a Michelin star. The setting is sumptuous, while the menu excels in meat dishes and local seafood. ◈ *C/Zaragoza 20 • Map L3 • 954 50 27 21 • €€€*

8 El Rinconcillo
The city's oldest *taberna* dates from 1670 and is an essential stop on your Seville itinerary. Traditionally the place where *tapa* was invented.
◈ *C/Gerona 40 • Map M2*

9 Eslava
This *tapas* bar offers specialities such as lamb with honey and courgette (zucchini) quiche.
◈ *C/Eslava 3-5 • Map L1*

10 Restaurante María Angeles
On the Triana side of Seville's oldest bridge, this place has superb views, as well as simple, traditional food. The riverside terrace offers the best panorama.
◈ *Puente de Isabel II • Map K4 • 954 33 74 98 • Dis. access • €–€€€*

Note: *Unless otherwise stated, all restaurants accept credit cards and serve vegetarian meals*

Left **El Rocío** Right **Palace wall painting, Écija**

Sevilla and Huelva Provinces

L EAVING BEHIND THE MAGNETIC ALLURE OF GLORIOUS SEVILLE, *the rest of Sevilla Province and neighbouring Huelva Province are among the least visited areas of Andalucía. Consequently, much of the zone has remained a rural hinterland, where time moves slowly and the old customs prevail. Some of the finest nature preserves are here, too, including the ecologically essential Coto de Doñana, mountainous reaches and pristine beaches, generally frequented by Spaniards rather than tourists. Culturally rich as well, each town and village shelters surprising art treasures and ancient marvels, where you may find yourself the only visitor – a welcome relief after the throngs encountered elsewhere in Andalucía.*

Sights

1. Parque Nacional Coto de Doñana
2. El Rocío
3. Huelva City
4. El Parque Minero de Río Tinto
5. Gruta de las Maravillas
6. Cazalla de la Sierra
7. Écija
8. Osuna
9. Carmona
10. Itálica

Necropolis, Carmona

Wetlands, Parque Nacional Coto de Doñana

Parque Nacional Coto de Doñana

Europe's largest nature reserve includes important wetlands and shifting dunes that are gradually moving inland. The fragile ecosystem can only be visited on guided tours *(see pp30–31)*.

El Rocío

The fact that this town resembles an Old West frontier outpost is no accident. The Spaniards who settled what are now the states of Texas, New Mexico and Arizona mostly came from this part of Spain and took their architectural style with them. Horses are still a normal way to get around here – hence the hitching posts. The place bursts into life during the annual Romería, one of Spain's largest festivals *(see p31)*. ✎ *Map B4*

Huelva City

Founded by the Phoenicians, Huelva was at its peak under the Romans – the Museo Provincial conserves remarkable archaeological finds. The city's other claim to fame is as the starting point of Columbus's epic voyage *(see p34)*. Huelva was the first port for New World trade, until Seville took over. ✎ *Map A4*
• *Museo Provincial: Alameda Sundheim 13, 959 25 93 00; Open 9am–8pm Tue–Sat, 9am–2pm Sun; Free*

El Parque Minero de Río Tinto

The Río Tinto (Red River) Mines, the world's oldest, have been exploited as a source of mineral wealth for some 5,000 years, and the gradual stripping away of the rich ore has left a weird moonscape shot through with coloured fissures. A museum details the mines' history. ✎ *Map B3 • Museo Minero: Plaza Ernest Lluch, 959 59 00 25; Open 10:30am–3pm, 4–7pm daily; Adm*

Gruta de las Maravillas

A guided tour of these marvellous caves – Spain's largest – will wind through beautiful chambers with naturally coloured formations and names such as the Hut, Organ, Cathedral, Quail and Twins. The last room is a notorious crowd-pleaser – the *Sala de los Culos* (Chamber of the Buttocks). In addition to the twelve caverns, there are also six underground lakes, which create stunning visual effects. The "Great Lake" lies under a 70 m (230 ft) high vaulted ceiling. ✎ *Pozo de la Nieve, Aracena, 959 12 83 55 • Map B3 • Open 10am–1:30pm, 3–6pm daily • Adm*

Gruta de las Maravillas

6 Cazalla de la Sierra

The main town in the Sierra Norte is a steep cluster of white-washed houses. It's a popular place for weekend getaways by *sevillanos* and particularly known for producing some of the area's famous anise-based tipples. Just 3 km (2 miles) outside of town is the magnificently situated former Carthusian monastery, now restored as part hotel, part arts centre with gallery. ◈ *Map C3 • La Cartuja de Cazalla arts centre: Open daily; 954 88 45 16; Adm*

7 Écija

Two nicknames for this town, in the plains east of Seville, render a clear idea of its chief glory and its biggest challenge. "The Town of Towers" refers to its 11 Baroque belltowers, all adorned with glazed tiles. "The Frying-Pan of Andalucía" is a reference to its searing summer temperatures, due to the fact that it's one of the few towns not built up a hill. Écija's archaeological museum is worth a visit. ◈ *Map D3 • Museo Histórico Municipal: Palacio de Benemejí, C/Cánovas del Castillo 4; Open 9am–2pm Tue–Sun (summer), 9:30am–1:30pm, 4:30–6:30pm Tue–Fri, 9am–2pm Sat–Sun (winter); Free*

La Campiña: Socialism versus Feudalism

The fertile Campiña valley has been in the hands of a few noble families since the Catholic Monarchs handed out huge tracts as fiefdoms. The people who worked the land were little more than serfs, a situation that still accounts for local poverty. In the village of Marinaleda, however, its mayor has created an island of social idealism, and has succeeded in wresting plots of property away from the landlords to be communally owned by the workers.

Palacio del Marqués de la Gomera, Osuna

8 Osuna

The enormously powerful Dukes of Osuna get the credit for endowing this town with exceptional architecture. The massive bulk of the Renaissance church, the Colegiata de la Asunción, dominates the scene; inside, there's an impressive painting of the Crucifixion by José de Ribera. The Universidad, also Renaissance, has tiled towers at its corners and a beautiful central courtyard. Elsewhere, fine mansions evoke the wealth of Spain's most powerful families *(see p38)*. ◈ *Map D4 • Collegiata: Plaza de la Encarnación; 954 81 11 21; Open May, Jun, Sep: 10am– 1:30pm, 4–7pm Tue–Sun; Jul–Aug: 10am– 1:30pm, 4–7pm Tue–Sat, 10am–1:30pm Sun; Oct–Apr: 10am–1:30pm, 3:30– 6:30pm Tue–Sun; Adm*

9 Carmona

The closest major town east of Seville has been continuously inhabited for more than 5,000 years. Its Roman remains are truly exceptional, especially the huge necropolis. The view from the originally Roman Puerta de Córdoba (Córdoba Gate) out over the sweeping plains also shouldn't be missed. Fine churches, palaces and *alcázares* adorn the site – one of the ancient castles is now restored as a spectacular parador *(see p140)*. ◈ *Map C3 • Necrópolis: Avda Jorge Bonsor 9; 954 14 08 11; Open 8:30am–2pm Tue–Fri, 10am–2pm Sat (summer); 9am–5pm Tue–Fri, 10am–2pm Sat–Sun (winter); Free*

10 Itálica

These wind-blown ruins were once the third largest city in the Roman empire, founded in 206 BC and home to some half a million people during the reign of Emperor Hadrian in the 2nd century. He was following in the glorious footsteps of his predecessor Trajan, who was another Itálica native. There's a huge amphitheatre to explore, as well as some fine mosaics amid the crumbling walls. Most of the wonders are still buried, however, while others have long since been quarried for their stone or moved to the Archaeological Museum in Seville *(see p76)*. ◈ *Avda de Extremadura 2, Santiponce; 955 99 73 76 • Map B3 • Open Apr–Sep: 8:30am–8:30pm Tue–Sat, 9am–3pm Sun; Oct–Mar: 9am– 5:30pm Tue–Sat, 10am–4pm Sun • Adm*

Roman ruins, Itálica

A Day in Columbus's Footsteps

Morning

🕐 The first stop on the tour is the Monasterio de Santa María de la Rábida, 9 km (5.5 miles) from **Huelva City** *(see p87)*, where a despondent Columbus found spiritual solace and practical help from the prior. The latter eventually persuaded Queen Isabel to sponsor the voyage that would discover America. The monks provide a tour *(10am–1pm, 4–7pm Tue–Sat; Adm)* showing visitors where Columbus stayed. It's also a pleasant place for refreshment or a meal in the shaded café.

Below the monastery, on the waterfront, la **Muelle de las Carabelas** sports lifesize replicas of the three boats that made the trip *(see p62)*.

Afternoon

Some 4 km (2.5 miles) northeast of La Rábida is the port, Palos de la Frontera, now silted up, from which Columbus set sail. More than half his crew also signed on here – the Iglesia de San Jorge is where the men heard mass before departing. Behind the church is La Fontanilla, the well that supplied them with water for the journey.

A further 7 km (4 miles) northeast is Moguer. Here, at the Convento de Santa Clara, Columbus gave thanks after his first voyage for having survived a storm in the Azores *(Tours 11am–7pm Tue–Sat; Adm)*.

At the end of your circuit, relax over a meal at La Parrala *(Plaza de las Monjas 22, Moguer • 959 37 04 52 • Closed Mon • €€)*.

If you don't have your own car, 10 bus trips make the Columbus circuit, from Huelva City to Moguer and back, Tue–Sat.

Left **Jabugo ham shop** Right **Almonaster La Real**

🔟 Best of the Rest

1 Aroche
Close to the Portuguese border, this town remains one of the best-preserved villages around. A wonderful oddity is the Museo del Santo Rosario, packed with rosaries that have belonged to Mother Teresa, John F Kennedy and General Franco, among others. ✎ *Map A2 • Museo del Santo Rosario: Paseo Ordoñez Valdés; Visit by appointment, 959 14 02 61; Free*

2 Niebla
Massive ramparts, built by the Moors in the 12th century, attest to the central role this town played in defending the land. The walls stretch for about 2.5 km (1.5 miles). ✎ *Map B4*

3 Cortegana
Dominated by a 13th-century castle, this is one of the largest towns in the area. ✎ *Map B3*

4 Almonaster La Real
A 10th-century mosque, a castle and a bullring are all clustered on the citadel overlooking the village *(see p42)*. ✎ *Map B3*

5 Jabugo
The "home of ham" produces Spain's most famous, known as *jamón ibérico* (cured Iberian ham), *jamón serrano* (mountain-cured ham) and *pata negra*, named after the black pigs that forage in the Sierra de Aracena. ✎ *Map B3*

6 Aracena
Capital of the sierra, this is an attractive town blessed with fresh air. The oldest town hall in the province offers information about the sierra. ✎ *Map B3*

7 Parque de la Sierra de Aracena y Picos de Aroche
This wild area provides plenty of inspiring views and fauna *(see p44)*. ✎ *Map B2*

8 Santa Olalla del Cala
Set off by a 13th-century castle, this village lies in the heart of the ham-curing area. The 15th-century parish church has a fine Baroque interior. ✎ *Map B3*

9 Alájar
A picturesque hamlet of whitewashed buildings, cobbled streets and a Baroque church *(see p42)*. ✎ *Map B3*

10 Zufre
This cliff-top community is like a mini-Ronda *(see pp24–5)*. The Paseo de los Alcaldes has rose and lime trees and a mirador with views across the terraced plain. ✎ *Map B3*

Ramparts, Niebla

Left **Mountain-cured ham** Right **Local ceramic dish**

🔟 Provincial Shopping

1 Aroche Markets
Thursday is the day the market stalls arrive in this Huelvan town. The market in Plaza de Abastos is a traditional produce spread, featuring the strong-flavoured goat's cheese favoured by the locals.

2 Souvenirs
In Aracena, head for the Calle Pozo de la Nieve, a cobbled street lined with souvenir shops. In El Rocío (see p87), souvenir stalls flank the church, hawking paraphernalia associated with the famous Romería (see p31).

3 Crafts
In addition to leather, Valverde del Camino is known for furniture and fine wooden boxes. Embroidery work from Aracena and Bollullos del Condado is worth seeking out, as well as linen tablecloths from Cortegana and Moguer. Nearer the coast it is also common to see Moroccan goods for sale.

4 Pottery
Pottery in this area has traditional patterns influenced by Moorish art. Items include jars, plates and water jugs, decorated in blue, green and white glazes.

5 Leather
The most notable leather goods come from Valverde del Camino. Choose botos camperos (cowboy boots) or the longer botos rocieros (Spanish riding boots). Many shops produce these items and other footwear, and a number of craftsmen make custom boots to order, taking three to four days to make a pair.

6 Huelva City
The provincial capital (see p87) boasts its own El Corte Inglés department store on Plaza de España, while the area around it and just off Plaza 12 de Octobre constitutes the main shopping district. The Mercadillo (open-air market) is held every Friday on the Recinto Colombino.

7 El Condado Wine District
The name refers to an area noted for its reliable white wine. Local finos include Condado Pálido and Condado Viejo.

8 Anise Liqueur
The liqueur of choice around this zone is anise-based. One of the best is Anis Cazalla from the eponymous town (see p88).

9 Ham
The Mesón Sánchez Romero Carvajal in Jabugo is one of the top producers of the local jamón ibérico (see p90).

10 Cured Fish
Considered a great delicacy and priced accordingly, raw wind-cured tuna (mojama) is an acquired taste. Isla Cristina is the main centre of production, but you can buy it in the Mercado del Carmen in Huelva City.

Left & Right **Casa Curro, Osuna**

Cafés and Tapas Bars

1 Bar Plaza, Carmona
In the heart of town, with terrace seating out in the square, this is a great little place for *tapas*. Go for the assortment menu if you want to be adventurous. One of the specialities is the rustic stew *pisto*, a concoction of vegetables with a poached egg. ⊗ *Plaza San Fernando 2; 954 19 00 67 • Map C3*

2 Bar La Reja, Écija
This local favourite offers a wide choice of *tapas* and *raciones* and the leisurely atmosphere invites sitting around and eavesdropping on local gossip. ⊗ *C/Elvira 1; 954 83 30 12 • Map D3 • Closed Sun*

3 Casa Curro, Osuna
A few blocks from the main square, this is a premier *tapas* bar. It's diminutive, but worth seeking out for the quality. ⊗ *Plazuela Salitre 5; 955 82 07 58 • Map D4*

4 El Martinete, Cazalla
This minuscule bar is part of the facilities for a camp site. The plus here is that along with your reasonably priced *tapas* there are woods and waterfalls to enjoy. ⊗ *Ctra Estación de Cazalla km12; 955 88 65 33 (information) • Map C3 • Closed Mon*

5 La Puerta Ancha, Ayamonte
A sociable place that purports to be the original town bar. There are tables on the square and good prices, too, for their line of drinks, *tapas* and other snacks. ⊗ *Plaza de la Laguna 14; 959 32 19 96 • Map A4*

6 Espuma del Mar, Isla Canela
This beachside establishment has *al fresco* tables so you can people-watch while sampling tasty *tapas*. The speciality is, of course, fresh fish and seafood. Try *raya* (skate) in one of its various manifestations. ⊗ *Paseo de los Gavilanes; 959 47 72 85 • Map A4*

7 Bar Chimbito, Punta Umbría
An unconventional *chiringuito* (beach bar) popular for drinks and snacks, including grilled and fried fish. On an old ferry boat on the river, downstream from Huelva City. ⊗ *Map A4*

8 Bar Lalo, Aroche
A little bar with balconies looking on to the plaza. For something different try the local liqueur made from *bellotas* (acorns). ⊗ *Plaza Juan Carlos • Map A2*

9 Café Bar Manzano, Aracena
On the south side of the town square this traditional bar is a classic Sierra place for coffee and a pastry. ⊗ *Plaza del Marqués de Aracena 22 • Map B3 • Closed Tue, last week Sep*

10 Hostería La Rábida
Next to an old monastery just east of Huelva where Columbus found spiritual retreat. You can have a drink or snack, or enjoy a full meal. ⊗ *Paraje de la Rábida; 959 350035 • Map A4 • Closed Mon, and Jan*

Price Categories

For a three-course		
meal for one with half	€	under €20
a bottle of wine (or	€€	€20–€30
equivalent meal), taxes	€€€	€30–€40
and extra charges.	€€€€	€40–€50
	€€€€€	over €50

Above **Local seafood**

🔟 Restaurants

1 Restaurante San Fernando, Carmona

Carmona's classiest choice occupies an old mansion and overlooks the eponymous plaza. Expect fine service and a well thought out menu that features a range of local game, lamb, duck and fresh fish. Great desserts. ◈ C/Sacramento 3 • Map C3 • 954 14 35 56 • Closed Sun D, Mon • €€

2 Restaurante Las Ninfas, Écija

Housed in the historic Palacio de Benameji this is a memorable restaurant. The cuisine is equally refined and light, with special dishes highlighting fresh fish. ◈ C/Elvira 1 • Map D3 • 955 90 45 92 • Closed Mon • €

3 Restaurante Doña Guadalupe, Osuna

A place to try *rabo de toro* (stewed bull's tail), game, or *Perdiz con Arroz*, (Partridge with Rice). Homemade desserts are a treat. ◈ Plaza Guadalupe 6–8 • Map D4 • 954 81 05 58 • Closed Tue, 1–15 Aug • €

4 Cambio de Tercio, Cazalla

This place is popular with devotees of rural cookery. Specialities include *somillo de cerdo ibérico en salsa de setas* (Iberian pork chops in wild mushroom sauce) and for dessert *tarta de castañas* (chestnut tart). ◈ C/Virgen del Robledo 53 bajo, Constantina • Map C3 • 955 88 10 80 • Closed Tue, last week Sep • €

5 Mesón Las Candelas, Aljaraque

This attractive restaurant is the best for perfect seafood and fish. ◈ Ctra Punta Umbria, Avda de Huelva • Map A4 • 959 31 83 01 • Closed Sun • €€

6 El Rinconcito, Huelva City

A neighbourhood establishment that serves honest regional dishes centring on seafood, fish and ham. Occasional flamenco performances. ◈ C/Marina 4 • Map A4 • 959 24 66 38 • No credit cards • €

7 Casa Luciano, Ayamonte

The place for tempting seafood and fish stews. Try the mouthwatering *atún al horno* (baked tuna). ◈ Avda La Palma 1 • Map A4 • 959 47 10 /1 • €€

8 Aires de Doñana, El Rocío

French windows provide panoramic views of the marshes here. The *Pato con Arroz* (Duck with Rice) is a treat. ◈ Avda La Canaliega, 1 • Map B4 • 959 44 27 19 • Closed Mon, 20 days in July • €€€

9 Asador Marisqueria Picos de Aroche, Aroche

A wide variety of meat (try the local Iberian pig!) and seafood is on offer at this lovely grillhouse. ◈ N433, km 127 Aroche • Map A2 • 959 14 01 87 • €

🔟 Casa El Padrino, Alájar

This rustic favourite is known for its tasty regional cuisine. ◈ Plaza Miguel Moya 2 • Map B3 • 959 12 56 01 • Closed Mon–Thu (except Aug) • €

 Note: Unless otherwise stated, all restaurants accept credit cards and serve vegetarian meals

Left **Arcos de la Frontera** Right **Sherry barrels, Jerez de la Frontera**

Málaga and Cádiz Provinces

THESE TWO ANDALUCÍAN PROVINCES *are a heady mix of cultural and recreational riches seldom equalled elsewhere in the world. Europe's oldest city, Cádiz, is located here, but the presence of history is balanced by the hedonistic delights of the Costa del Sol and its fine beaches. Some of the region's most dramatic landscapes lure nature-lovers, while others are drawn by the charms of the famed* pueblos blancos *(white villages), the most renowned being stupendous Ronda, birthplace of that strongest of Spanish traditions, the bullfight. This is also the area that produces the world-famous fortified wines known as sherry, as well as the celebrated sweet wines of* Málaga. *Finally, Europe's southernmost point is located here, Tarifa, with views over to North Africa, and a stone's throw away, the Rock of Gibraltar, an eccentric enclave of Britishness on the Mediterranean coast.*

Sights

1. Cádiz
2. Ronda
3. Costa del Sol
4. Málaga
5. Antequera
6. Pueblos Blancos
7. Gibraltar
8. Arcos de la Frontera
9. Jerez de la Frontera
10. Costa de la Luz

Antequera

Around Andalucía – Málaga & Cádiz Provinces

1 Cádiz

At the apex of the Atlantic's untamed Costa de la Luz *(see p98)*, this city floats like an ancient dream on what was originally its own island. With good claim to being Europe's oldest city, it's thought to have been founded by the ubiquitous Phoenicians in around 1104 BC. Much of what can be seen today, however, dates from the 18th century, the city having been almost completely razed by an Anglo-Dutch raid in 1596. The vast Catedral Nueva (1722) is one of Spain's largest churches, and many Baroque edifices enhance this unpretentiously beautiful provincial capital and, apart from two weeks in February when it stages Spain's most celebrated Carnaval bash *(see p60)*, it remains very much under-visited *(see pp22–3)*.

2 Ronda

To many visitors over the centuries, this town evokes the "real" Andalucía, at its wild and spectacular best. This mountain rock eyrie is quite literally

Nerja, Costa del Sol

breathtaking, being dramatically sliced down the middle by El Tajo, a fantastically deep and narrow limestone ravine, formed over thousands of years by the Río Guadalevín. The town itself is essentially two in one – the ancient half being steeped in rich Moorish history, with lovely cobbled streets, while the more modern part on the north side of the gorge sees to contemporary everyday needs *(see pp24–5)*.

3 Costa del Sol

Still living up to its well-earned reputation as one of the world centres for sun, surf and cheap, superficial fun, this string of former Mediterranean fishing villages nevertheless retains more than at first meets the eye. To those who care to look beyond the brash tourist enclaves, there is still much authentic charm on offer here – and even a good share of places that offer the chance of tranquil reflection – especially in the towns of Estepona, Nerja, Mijas and ultra-classy Marbella *(see p48)*. Year-round golf makes the whole area a great attraction for international lovers of the sport *(see p103)* and, in high season in particular, Torremolinos is the place to find some of Spain's liveliest nightlife *(see pp26–7)*.

Puente Nuevo, Ronda

In early September Ronda's bullring stages the Corridas Goyescas, in which matadors fight in 19th-century style costumes.

Málaga

4 Despite being home to the main airport bringing holiday-makers to the Costa del Sol, this provincial capital has been bypassed by the brunt of the "sun coast" development, and thus also by the swarms of foreign tourists. It has managed to hold onto its Spanish-ness quite admirably – despite recent attempts to bring it up to speed with the buzzing Costa lifestyle. An important trading port since ancient times, it was the favourite city of poet Garcia Lorca *(see p57)*, who loved it for its rawness. But its even greater claim to artistic fame is that it was the birthplace of Pablo Picasso, a fact that has now, at long last, been acknowledged by the presence of a Picasso museum, the third largest in the world dedicated to the modern master *(see p55)*. Málaga's alcázar, built between the 8th and 11th centuries, includes a Roman amphitheatre. ◈ *Map E5*
• *Museo Picasso: C/San Agustín 8; 952 60 27 31; www.museopicassomalaga.org; Open Tue–Sun; Adm*

Setenil, a pueblo blanco

Antequera

5 So ancient that even the Romans called it Antiquaria, this market town presents a wonder-fully condensed architectural history of the entire area, beginning with Neolithic dolmens dating from between 4500 and 2500 BC. In addition, there are significant Roman ruins, including villas with outstanding mosaics, a Moorish Alcazaba (closed to the public), the 16th-century Arco de los Gigantes, and fine Renaissance palaces and churches to explore. Many treasures originally found in the town – including the exquisite Ephebe of Antequera, a rare, life-size Roman bronze of a young boy – are displayed in the Municipal Museum, housed in an 18th-century palace. ◈ *Map D4*
• *Museo Municipal: Palacio Nájera, Plaza del Coso Viejo, 952 70 40 51; Open Oct–May: 10am–1:30pm, 4:30–6:30pm Tue–Fri, 10am–1:30pm Sat, 11am–1:30pm Sun, evening hours vary in summer; Adm*

Pueblos Blancos

6 The term "white villages" refers to the profusion of whitewashed hillside hamlets in the Serranía de Ronda, the mountainous territory around Ronda. Many of them are truly spectacular and it's well worth spending several days driving from one to the other, and then striking out on foot to take in some of the views *(see p52)*. Towns not to miss include Grazalema, Zahara de la Sierra, Gaucín, Casares, Setenil, Jimena de Libár and Manilva. Villagers, who originally settled on these plains to protect themselves from potential bandits in the lowlands, have lived the same way of life for centuries, and retain a strong agricultural tradition. Between Grazalema

Gibraltar

and Zahara, you'll go through Andalucía's highest mountain pass, the breathtaking Puerto de las Palomas (The Pass of the Doves). ◈ *Map C5*

7 Gibraltar

This gargantuan chunk of limestone rising up from the Mediterranean was one of the mythic Pillars of Hercules. Yet, despite being nicknamed "The Rock", as a worldwide symbol of stability and security, this fortress is actually a serious political football these days. Taken by the English in 1704 as part of the War of the Spanish Succession, today it is still very much a part of the British ethos, and only grudgingly do the Spaniards who live around it even acknowledge its existence. The Spanish government meanwhile most definitely wants it back. Legend has it that Britain will retain sovereignty of the rock as long as its most famous residents, the wild Barbary apes, remain, but their increasing number does not prevent on-going diplomatic arguments. Still, if you're homesick for Englishness, cross over the frontier at La Línea to enjoy some fish and chips or a pint of ale. ◈ *Map C6*

A Morning Walk in Jerez de la Frontera

Begin your tour at the impressive alcázar, with its many Moorish remains, including restored gardens, a mosque and a *hammam* (baths), as well as a *camera obscura* providing views of the city and beyond. Beside it is the stunningly decorated cathedral, extravagantly rich inside and out. Note the fine painting of *The Sleeping Girl* by Zurbarán in the sacristy.

Next take the tour – with tastings – of the **González-Byass bodega** *(see p66)*, featuring possibly the oldest cellars in Jerez, with one designed by Gustave Eiffel. Don't miss the many signatures of famous people on the barrels (called "butts"), including Queen Victoria, Cole Porter, Martin Luther King and General Franco, among others.

Continuing on north, the **Pedro Domecq bodega** *(see p66)* also offers tours and is distinctively Moorish in style. A block further north, pop into the Museo Arqueológico to see the prized Greek bronze helmet from the 7th century BC, and then enter the Barrio de Santiago. This gently dilapidated neighbourhood of maze-like alleyways is home to a sizeable gypsy community and numerous flamenco venues.

To cap off your walk, continue straight out of the *barrio* to the east, past the Church of San Juan, to Restaurante Gaitán *(C/Gaitán 3 • 956 34 58 59 • €)* for a lunch of excellent Andalucían and Basque food.

Around Andalucía – Málaga & Cádiz Provinces

Sherry, Brandy and Wine

The famed "Sherry Triangle" is comprised of the towns of Jerez, Sanlúcar de Barrameda and El Puerto de Santa María. The rich, nutty fortified wine has been produced here since ancient times, using vines imported by the Phoenicians some 3,000 years ago. In Roman times it was exported all over the empire, and it has been popular in England since the Elizabethan age. Sherry comes in a number of variants, to do with degrees of dryness or sweetness. The *fino* and *manzanilla* are dry and light, while the *amontillado* and *oloroso* are more robust. Brandy de Jerez is darker, richer and sweeter than brandy from France.

8 Arcos de la Frontera

Another town built atop a sheer cliff, this is probably the most dazzling of the *pueblos blancos* and the one situated furthest west. As ancient as any town in the region, little remains of the period before the *reconquista*, when it received its "de la Frontera" appellation, meaning it was a bastion "on the frontier" between Christian and Moorish Spain. The Galería de Arte Arx-Arcis crafts museum and shop displays locally fashioned carpets, blankets, baskets and pottery *(see p102)*.
◈ *Map C5 • Galería de Arte Arx-Arcis: C/Marques de Torresoto 11, 956 70 39 51; Open 10:30am–2:30pm, 5–9:30pm Mon–Sat; Free*

9 Jerez de la Frontera

The largest city in Cádiz province *(see p97)* is synony-mous with the production of "sherry", which is simply a corruption of "Jerez" – itself a corruption of the original Phoenician name of Xeres *(see p67)*. Before that, it was part of the fabled Tartessian civilization (8th century BC). Sights include an array of religious edifices, various palaces and a rather academic archaeological museum. However, flamenco and horses also get the credit for bringing the city international fame. It has a renowned centre for equestrian art, Andalucían style, and is home to one of the largest remaining gypsy populations, a determining force in flamenco tradition *(see pp58–9)*. ◈ *Map B5*

10 Costa de la Luz

This stretch of Atlantic coast, named after its charac-teristic bright light *(luz)* and covering the area from Chipiona to Tarifa, is still off the beaten path despite recent attempts to exploit its wild loveliness. Part of what protects it are the prevailing winds, wonderful for windsurfers but wretched for sunbathers, who may have to face wind-tossed sands travelling at fairly high speeds. Still, there are excellent beaches that can be enjoyed, often backed by cliffs, and modest resorts, such as Chipiona *(see p99)*, mostly frequented by Spaniards.
◈ *Map B5–C6*

Costa de la Luz

Left **El Chorro gorge** Right **El Puerto de Santa María**

🔟 Best of the Rest

1 El Torcal
A mountain nature reserve, great for hiking. The bizarre limestone rock formations are the big draw *(see p44)*. ✎ *Map D4*

2 El Chorro
The Chorro Gorge is a deep ravine, worn through a mountain of sheer rock by the Río Guadalhorce. You can walk up to the rail bridge and through the tunnel to get the best views. ✎ *Map D4*

3 Alcázar de Jerez
Jerez's Moorish fortress was originally part of a 4-km (2.5-mile) wall. A well-preserved mosque, now the Santa María La Real chapel, features an octagonal cupola over the *mihrab* (prayer niche). ✎ *Alameda Vieja, 956 31 97 98 • Map B5 • Open May–mid-Sep: 10am–7:30pm Mon–Sat, 10am–2:30pm Sun; mid-Sep–Apr: 10am–5:30pm daily • Adm*

4 Tarifa
The most southerly point of Europe, 11 km (7 miles) from Africa. Tarifa was the first town taken by the Moors in AD 710. Today it is a favoured spot for windsurfing. ✎ *Map C6*

5 Algeciras
Although the town of Algeciras is industrial and polluted, its port is the best in Spain; it is from here that you can catch the ferry to Morocco. It is fun to peruse the Moorish bazaars while waiting for the boat to take you across to the real thing. ✎ *Map C6*

6 El Puerto de Santa María
One of the towns of the Sherry Triangle. Three *bodegas* can be visited for tours and tastings *(see pp66–7)*. ✎ *Map B5*

7 Sanlúcar de Barrameda
Famed for its *manzanilla* sherry and superb seafood, the town also offers beautiful churches, palaces and a tour of a *bodega*. ✎ *Map B5*

8 Chipiona
This pretty resort town is crowded with Spanish beach enthusiasts in high season. The pace of life is leisurely, consisting of surf and miles of golden sand during the day, then strolls and ice cream until late in the evening. ✎ *Map B5*

9 Vejer de la Frontera
Of all the *pueblos blancos (see p96)*, this one has kept its Moorish roots most intact. Its original four Moorish gates still stand and its labyrinthine streets seem barely to have changed in 1,000 years. ✎ *Map C6*

10 Medina Sidonia
The most important edifice here is the 15th-century church of Santa María la Coronada, built over an earlier mosque. The interior features a 15-m (50-ft) high *retablo*. ✎ *Map C5 • Iglesia de Santa María la Coronada: Plaza Iglesia Mayor; Open 10am–2pm, 4–8pm daily (summer), 10:30am–2pm, 4:30–7:30pm (winter); Adm*

Following pages: Cádiz Cathedral

Left **Hecho en Cádiz** Right **Mediterráneo**

Provincial Shopping

Málaga Wines
1 The Bodega El Pimpi in Málaga's old town is decorated like a traditional Andalucían house, together with wine barrels and pots of geraniums in the windows, while the walls display photos of all the celebrities who have been here. Choose from among the sweet wines of the Málaga area, based on the Moscatel and Pedro Ximénez grapes *(see p67)*. ✎ *C/Granada 68 • Map R5*

Leather
2 In the shops of Ronda *(see pp24–5)* you'll find some of the best prices on leather goods of anywhere in Spain. Many of the items have well-known labels, since fashion houses often have contracts with leather factories in this area.

Mediterráneo, Cádiz
3 This is the best place in Cádiz to find provincial crafts. There's an excellent array of practical and decorative ceramics, rugs, blankets, ponchos, candles, jewellery and lots more, all at very affordable prices. ✎ *C/San Pedro 12 • Map B5*

Hecho en Cádiz, Cádiz
4 Paintings and sculptures by local artists are available here, but they also carry a full line of gastronomic specialities from the area, including honey, wine, olive oil, as well as crafts of all sorts. ✎ *Plaza Candelaria, 956 25 99 08 • Map B5*

Los Duros Antiguos, Cádiz
5 This is the place for CDs of Carnaval music, videos of the zany goings-on, commemorative shirts and posters *(see p60)*. ✎ *C/Beato Diego de Cádiz, 956 21 11 68 • Map B5*

Flamenco Costumes
6 One of the very best places to find genuine flamenco gear is Jerez de la Frontera. Head for Calle del Flamenco. ✎ *Map B5 • Francos 49, Jerez, 956 34 01 39*

Equestrian Equipment
7 Jerez is also one of the best places in the world for refined horseriding gear. Arcab is a good starting point. ✎ *Map B5 • Arcab: Avda Duque de Abrantes, Jerez, 956 32 41 00*

Sherry
8 Jerez de la Frontera is, of course, also the prime spot to savour the finer points of a *fino*, a *manzanilla*, an *amontillado* or an *oloroso (see pp66–7)*.

Traditional Textiles
9 The villages of Grazalema and Arcos de la Frontera *(see p98)* are known for their blankets, ponchos, rugs and other woven textiles.

Gibraltar Shopping
10 The shopping draw here is twofold: there's no sales tax and it's mostly duty-free and most of the leading UK high street names are represented, such as Marks & Spencer and The Body Shop. ✎ *Map C6*

Left & Right **Costa del Sol golf courses**

ᵀᴼᴾ10 Costa del Sol Golf Courses

1 Valderrama
Of the 60-odd golf clubs along the Costa, this is the most famous – it hosted the Ryder Cup in 1997. A Robert Trent Jones masterpiece and rated number one in continental Europe. ◊ *Ctra Cádiz-Málaga km132, Sotogrande • Map D6 • 956 79 12 00*

2 Real Club de Golf Sotogrande
Royal Sotogrande opened in 1964 and is still one of Europe's top 10 courses. Green-fee-paying visitors are welcome if they book in advance. The Robert Trent Jones design features mature trees and plenty of water obstacles. ◊ *Paseo del Parque, Sotogrande • Map D6 • 956 78 50 14*

3 San Roque
Opened in 1990, San Roque is a Dave Thomas design. The course was planned so that the holes are located in the same direction as the prevailing wind. ◊ *N-340 km126.5, San Roque • Map C6 • 956 61 30 30 • www.sanroqueclub.com*

4 Real Club Las Brisas
Las Brisas is recognized as one of the finest courses in Europe. Also designed by Robert Trent Jones and opened in 1968, it has hosted the World Cup on two occasions and the Spanish Open three times. It features raised greens, numerous sand traps and water features. ◊ *Urb. Neuva (Andalucia), above Puerto Banús, Marbella • Map D5 • 952 81 08 75*

5 Alcaidesa Links
The only links course in Spain opened in 1992, designed by Peter Alliss and Clive Clark. ◊ *N-340 km124.6, La Línea • Map C6 • 956 79 10 40 • www.golf-andalucia.net*

6 Golf El Paraíso
This British-style golf club was designed by Gary Player. ◊ *Ctra N-340, km167, Estepona • Map D5 • 952 88 38 35*

7 Los Arqueros
This was the Costa's first course to be designed by Spanish champ Seve Ballesteros. It offers a stiff test even for professionals. ◊ *Ctra de Ronda km163.5, Benahavis • Map D5 • 952 78 67 07*

8 Miraflores
Designed by Folco Nardi, Miraflores has many challenging holes. ◊ *Riviera del Sol, Ctra de Cadiz km198, Mijas • Map D5 • 952 93 19 60*

9 La Duquesa
A Trent Jones design. The front nine holes begin in a westerly direction then finish with a long par five. ◊ *Urb. El Hacho, N-340 km143, Manilva (west of Estepona) • Map D5 • 952 89 04 25*

10 La Cañada
Here the long 1st hole sets the tone for a tough round of golf – the 4th is a trek into the unknown with no view of the green until the third shot. ◊ *Ctra Guadiaro km1, Guadiaro, San Roque • Map C6 • 956 79 41 00*

All of the golf courses charge a green-fee admission that varies between €50 and €300. Some offer day packages.

Left **Dreamers** Right **Olivia Valere**

Costa del Sol Nightlife

1 Olivia Valere, Marbella
This club is the Costa hot spot of the moment. Designed by the same creative genius who did Paris's famous Buddha Bar, it attracts the rich and beautiful like moths to the flame. Very exclusive and expensive. ⊗ Crta de Istán, km0.8 • Map D5

2 La Comedia, Marbella
Puerto Banús's party palace is where the young and beautiful dance into the early hours. It gets going at around 3am. ⊗ Plaza de la Comedia, Local 2 • Map D5

3 Dreamers, Marbella
Another choice with a youthful atmosphere, this disco features go-go dancers and live acts. Summer nights are brightened up by international DJs who come to spin the latest sounds. ⊗ Ctra N-340 km175, Rio Verde, Nueva Andalucía • Map D5

4 Kiu, Benalmádena
This is the largest of the discos on this busy square. The Atlantis room is the best area for banging club tunes. ⊗ Plaza Sol y Mar • Map D5

5 Casino Torrequebrada, Benalmádena Costa
Located in the Hotel Torrequebrada, the casino has tables for blackjack, chemin de fer, punto y banco and roulette. The nightclub offers a flamenco show. Smart dress. ⊗ Ctra de Cádiz • Map D5

6 Aqua, Torremolinos
Top spot in the port. A large club with a spacious outdoor terrace and tropical ambience. Smart dress. ⊗ Pueblo Marinero s/n • Map E5

7 Mango, Benalmadena
Popular with the younger crowds, this club has an electric atmosphere. Most of its bars have a small dance floor and throbbing music. ⊗ Plaza Solymar • Map D5

8 The Palladium, Torremolinos
This popular disco is on two floors and boasts a huge indoor swimming pool. Strobes, a great sound system, and go-go dancers complete the scene. ⊗ Avda Palma de Mallorca 36 • Map E5

9 La Taberna de Pepe Lopez, Torremolinos
This flamenco venue is highly touristy, but fun. Shows take place here between 10pm and midnight every night. ⊗ Plaza de la Gamba • Map E5

10 Gay Torremolinos
One of the most popular gay spots is Abadía (No. 521). Tensión (No. 524) is good too, although names are always shifting along this gay-orientated street. Another venue of interest is Minogues (in Montemar, near Benalmadena Marina), which hosts live drag shows. ⊗ All along C/La Nogalera • Map E5

Price Categories

For a three-course meal for one with half a bottle of wine (or equivalent meal), taxes and extra charges.

€	under €20
€€	€20–€30
€€€	€30–€40
€€€€	€40–€50
€€€€€	over €50

Above **Bar Altamirano**

🔟 Costa del Sol Places to Eat

1 La Posá Dos, Estepona
Great Spanish food is featured here, with specialities such as roast lamb and the chef's own special creations. A romantic dinner choice. ◈ *C/Caridad 95 • Map D5 • 952 80 00 29 • Closed L • €€*

2 Bar Altamirano, Marbella
Despite Marbella's glitzy image there are several afford-able and traditional *tapas* bars. This is one of them, just south-east of Plaza Naranjos; it even has its seafood specialities listed on ceramic menus. ◈ *Plaza Altamirano 4 • Map D5 • 952 82 49 32 • Closed Wed, mid-Jan–mid-Feb • €*

3 El Estrecho, Marbella
Another winning *tapas* bar and a local favourite. There's a pleasant terrace, fish and sea-food treats and nice *fino*. Try the *Roqueron al Limon* (Anchovies in Lemon). ◈ *C/San Lázaro • Map D5 • 952 77 00 04 • Closed Sun, first 2 weeks in Jun & Christmas • €*

4 La Sirena, Benalmádena Costa
On the beachfront, and the paella is one of the best in the area. ◈ *Paseo Marítimo • Map D5 • 952 56 02 39 • Dis. access • €€*

5 Bodegas Quitapenas, Torremolinos
An excellent seafood *tapas* bar amid all the fast-food joints. Spanish seafood, including *pulpo* (octopus). ◈ *C/Cuesta del Tajo 3 • Map E5 • 952 38 62 44 • No credit cards • €*

6 Restaurante La Escalera, Torremolinos
A great little choice, with dreamy views from its terrace. The inventive international menu includes curry soup with green peas. ◈ *C/Cuesta del Tajo 12 • Map E5 • 952 05 80 24 • Closed Sun • Dis. access • €€*

7 Las Acacias, Málaga
This open-air beach café serves the coast speciality – *sardinas ensartadas* (sardines grilled on a skewer). ◈ *Paseo Marítimo, El Pedregal 90 • Map E5 • 952 29 89 46 • €*

8 El Tintero II, Málaga
Another open-air restaurant on the beach. There's no menu, so the waiter will tell you what's on offer – all fish, of course. ◈ *Ctra Almería 99, Playa Del Dedo • Map E5 • 952 20 44 64 • Dis. access • €*

9 Café Carabeo, Nerja
This café has been cut into the cliff, so you have views of the sea while protected under palm frond umbrellas. ◈ *Beneath Plaza Cueva del Bendito • Map E5*

10 El Ancladero, Nerja
With another superb location on the cliff affording panoramic views of the sea, this place is a popular spot with photographers. The menu is eclectic, with the emphasis on steak and seafood. ◈ *Capistrano Playa • Map E5 • 952 52 19 55 • Dis. access • Closed 21 Nov–7 Dec, 1–15 Jan • €*

Note: Unless otherwise stated, all restaurants accept credit cards and serve vegetarian meals

Left **Las Bridas**, Ronda Right **Anfiteatro, Cádiz**

Nightlife in the Region

1 Varsovia, Málaga
This old-town disco attracts people of all ages. The music is a mix of 1980s feel-good, with some current hits thrown in. ⊗ C/José Denis Belgrado 5 • Map R5

2 ZZ Pub, Málaga
Mostly university students come to this modest establishment in the old part of town, to hear the two regular bands that play here on Mondays and Thursdays. A DJ fills in the quiet moments every night. ⊗ C/Teján y Rodríguez 6 • Map Q4

3 Ronda After Dark
Café Las Bridas offers imported brews, with live music on weekends from midnight. Café Pub Siete Locos is a good place to dance to the latest Spanish electro-pop. ⊗ Map D5 • Café Las Bridas: C/Remedios 18 • Café Pub Siete Locos: C/Carlos Lobo 4

4 Nerja by Night
Funky beats and House music make Narixa a popular place to party. Coconut, on the other hand, is more laid back and is where you'll find the salsa crowd hanging out. ⊗ Map E5 • Narixa: C/Tajillo • Coconut: C/Antonio Millón

5 Cádiz Pop
The zone around the harbour is loaded with venues and Anfiteatro is one of the best. Open Friday and Saturday only. ⊗ Map B5 • Anfiteatro: Paseo Almirante Pascual Pery Junquera, 956 22 45 19

6 Cádiz Flamenco
The flamenco clubs burst with life in Cádiz. Good bets include Peña La Perla and Peña Enrique el Mellizo. ⊗ Map B5 • Peña La Perla: C/Carlos Ollero • Peña Enrique el Mellizo: Punta San Felipe

7 Flamenco in Jerez
Here you will find genuine flamenco at its impassioned best. The gypsy quarter of Santiago is the place to make for, where you will find a number of peñas (clubs), but don't expect much before 10pm. ⊗ Map B5

8 Tarifa Nights
You don't even have to leave the beach to check out the open-air Il Balneario. The floor is sand and the feel is tropical. In town, Tanakas can accommodate about 1,000 people. ⊗ Map C6 • Il Balneario: Playa Chica • Tanakas: Plaza de San Hiscio

9 Gibraltar Nightlife
More than 360 pubs here keep British hours (closing time 11pm). For devotees of later doings, Queensway Quay, Marina Bay and Casemates Square have a wide selection of bars, often with live entertainment. ⊗ Map C6

10 Gibraltar Gambling
In addition to the bar scene, the Rock boasts the Ladbroke International Casino Club, which offers spectacular views over the bay and live entertainment. ⊗ 7 Europa Road • Map C6

Price Categories

For a three-course	€ under €20
meal for one with half	€€ €20–€30
a bottle of wine (or	€€€ €30–€40
equivalent meal), taxes	€€€€ €40–€50
and extra charges.	€€€€€ over €50

Above **El Faro, Cádiz**

🔟 Places to Eat in the Region

1 Ventorrillo del Chato, Cádiz

The oldest restaurant in Cádiz (1780), this inn on the Playa de Cortadura is also one of the best. Try *salmorejo*, a thick tomato soup served as a dip or side dish, and *dorada a la sal*, a local fish baked in a salt crust. ◈ *Ctra Cádiz-San Fernando 2km (Via Augusta Julia) • Map B5 • 956 25 00 25 • Closed Sun • €€€*

2 El Faro, Cádiz

Cádiz is renowned for its fresh fish and this is probably the best place to experience such delights. *Lubina* (sea bass) is a perennial favourite, as are *cigalas* (giant crayfish). ◈ *C/San Felix 15 • Map B5 • 956 21 10 68 • €€€*

3 El Bosque, Jerez

In a town noted for elegance, its best restaurant is formal, as you would expect. It serves excellent seafood. ◈ *Avda Alcalde Alvaro Domecq 26 • Map B5 • 956 30 70 30 • Closed Sun, Mon D • €€€€*

4 Bar Juanito, Jerez

This bar is famous for the best *tapas* in town. Try *fideos con gambas* (noodles with prawns). ◈ *C/Pescadería Vieja 8 & 10 • Map B5 • 956 33 48 38 • €*

5 Casa Flores, El Puerto de Santa María

A stunning setting and the finest fresh seafood makes this one of the best choices in this port town. ◈ *C/Ribera del Río 9 • Map B5 • 956 54 35 12 • €€€€*

6 Tragabuches, Ronda

Probably the best restaurant in Andalucía. The chef has re-thought provincial cuisine and come up with a unique post-modern fusion. Choices include gazpacho ice cream and garlic soup with herring, egg and figs. ◈ *C/José Aparicio 1 • Map D5 • 952 19 02 91 • Closed Sun D, Mon • €€€€*

7 Tetería Al-Zahra, Ronda

In this authentic Moroccan-style tearoom sip mint tea – or slurp a milkshake – and delve into delicious Arab pastries. ◈ *C/Las Tiendas 19 • Map D5 • 607 74 51 73 • Closed Tue • No credit cards • €*

8 Bar La Farola, Ronda

This traditional *tapas* bar serves wonderful *chipirones* (baby squid), *berenjenas* (aubergine/eggplant) and mouth-watering *chorizos* (paprika sausages). ◈ *Plaza Carmen Abela 10 • Map D5 • 952 87 15 47 • Closed Sun • €*

9 Antigua Casa de Guardia, Málaga

The city's oldest *taberna*, dating from 1840. Some 20 barrels of local wine line the bar. The steamed mussels *(mejillones)* are great. ◈ *Alameda Principal 18 • Map Q5 • 952 21 46 80 • Closed Sun • €*

10 Antonio Martín, Málaga

The city's premier fish restaurant. *Fritura malagueña* (fish-fry Málaga-style) is popular. ◈ *Plaza de la Malagueta s/n • Map E5 • 952 22 73 98 • €€*

 Note: Unless otherwise stated, all restaurants accept credit cards and serve vegetarian meals

Left **Monasterio de la Cartuja, Granada** Right **Cave dwellings, Guadix**

Granada and Almería Provinces

SO TAKEN ARE THEY WITH THE LEGENDARY PALACES OF THE ALHAMBRA, most tourists discover little else in these two provinces. However, besides numerous important and unique attractions in the enchanting city of Granada itself, the entire region is worth exploring, being especially rich in natural wonders. Spectacular mountains and superbly untouched coastal areas are the pride of both provinces, while inland some of the remote villages are among Andalucía's most fascinating and historic. Finally, film buffs will be delighted with the old "Spaghetti Western" movie sets that have been turned into endearingly quirky theme parks.

🔟 Sights

1. Sierra Nevada
2. Moorish Granada
3. Cathedral & Capilla Real, Granada
4. Monasterio de la Cartuja, Granada
5. Museo-Casa Natal Federico García Lorca
6. Alhama de Granada
7. Almuñécar & Around
8. Guadix
9. Almería City & Around
10. "Wild West" Towns

Moorish arch, Granada

1 Sierra Nevada

Spain's tallest peaks – and, after the Alps, Europe's second loftiest chain – make Andalucía home to some excellent skiing in winter, robust trekking in spring and summer, and a favourite with naturalists who come to marvel at the abundant wild-flowers and wildlife. For the more culturally inclined, the historic villages of the Alpujarras, on the dramatic southern slopes, are a fascinating study in an age-old way of life *(see pp32–3)*.

2 Moorish Granada

The fairytale "Arabian Nights" palace of the Alhambra, together with its equally evocative gardens, constitute one of Spain's principal attractions, drawing millions of visitors each year. In the city down below, the ancient Albaicín district embodies a microcosm of a North African village, a "Little Morocco", with colourful market streets and tearooms. Above and behind the area stands Sacromonte, the traditional home of cave-dwelling gypsies *(see pp8–13)*.

3 Cathedral & Capilla Real, Granada

To unequivocally establish Christian rule, these triumphalist structures were built by some of the greatest architects of the age and adorned with important works of sculpture and painting, much of it Renaissance. The towering, light-suffused interior of Granada's cathedral is one of the most spectacular achieve-ments of the period, while the façade, by Alonso Cano, echoes the ancient triple arch favoured by Roman emperors. The Capilla Real (Royal Chapel) is Granada's finest Christian building and a repository of rare treasures,

Cathedral, Granada

including a *reja* (gilded grille) by Bartolomé de Jaén, priceless crown jewels, and paintings by Roger van der Weyden and Sandro Botticelli *(see p41)*. ◈ *Map Q2 • Catedral: C/Gran Vía de Colón 5; Open 10am–1pm, 4–8pm Mon–Sat, 4–8pm Sun (until 7pm Nov–Mar); Adm • Capilla Real: C/Oficios 3; Open Apr–Oct: 10:45am–1pm, 4–7pm Mon–Sat, 11am– 1pm, 4–7pm Sun; Nov–Mar: 10:30am– 1pm, 3:30–6:30pm Mon–Sat, 11am–1pm, 3:30–6:30pm Sun; Adm €3.00*

4 Monasterio de la Cartuja, Granada

Don't let the austere exterior fool you – inside the church and sacristy of this Carthusian monastery lurk some of the most flamboyant Spanish Baroque architecture and detailing you'll ever encounter. So busy are the arabesques, flourishes and excrescences of gilded and polychromed stucco that the architectural lines are all but swallowed up in ravishing visual commotion. ◈ *Paseo de la Cartuja • Map F4 • Open Apr–Oct: 10am–1pm, 4–8pm Mon–Sat, 10am–noon, 4–8pm Sun; Nov–Mar: 10am–1pm, 3:30–6pm Sun, 10am–noon, 3:30–6pm Sun • Adm €3.00*

5 Museo-Casa Natal Federico García Lorca

Sadly, the many depths of Granada's talented native son – playwright, poet, artist, musician, impresario – were denied to the world when he was murdered at the age of 38 by Fascists at the beginning of the Spanish Civil War. His birthplace, in a village near Granada, has been turned into a museum devoted to his memory (see p57). ✆ C/Poeta García Lorca 4, Fuente Vaqueros • Map F4 • Open Apr–Jun & Sep: 10am–1pm, 5–7pm Tue–Sun; Jul–Aug 10am–2pm Tue–Sun; Oct–Mar: 10am–1pm, 4–6pm Tue–Sun • www.museogarcialorca.org • Adm

6 Alhama de Granada

Clinging precariously to the edge of a breathtaking gorge, this whitewashed village has been known since Moorish times for its beauty and natural thermal waters (al-hamma means "hot spring" in Arabic). The Hotel Balneario preserves the 11th-century aljibe (cistern), graced by Caliphal arches. In the 16th-century Iglesia de la Encarnación some of the priestly vestments on display are said to have been embroidered by Queen Isabel the Catholic. ✆ Map E4

Plasticultura

If you approach the coastal area of these provinces from the west, you will notice the extent of plastic tenting, a phenomenon that reaches a sea-like peak before Almería City. This agricultural technique is known as plasticultura, and is the last word in how to squeeze out every drop of moisture from these desert lands in order to produce crops. The process is anything but organic, but this huge agribusiness does provide jobs, mostly for itinerant North Africans.

Castle overlooking Almuñécar

7 Almuñécar & Around

The Costa Tropical is perhaps Spain's most spectacular coast, where towering mountains rise from the shore. Almuñécar is the chief town along this stretch and it is now given over almost entirely to resort life. Yet it has an ancient heritage, dating back to the Phoenicians, and was an important port under the Moors. The intriguing Museo Arqueológico Cueva de Siete Palacios has a unique Egyptian vase dating from the 7th century BC (see p55). ✆ Map F5 • Museo Arqueológico Cueva de Siete Palacios: Barrio de San Miguel; Open 10:30am–1:30pm, 6:30–9pm Tue–Sat, 10:30am–1:30pm Sun; 958 63 37 46; Adm

8 Guadix

This ancient town is famous for its cave dwellings, inhabited for centuries. They were developed after the reconquista by local Moors who had been cast out of society by the Christians. The Barrio de las Cuevas is a surreal zone of brown hills with rounded whitewashed chimneys sprouting up here and there. To learn more, visit the Cueva-Museo or instead stay in a cave hotel (see p145). ✆ Map F4 • Cueva-Museo: Plaza Padre Poveda, 958 66 90 02; Open 10am–2pm, 6–8pm Mon–Sat, 10am–2pm Sun (summer); 10am–2pm, 4–6pm Mon–Sat (winter); Adm

9 Almería City & Around

Notwithstanding its poetic Arabic name (*al-mariyat* means "mirror of the sea"), this town has lost much of its appeal due to modern development. Still, it does have a most impressive 10th-century Alcazaba, one of the most massive of the extant Moorish fortresses, and an engaging old quarter that still seems North African in essence. ◉ *Map G4 • Alcazaba: C/Almanzor; Open Apr–Oct: 9am– 8:30pm Tue–Sun; Nov–Mar: 9am–6:30pm Tue–Sun; Adm*

10 "Wild West" Towns

The interior of Almería Province resembles the deserts and canyons of the American Southwest: it was the perfect spot for filming the Wild West epics known as "Spaghetti Westerns" in the 1960s and 1970s. Three of the sets are now theme parks: Mini Hollywood *(see p63)*, Texas Hollywood and Western Leone offer stunt shows and memorabilia. ◉ *Mini Hollywood: Ctra N340 km 364, Tabernas; Map G4; Open 10am–9pm daily (summer), 10am–6pm Sat–Sun & pub. hols (winter); 950 36 52 36; Adm • Texas Hollywood: Ctra N340 km 468, Paraje de Lunhay, Tabernas; Map G4; Open Nov–Feb: 10am–6pm daily (to 9pm Mar–Oct); 950 16 54 58; Adm • Western Leone: Ctra A92, Tabernas; Map G4; Open 9:30am–dusk daily (summer); 9:30am–dusk Sat–Sun (winter); 950 16 54 05; Adm*

Plaza Vieja, Almería City

A Morning in Granada

Begin your walk at Plaza Bib-Rambla, enhanced with flower stalls and the Neptune fountain. Fronting the western side of the square is the warren of ancient shopping streets called the **Alcaicería** *(see p114)*. Don't miss the 14th-century Moorish Corral del Carbón, which now houses craft shops and a tourist office.

Once the **cathedral** *(see p109)* opens, it's time for a visit there; be sure to see the enormous Santiago el Matamoros (the Moor-slayer) on horseback, by Alonso de Mena, adorning the altar of St James. The next stop is the **Capilla Real** *(see p109)*; you should visit the crypt under the ostentatious marble sarcophagi of the kings and queens, where their bodies repose in plain lead boxes. On the carved Renaissance sepulchres, note the split pomegranate, symbol of a defeated Moorish Granada.

Continue on across the busy thoroughfares until you get to the river and the long expanse of the **Plaza Nueva** *(see p47)*. Choose an outside table (the cafés here are all similar), order a drink and take in the street life.

Now it's time to enter the labyrinth of the **Albaicín** *(see p12–13)*. Take Calle Elvira up to Calle Calderería Vieja for the vibrant bazaar of the Moorish Quarter. Following the old steep streets, keep going until you reach the fanciful **La Tetería del Bañuelo** *(see p116)*, an inviting place to sip some mint tea and sample Moroccan sweets.

Following pages: Albaicín quarter, Granada

Left **Marquetry box, Granada** Right **Moroccan goods, Albaicín**

🔟 Traditional Handicrafts

1 La Alcaicería, Granada
In Moorish times this was the silk market, although the horseshoe arches and stucco work are a modern re-creation. The narrow alleyways are bursting with colourful wares of every description. Silver jewellery, embroidered silk shawls and ceramics are top buys. ❧ Map Q2

2 Albaicín, Granada
The authentic Moroccan shops in this ancient quarter are all concentrated on two sloping streets off Calle Elvira – Calderería Vieja and Calderería Nueva *(see pp12–13)*.

3 La Alacena, Granada
This is a tempting place to come for regional foodstuffs. You'll find some of the finest olive oils, local and national wines and ham from the southern slopes of the Sierra Nevada. ❧ C/San Jerónimo 3, 958 20 68 90 • Map F4

4 Artesania Carazo Ortiz E, Granada
In this mystical place you can find the likes of handmade ceramics and natural stones, and you may even stumble upon some archeological items for sale. ❧ C/Zacatín 11, 958 22 62 60 • Map R2

5 Manuel Morillo Castillo, Granada
Arab-style furniture and *taracea* (marquetry) boxes are made and sold here *(see p64)*. ❧ Cuesta de Gomérez 20, 958 22 97 57 • Map R2

6 El Rocío, Granada
The complete outfitter for *romería* and festival-going gear. All the frills, polka dots and bright colours will dazzle your eye, and it all comes in every size, so even babies can have a flounce or two. ❧ C/Capuchinas 8 • Map Q2

7 Artesania Kandossi, Granada
Classic Granada pottery, ranging from plates and bowls to jars and crockery as well colourful Moroccan items. ❧ Officios 4 • Map Q2

8 Artesania El Suspiro, Granada
A good array of all the traditional crafts that have survived in this city. Particularly appealing are the glazed tiles and the carpets in multicoloured designs. ❧ Plaza Santa Ana 1, 958 22 99 96 • Map R2

9 Alpujarras Crafts
The hill towns of this zone are rich in traditional crafts, including ceramics and weaving. Local *jarapas* (rugs) are particularly prized. Bags, ponchos and blankets, too, are hand-loomed in age-old patterns. They're all offered at weekly markets throughout the area. ❧ Map G4

10 Níjar, Almería Province
This coastal town is known for its distinctive pottery and *jarapas*. Head for Calle Las Eras, in the Barrio Alfarero, just off the principal street, where you'll find the genuine article. ❧ Map H4

Left **Babylon** Right **Planta Baja**

Nightlife

1 El Camborio, Granada
This is a popular disco in the caves of Sacromonte *(see p13)*. Music echoes from four dance floors to the rooftop terraces, offering a striking view of the Alhambra at sunrise. Weekends are the time to go, unless you want the place to yourself.
§ *Camino del Sacromonte 48 • Map S1*

2 Granada 10, Granada
An opulent disco set in a 1930s theatre whose decor has been preserved. You can dance under crystal chandeliers, Neo-Classical-style plasterwork and plush private boxes. The music consists mainly of chart hits that attract people of all ages and styles. § *C/Carcel Baja 3 • Map Q2*

3 Babylon, Granada
If you're looking for somewhere basic and relaxed, this place might be for you. The music is reggae, hip-hop, rap, funk and R&B, and the only concession to design is a Bob Marley poster or two and a few coloured lights. If it's your birthday, two bottles of bubbly are on the house.
§ *C/Sillería 5 • Map F4*

4 Sala Príncipe, Granada
In this two-storey disco the music consists mainly of Spanish pop and salsa but the DJ takes requests. It's a popular place, decorated in rather vulgar imitation of the Nasrid palaces on the hill above. § *Campo del Príncipe 7 • Map R3*

5 Planta Baja, Granada
A two-storey venue: the upper floor is a quiet bar; downstairs, the DJs play chart hits and everyone dances. § *C/Horno de Abad 11 • Map F4*

6 Pie de la Vela, Granada
The crowd here is mostly male, young and cruisy, but it isn't exclusively gay, drawing a mixed crowd of locals and foreigners. § *C/del Darro 35 • Map R2*

7 El Ángel Azul, Granada
This gay bar has a basement dance floor and curtained booths, as well as monthly drag shows and striptease contests.
§ *C/Lavadero de las Tablas 15 • Map F4*

8 Jardines Neptuno, Granada
You can see a spectacular show of flamenco and Andalucían folk music here at the same time as dining on typical local dishes.
§ *C/Arabial • Map F4*

9 Eshavira, Granada
This atmospheric club hosts flamenco, jazz and ethnic music concerts on Thursdays and Sundays. Decorated in Moorish style, the centuries-old water cistern has been transformed into a stage. § *Postigo de la Cuna 2 • Map Q1*

10 Peña El Taranto, Almería
For lovers of real flamenco without tourist kitsch, this is the best place in the city *(see p59)*.

Left **Kasbah** Right **La Tetería del Bañuelo**

Tearooms and Tapas Bars

1 La Tetería del Bañuelo, Granada

A more relaxed and inviting place is hard to imagine. The little rooms and intimate niches are suffused with a gentle light, the air with the aromas of tea and flowers and the sound of song-birds. Try some exotic brews and sweets and enjoy unsurpassed views. ◎ *C/Bañuelo 5 • Map R2*

2 Kasbah, Granada

Relax amid the comforts of this candlelit café. Silky pillows and romantic nooks abound. You can try Arab pastries and a selection of Moroccan teas.
◎ *C/Calderería Nueva 4 • Map Q2*

3 Pervane, Granada

Near the top of this hilly street, this tearoom feels authentically Moroccan. Sit on cushions on the floor at one of the upper windows, sip your mint tea, and take in the colour-ful street life down below.
◎ *C/Calderería Nueva 24 • Map Q2*

4 La Esquinita, Granada

Small, atmospheric and sometimes claustrophobic. A speciality here is fried fish.
◎ *Campo del Príncipe • Map R3*

5 El Bodegas Castañeda, Granada

Rows of antique wine barrels create the atmosphere here. The cheese boards are a good bet, as well as *montaditos* (small open sandwiches). ◎ *C/Elvira 5 • Map Q2*

6 Casa Enrique, Granada

This is another wonderfully old-fashioned hole-in-the-wall lined with antique barrels. Try the platters of mussels steamed with herbs and white wine.
◎ *C/Acero de Darro 8 • Map Q3*

7 Cafetería Acapulco, Granada

This place is heaven on earth for those with a sweet tooth. The decadent chocolates and sweets will satisfy even the most discern-ing of chocaholics and cake lovers.
◎ *Avda Obisfo Medina Olmos s/n, Guadix • Map F4*

8 Bodega Francisco, Almuñécar

A forest of ham shanks hanging from the ceiling greets the eye, along with barrels of *fino* behind the bar in this traditional *tapas* bar. The attached restaurant next door, Francisco II, serves full meals. ◎ *C/Real 14 • Map F5*

9 Casa Puga, Almería

One of the city's best *tapas* bars. The wine list is exhaustive, as you might guess from the many wine racks on view.
◎ *C/Jovellanos 7 • Map G4*

10 El Quinto Toro, Almería

The name derives from the tradition that the best bull of a *corrida* is chosen to fight in the fifth *(quinto)* confrontation of the day. This *tapas* bar is favoured by local aficionados of the bullfight.
◎ *Juan Leal 6 • Map G4*

Price Categories

For a three-course meal for one with half a bottle of wine (or equivalent meal), taxes and extra charges.

€	under €20
€€	€20–€30
€€€	€30–€40
€€€€	€40–€50
€€€€€	over €50

Above **Arrayanes**

🔟 Restaurants

1 Cunini, Granada
The fresh seafood, brought in daily from Motril, is highly recommended. It's a big hit with the food critics – so it must be good. ✆ Plaza Pescadería 14 • Map F4 • 958 25 07 77 • Closed Sun D, Mon • €€

2 Arrayanes, Granada
The most authentic and sophisticated of the North African restaurants in the little Moroccan quarter. Only *halal* meat is served, and no alcohol. ✆ Cuesta Marañas 4 • Map Q2 • 958 22 84 01 • Closed Tue • €€

3 Mirador de Aixa, Granada
With its position at the top of the Albaicín there are views of the Alhambra from the terrace. The food, too, is an adventure in local culture, featuring recipes such as *habas con jamón* (broad beans with ham). ✆ Carril de San Agustín 2 • Map Q2 • 958 22 36 16 • €€

4 Restaurante El Ventorro, Alhama de Granada
In this lovely rural restaurant you can try *tortilla Sacromonte* – an omelette with calves' brains and bull's testicles – if you have the nerve. ✆ Ctra de Jatar, km2 • Map E4 • 958 35 04 38 • Closed Mon • €€

5 Restaurante González, Trevélez
In this famous ham town you'll get what you came for – the dining room is hung with legs of meat. ✆ Plaza Francisco Abellán • Map F4 • 958 85 85 33 • €€€

6 Chez Jacquy, Playa Cotobro, Almuñécar
One of Andalucía's finest restaurants. Belgian chef Jacques Vanhoren blends the best of his native cuisine with high points of Spanish cookery. ✆ Edificio Río Playa Cotobro 1 • Map F5 • 958 63 18 02 • Closed Mon (winter) • €€€

7 El Tinao del Mar, La Herradura
Regional cooking at its simple best, which means seafood at this beach location. ✆ Edificio Bahía II, Paseo Marítimo de Don Andrés Segovia 17 • Map F5 • 958 82 74 88 • €€€

8 Pesetas, Salobreña
Absorb the ambience of the old quarters of Salobreña and the excellent views of the coast while dining here. The Choco A La Mariñera (Squid In Tomato Sauce) is a speciality. ✆ C/Bóveda 11 • Map F5 • 958 61 01 82 • €€

9 Restaurante Valentín, Almería
Specialities include *arroz negro* (rice in squid ink) and *pescado en adobo* (clay-baked fish). ✆ C/Tenor Iribarne 19 • Map G4 • 950 26 44 75 • Closed Mon • €€€€

🔟 La Goleta, San Miguel del Cabo de Gata
All the seafood is at its freshest here, of course, since this village is located right in the middle of Andalucía's most unspoilt coast. ✆ Beachfront • Map H5 • 950 37 02 15 • Closed Nov & Mondays, Dec– May • €€

 Note: Unless otherwise stated, all restaurants accept credit cards and serve vegetarian meals

Left **Castillo de Almodóvar del Rio** Right **Montilla vineyards**

Córdoba and Jaén Provinces

THESE TWO PROVINCES ARE AN ATTRACTIVE BLEND *of exquisite urban architecture, famed agricultural zones and great wildlife reserves within rugged mountain ranges. The ancient treasure-trove of Córdoba City is the star, of course, but the Renaissance towns of Baeza and Úbeda are among the region's most beautiful. For wine-lovers and those who appreciate delicious ham and perfect olive oil, the areas around Montilla, Valle de los Pedroches and Baena should not be missed. Meanwhile, along the northern zones, nature lovers can hike for days and days amid the pristine wilds of the Parque Natural de la Sierra de Cardeña y Montoro in Córdoba Province and the Sierra de Cazorla in Jaén Province.*

TOP 10 Sights

1 Córdoba City
2 Úbeda
3 Baeza
4 Medina Azahara
5 Castillo de Almodóvar del Rio
6 Montoro
7 Valle de los Pedroches
8 Montilla
9 Jaén City
10 Alcalá La Real

Medina Azahara

1 Córdoba City

This town, wonderfully rich in history and cultural importance, is also small enough to cover easily and enjoyably on foot. It has a delightfully contrasting mix of sights, from the architectural splendour of the great mosque – with a Christian church oddly sprouting out of

Alcázar, Córdoba City

its centre – to the whitewashed glories of the old Jewish quarter, the splendid Alcázar, and the frankly morbid museum dedicated to the bullfight. There are other engaging museums as well, featuring works of art by both Old Masters and local artists, and ancient artifacts evoking the area's influential past *(see pp18–21)*.

2 Úbeda

Ignore the downtrodden outskirts as you approach this town – once you get to the historic centre you will realize that it is one of Andalucía's most remarkable splendours. The keynote here is architecture – an entire district of mostly Renaissance edifices built for local nobility in the 16th century. One of Andalucía's greatest architects, Andrés de Vandelvira, was the genius who gave most of these structures their harmonious forms *(see pp28–9)*.

Renaissance church altar, Úbeda

3 Baeza

Like nearby Úbeda, this smaller town is also a jewel of Renaissance glory, but includes earlier remains dating back to the Moors and, before them, the Romans. The town radiates a sense of tranquillity as you walk from one cluster of lovely buildings to another. Again, much of the beauty owes its existence to Vandelvira *(see pp28–9)*.

4 Medina Azahara

The building of the first palace here dates from AD 936, commissioned by Caliph Abd el-Rahman III, the Emir of Córdoba and the man who brought the city to glory. He named it after his favourite wife, Az-Zahra (the Radiant). Though it is little more than a ruin now – sacked in 1009 and rediscovered only in 1910 – at one time this pleasure-dome incorporated a zoo, ponds and gardens, baths, houses, weapons factories and barracks, markets, mosques, a harem of 6,000 women and accommodation for 4,000 slaves. Decorated with ebony, ivory, jasper and marble, it even had a pool of mercury that created dancing lights on the walls and ceiling. ◈ *Ctra Palma del Río, W of Córdoba • Map D3 • Open 10am–8:30pm (to 6:30pm in winter) Tue–Sat, 10am–2pm Sun • 937 32 91 30 • Adm*

Baena Olive Oil

It was the Romans who brought cultivation of the olive here, and the Moors who carried the tradition forward. This Córdoba Province town is famed for its olive oil, and you can catch its unmistakable fragrance as you enter the district. The Nuñez de Prado factory *(Avda de Cervantes 15 • Open Nov–Jun: daily; Jul–Oct: Mon–Fri • Free)* is one of the most traditional. Each organically grown olive is carefully kept from bruising and the paste is extracted by the process of stone-crushing, the oil then being bottled and sealed in with wax.

5 Castillo de Almodóvar del Río

Originally the site of a Roman fortification, the present fairytale castle goes back to the 14th century, when it was embellished in Gothic style. Before that, it had been a Moorish structure dating from AD 740 that had survived four centuries of Christian sieges. Magnificent views from the battlements take in the whitewashed town below. Legend holds that ghosts of those who died while imprisoned here haunt the eight monolithic towers. ✆ *25 km (16 miles) W of Córdoba; 957 63 40 55 • Map D3 • Open 11am–2:30pm, 4–8pm daily • Adm*

Local produce, Valle de los Pedroches

6 Montoro

Attractively laid out on an undulating series of five hills at a bend in the river, this ancient town sports a Baroque tower and a handsome 15th-century bridge. Other sights include a good Museo Arqueológico Municipal and the eccentrically kitsch Casa de las Conchas, a shell-encrusted folly that the owner will be happy to show you around. ✆ *Map E2 • Museo Arqueológico: Plaza de Santa María de la Mota; Open 11am–1pm Sat–Sun (& public holidays); Free • Casa de las Conchas: C/Criado 17; Adm*

7 Valle de los Pedroches

The far north of Córdoba Province is fertile grazing land for farm animals, as well as deer and wild boar. Most importantly, it is a "land of acorns", densely clad with holm oaks and therefore a prime zone for raising the famed Iberian black pig. In October, the creatures are fattened up on acorns and their meat is elaborately cured to produce succulent *jamón ibérico* or *pata negra*, the local product rivalling that of Jabugo in Huelva Province. ✆ *Map D2*

8 Montilla

This town is the centre of Córdoba's wine-making region, where the word *amontillado* originates, meaning "in the style of Montilla". The wine produced here is like sherry, but nuttier and more toasted – and since the region is hotter than around Jerez, the grapes ripen more intensely and the wines need no fortifying. You can taste the difference for yourself at Bodegas Alvear *(see p66).* ✆ *Map D3 • Bodegas Alvear: Avda de María Auxiliadora 1, 957 66 40 14; Open Jul–Aug (English tours by appointment); Adm*

Cathedral, Jaén City

9 Jaén City

This modern provincial capital is set off by the dramatically placed ramparts of the mighty Castillo de Santa Catalina *(see p39)*, originally Moorish, and the immensity of its double-towered cathedral by Vandelvira *(see p41)*. You can fully experience the castle and its spectacular views of the city and surrounding olive groves, as it now houses a parador *(see p140)*. Another rewarding stop is the Museo Provincial, especially to see the country's finest collection of 5th-century BC Iberian sculpture. ⊗ *Map E3*
• *Cathedral: Plaza Santa María; Open 8:30am–1pm, 5–8pm daily (from 9am Sun); Free* • *Museo Provincial: Paseo de la Estación 27; Open 3–8pm Tue, 9am–8pm Wed–Sat; 9am–2:30pm Sun; Adm*

10 Alcalá La Real

The Fortaleza de la Mota that dominates this once strategic town is unique in Jaén Province in that its original Moorish castle was built by the rulers of Granada. It is mostly in ruins now, but it still preserves the original seven gates. Inside, built on the remains of a former mosque, is the Gothic-Mudéjar church of Santo Domingo, which uses the former minaret as a belltower *(see p38)*. ⊗ *Map E3* • *Fortress: Open 10:30am–1:30pm, 5–8pm daily (summer); 10:30am–1:30pm, 3:30–6:30pm daily (winter); 639 64 77 96; Adm*

A Morning Walk Through Baeza

🕐 Start your tour of this Renaissance town at the lovely **Plaza del Pópulo** *(see p28)*, where the tourist office is located in a fine Plateresque palace, the Casa del Pópulo. Next to it are the arches of the **Puerta de Jaén** *(see p28)* and the Arco de Villalar, while adorning the centre of the plaza is the Fuente de los Leones. The ruined lions and their eroded mistress, said to be a statue of Hannibal's wife, still manage to convey an undeniable elegance.

Exiting the square to the left of the tourist office, continue southeast to the **Plaza Santa María** *(see p28)* and the cathedral. Note the graffiti in bull's blood on the old seminary wall. Inside the cathedral, don't miss the extravagant choir screen by Bartolomé de Jaén.

Next stop, to the north, is the **Palacio de Jabalquinto** *(see p29)*, with one of the most eccentric façades in the region, an example of Isabelline Plateresque style. Visit its inner patio and then that of the Antigua Universidad next door. Down the street, you can see the 1,000-year-old Moorish Torre de los Aliatares and around the corner, facing **Paseo de la Constitución** *(see p29)*, La Alhóndiga, the old corn exchange, with its triple-tiered façade.

🍴 Have lunch at an outdoor table of the Restaurante Sali across from the town hall, which offers a range of choices from local farms *(Pasaje Cardenal Benavides 15 • 953 74 13 65 • Closed Wed D • €)*.

Around Andalucía – Córdoba and Jaén Provinces

Left **Arte Cordobés** Right **La Tienda del Olivo**

🔟 Shops and Markets

1 Arte Cordobés, Córdoba
A good choice for traditional Córdovan silver. Everything from small sculptures to filigree jewellery is on offer. Gold filigree creations are available as well. ✪ *C/Deanes 17 • Map D3 • 957 47 76 87*

2 Ghadamés, Córdoba
Here, Córdoba leather is worked and coloured into traditional patterns and images, most of them relating to the area's Moorish history, although some are on religious themes and others pertain to local customs. ✪ *Corregidor Luis de la Cerda 52 • Map D3 • 957 48 16 07*

3 Bodegas Mezquita, Córdoba
This is an excellent place for finding local foodstuffs. Slow-cured hams, fine wines, olive oils and other delectables will tempt your palate. ✪ *Corregidor Luis de la Cerda 73 • Map D3*

4 Baraka, Córdoba
For good-quality souvenirs this is likely spot. Choose from ceramics, leather goods, glassware and other accessories, all handmade. ✪ *C/Manriquez • Map D3*

5 Nucra, Córdoba
For more contemporary silver jewellery, all designed by local artisans. Many creations start with traditional Córdovan ideas but branch out into stylish variations that better suit modern tastes. ✪ *C/Lucano 22 • Map D3 • 957 48 83 01*

6 La Tienda del Olivo, Córdoba
This shop specializes in products relating to the venerable olive. Olive oil here comes in every variety, from light ones for cooking, to rich rare pressings. Other olive products include skin creams and handmade soaps. ✪ *C/San Fernando 124B • Map D3 • 957 47 44 95*

7 Nuñez de Prado, Baena
One of the premier olive oil factories in this historic town *(see p120)*. Their production methods have not compromised with modernity, so their oil remains rich and flavourful. ✪ *Avda de Cervantes • Map E3 • 957 67 01 41*

8 Galería de Vinos Caldos, Jaén
One of the region's best wine shops. Featured, of course, are regional wines, including those from Montilla *(see p120)*. ✪ *C/Ceron 12 • Map F3 • 953 23 59 99*

9 Flea Market, Jaén
Thursday mornings see this street come to life with a catch-all market that can net you anything from pure junk to a rare treasure. ✪ *Recinto Ferial, Avda de Granada • Map F3*

10 Pottery Quarter, Úbeda
Úbeda is famous for its dark green pottery, fired in wood kilns over olive stones. Its intricate pierced designs are Moorish-inspired and the workmanship superb. ✪ *C/Valencia • Map F2*

Price Categories

For a three-course meal for one with half a bottle of wine (or equivalent meal), taxes and extra charges.		
€	under €20
€€	€20–€30
€€€	€30–€40
€€€€	€40–€50
€€€€€	over €50

Above **El Churrasco**

🔟 Places to Eat

1 Tene2Ores, Córdoba
This restaurant is part of a hotel complex in the heart of Cazorla. Regional fare is served, with samplings of local game and fish ◉ *Magistrado Ruiz Rico 3, Cazorla (Jaén)* • *Map D3* • *953 72 40 34* • *€*

2 Taberna Sociedad de Plateros, Córdoba
Housed in a former convent, this *taberna* has a skylit patio decorated with *azulejos* (glazed tiles) and hanging plants. ◉ *C/San Francisco 6* • *Map D3* • *957 47 00 42* • *Closed Sun (summer), Mon (winter)* • *No credit cards* • *€*

3 Taberna Salinas, Córdoba
A bustling place, with dining rooms around a patio. Try the *bacalao* (cod) with orange and olive oil. ◉ *C/Tundidores 3* • *Map D3* • *957 48 01 35* • *Closed Sun, Aug* • *€*

4 Casa Rubio, Córdoba
Built into the old city wall, just inside the Judería, with Moorish arches and a stone floor, this atmospheric bar offers a good range of *tapas*. ◉ *Puerto Almodóvar 5* • *Map D3* • *957 42 08 53* • *No credit cards* • *€*

5 El Churrasco, Córdoba
One of the city's smartest eateries, serving traditional fare in a sumptuous setting. Try the eponymous *churrasco* (grilled pork loin with spicy red pepper sauce). ◉ *C/Romero 16* • *Map D3* • *957 29 08 19* • *Closed Aug* • *€€€*

6 Almudaina, Córdoba
Set in a 16th-century mansion, this is another great place to try traditional dishes, such as *pechuga de perniz en salsa* (partridge breasts in sauce). ◉ *Plaza Campo Santo de los Martires 1* • *Map D3* • *957 47 43 42* • *Closed Sun D* • *€€€*

7 Las Camachas, Montilla
Fish dishes are a speciality here, such as *pez spada* (swordfish) with Montilla sauce. Wash it all down with a bottle of the delightful local wine. ◉ *Ctra Madrid-Málaga, Avda de Europa 3* • *Map D3* • *957 65 00 04* • *€€€*

8 Taberna La Manchega, Jaén
An animated and authentic *tapas* bar. Downstairs they serve full meals, highlighting local meats. ◉ *C/Bernardo López 8 & Arco de Consuelo* • *Map F3* • *953 23 21 92* • *Closed Tue* • *No credit cards* • *€*

9 Restaurante Andrés de Vandelvira, Baeza
Housed in a section of the eponymous architect's 16th-century Convento de San Francisco, dishes include *trucha escabechada* (marinated trout). ◉ *C/San Francisco 14* • *Map F2* • *953 74 81 72* • *Closed Mon* • *€€*

10 Mesón Navarro, Úbeda
Something of a local institution. Free *tapas* come with each glass of *fino*. ◉ *Plaza Ayuntamiento 2* • *Map F2* • *953 79 06 38* • *€*

 Note: *Unless otherwise stated, all restaurants accept credit cards and serve vegetarian meals*

STREETSMART

Planning your Trip
126

Specialist Holidays
127

Getting to Andalucía
128

Getting Around
Andalucía
129

Things to Avoid
130

Budget Tips
131

Banking and
Communications
132

Security and Health
133

Special Concerns
134

Tips for Families
135

Eating and
Drinking Tips
136

Accommodation Tips
137

Places to Stay
138

ANDALUCÍA'S TOP 10

Left **Tourist office** Right **Enjoying the warm climate**

🔟 Planning Your Trip

1 Internet Information

There are several sources of information on the Internet. If you're interested in a particular place or aspect of the region, see the following websites for more information. ⑤ www.andalucia.com • www.andalucia.org • www.okspain.org • www.spainlive.com • www.spain.info

2 Climate

The region enjoys a very mild climate. The year-round average temperature is 18–20°C (64–68°F) with some 320 sunny days. Coastal areas have highs fluctuating between 15°C (59°F) and 30°C (86°F). Inland, average city highs vary from 12°C (54°F) in January to 36°C (97°F) in August.

3 When to Go

Every season offers its reasons to come here: summer for nightlife, spring and autumn for nature, winter for skiing. But autumn is the best time – the weather is still good, the water is warm, the crowds have gone, prices are lower and there are lots of local festivals.

4 Passports & Visas

Britons, Americans, Australians, New Zealanders, Canadians and EU citizens need only a valid passport to stay for 90 days. Other nationalities must get a visa from their Spanish consulate.

5 Spanish Embassies & Consulates Abroad

If you have any questions, your local Spanish embassy or consulate is well equipped to help you. ⑤ Australia: 15 Arkana St, Yarralumla, Canberra; 02 6273 3555 • Canada: 74 Stanley Ave, Ottawa; (613) 747 2252 • Ireland: 17a Merlyn Park, Dublin 4; 353(0) 1283 9900 • UK: 39 Chesham Place, London; 020 7235 5555 • USA: 2375 Pennsylvania Ave NW, Washington, DC; (202) 728 2330

6 Foreign Consulates in Andalucía

For any further questions whilst in Spain, contact your country's consulate. ⑤ Canada: Edificio Horizonte, Plaza de la Malagueta 3, Málaga; 952 22 33 46 • Ireland: Avda de los Boliches 15, Fuengirola; 952 47 51 08 • UK: Edificio Eurocom Sur, C/Mauricio Moro Pareta 2, 2°, Málaga; 952 35 23 00 • USA: Paseo de las Delicias 7, Seville; 954 23 18 85

7 Spanish National Tourist Offices

This service (see box) will provide maps and brochures on request.

8 General Information

The time zone is that for Western Continental Europe (GMT +1 hour). Voltage is 220, and round-pronged plugs are used. UK gadgets need an adapter; US counterparts also require a transformer. The minimum age for driving is 18.

9 Insurance

It is always a good idea to obtain private medical insurance. Then, if you require treatment while on holiday, you pay for the care, keep the receipts and are reimbursed according to the terms of your policy. General travel insurance is also recommended.

10 What to Take

Casual dress is generally acceptable throughout Andalucía – linens or cottons are the best way to beat the summer heat. A hat will also be useful, and don't forget a high-factor sunscreen.

Spanish National Tourist Offices

Canada
2 Bloor St W, 34th Floor, Toronto • (416) 961 1992

UK
2nd Floor
79 New Cavendish St London W1W 6XB • 020 7486 8077

USA
666 5th Ave, 35th Floor, New York • (212) 265 8822

ONLINE INFO
www.spain.info

If planning via the Internet, be aware that Andalucíans, if they have a website, tend not to update them very regularly.

Left **Cultural tour** Right **Andalucían bodega**

🔟 Specialist Holidays

1 Walking & Hiking Tours

Walking and hiking are up-close ways to explore the countryside, and many companies offer well-organized groups. ◉ *Federación Española de Deportes de Montaña, Granada; 958 29 13 40 • Explore Worldwide, 1 Frederick St, Aldershot, Hants; 01252 760 144 • Nevadensis, C/Verónica, Pampaneira (Granada); 958 76 31 27*

2 Horse-Riding & Nature Tours

Nature lovers can take to trails on horseback, peer at the local birdlife from special hides, see the dolphins at the Straits of Gibraltar, or go on a nature safari. ◉ *Bird Holidays, 10 Ivegate, Yeadon, Leeds; 0113 391 0510 • Dolphin Safari, Marina Bay, Gibraltar; 956 77 19 14 • Rancho Los Lobos, Estación de Jimena (Cádiz); 956 64 04 29 • Safari Andalucía, Apartado 20, Gaucín (Málaga); 952 15 11 48*

3 Bodega Tours

Tours of the famous wine cellars *(bodegas)* in the Sherry Triangle and Málaga can be arranged either on the spot or in advance. Tours often feature samplings of great wines as well as gastronomic delights. ◉ *Mundicolor Holidays, 276 Vauxhall Bridge Rd, London; 020 7828 6021 • Saranjan Tours, Kirkland, Washington, USA; 800 858 9594*

4 Flamenco Tours & Salsa Holidays

Learn to dance, Spanish-style. The flamenco-based *sevillana* is a must for fiesta-goers, while the salsa is popular at clubs. ◉ *Taller Flamenco, C/Peral 49, Seville; 954 90 74 51; www.tallerflamenco. com • Spanish Fiesta, Urb. Lindaraja 12, Almuñecar; 680 22 69 30 • Dance Holiday, 24–32 Stephenson Way, London; www.dance holidays.com*

5 Spanish Language Holidays

Combining a holiday with courses in Spanish is a popular choice. Schools often offer a range of other activities. ◉ *Instituto Cervantes, 102 Eaton Sq, London; 020 7201 0750 • Don Quijote, Azhuma 5, Granada, or Conde de Ibarra 2, Seville; 958 25 42 12 • Instituto de Español Picasso, Plaza de la Merced 20, Málaga; 952 21 39 32*

6 Cultural Study Holidays

Many companies organize art, architecture and archaeology tours, or courses on regional cookery, painting and more. ◉ *Instituto Internacional Gibralfaro, Duque de la Victoria 8, Malaga; 952 21 54 11 • Prospect Music & Art Tours, 36 Manchester St, London; 020 7486 5704 • The Spirit of Andalucía, c/o Sally von Meister, Apartado 20, El Nobo, Gaucín (Málaga); 952 15 13 03*

7 Golfing Holidays

With more than 50 courses on the Costa del Sol *(see p103)* and ideal weather it's little wonder that the world comes here to play golf. Many hotels cater specifically to the golfer, and there are many specialist operators. ◉ *Longshot Golf Holidays, Meon House, College St, Petersfield, Hants; 0870 6090995*

8 Extreme Sports Tours

Scuba-diving, paragliding, hot-air ballooning, snowboarding – these are just a few of the more extreme sports you can find in Andalucía. ◉ *Aviación del Sol, Apartado 344, Ronda; 952 87 72 49 • Club Parapente Valle de Abdalajís, C/Sevilla 2, Valle de Abdalajís (Málaga); 952 48 91 80*

9 Luxury Tours

The luxury-minded traveller has plenty of options, including a train tour on the opulent Al-Andalus Expreso. ◉ *Al-Andalus Expreso, Cox & King's Travel Ltd., Gordon House, 10 Greencoat Place, London; 020 7873 5000*

10 Pilgrimages

Andalucíans take their religious pilgrimages seriously. If you want to join a *romería*, contact the local tourist board for exact dates, as all of them shift according to the lunar calendar or when weekends fall.

Left **Seville airport** Right **AVE high-speed trains in Seville**

Getting to Andalucía

1 By Air from Europe

Málaga is the main airport in Andalucía, but many other cities in the region also have airports – European flights also come into Seville, Jerez, Almería and Gibraltar. All airports have both bus and taxi services to city centres, except for Jerez, which only has taxis.
◈ *Air France: www. airfrance.fr • British Airways: www. britishairways.com; UK 0870 850 9850; USA 800 247 9297 • Iberia: www. iberia.com; UK 0845 850 9000, USA 800 772 4642 • KLM: www.klm.com • Lufthansa: www. lufthansa.com*

2 By Air from outside Europe

Most international flights land at Málaga and the list of carriers is vast. The airport is 6 km (4 miles) southwest of the city. There is a train service to the east and west of the region, as well as buses. Taxis are also an option.
◈ *American Airlines, www. aa.com; USA 800 433 7300*

3 Charter & Budget Flights

Most air traffic to Andalucía is made up of charter flights, which are cheaper than scheduled flights. For budget flights to the region, try those recommended below:
◈ *www.easyjet.com
• www.ryanair.com
• www.vueling.com*

4 Packages

Most travel agencies will have slick, full-colour brochures touting these complete getaway deals, and the prices often include full- or half-board accommodation as well as transport. Be aware, however, that these packages are usually centred in the most congested and touristy resorts on the coast, and you may not get a true impression of Andalucía.

5 By Car

From Madrid, it is a day's drive down to Andalucía. To get to Spain with your own car from the UK, options include ferries to France or to the north of Spain itself. Another alternative is to load your car on to an overnight train from Paris and collect it in Madrid the next morning. ◈ *P&O European Ferries: 08705 980 333; www.poferries. com • Brittany Ferries: 8703 665 333; www.brittany ferries.com • Motorail, SNCF France: (+33) 145 820 841*

6 By Sea

The ferries from the UK connect with trains to Córdoba and Málaga direct from Bilbao, another with connections in Madrid from Santander. If you're coming to Andalucía from the Balearic Islands, there are ferries from Palma to Barcelona and Valencia, from which you can take the train down to the south.

7 By Bus

This option works out, in most cases, to be more expensive than a low-cost flight. And from the UK, the prices can be a gruelling 35-hour trip. Consider it as a last resort. ◈ *Eurolines: 020 7730 8235; www. eurolines.com*

8 By Train

From Madrid there are 20 high-speed AVE trains daily to Seville. The journey takes 2 hours 20 minutes, with a stop in Córdoba. From Barcelona, the train trip to Seville is about 9 hours. ◈ *RENFE: www.renfe.es*

9 Car Rentals

Renting a car in Andalucía is comparatively cheap. Local firms will generally treat you better, even delivering and picking up the vehicle. Most companies require that drivers be at least 25 years old, with a valid licence and credit card. Make sure there are no hidden charges.
◈ *Hertz: www.hertz.com
• Avis: www.avis.com
• Europcar: www.europcar. com • Málaga companies: Autopro 952 17 60 30; Dany Car 952 79 02 37; Helle Hollis 952 24 55 44*

10 By Motorcycle

The same options as for cars apply for motorcycle travel. And, once in Andalucía, it's a great way to get around, especially for the hinterland.

Left **Seville bus station** Right **Taxis**

🔟 Getting Around Andalucía

1 By Bus
If you don't have your own wheels, the bus system is the best way to get around. Buses go to almost every village, sooner or later, and the roads have improved in recent years, shortening routes. There are dozens of companies dividing up the market, with multiple bus stations in some towns. You can buy tickets on board. ✆ Seville: Prado de San Sebastian, 954 41 71 11 • Granada: Ctra de Jaén, 958 18 50 10 • Córdoba: Glorieta de Tres Culturas s/n, 957 40 40 40 • Málaga: Paseo de los Tilos, 952 35 00 61

2 By Train
Train connections between major towns are fairly developed and there are some regional routes as well. Recently built stations in Seville and Córdoba are efficient and user-friendly. However, expect many stops along the way. ✆ Seville: Santa Justa, Avda Kansas City, 902 24 02 02 • Granada: Avda Andaluces, 902 24 02 02 • Córdoba: Glorieta de las Tres Culturas, 902 24 02 02 • Málaga: Explanada de la Estación, 902 24 02 02 • www.renfe.es

3 By Metro
During 2006 a new subway system is being introduced in Seville. City centre stations will branch out to the surrounding suburbs, providing a cost effective and efficient means of transport.

4 By Car
Many of the main roads in the region are less than 10 years old and in great condition. The problem is that, as a result, older maps can be confusingly out of date. Expect chaotic driving conditions, as locals pay little attention to rules and signs. Parking in towns and cities can be a real problem – leave the car in a car park and walk.

5 By Motorcycle
This is an excellent way to visit the out of the way areas and to discover a side of the region that most pass by. For steep inclines you'll need a good-sized bike, but if you're on the coast a scooter will do. Helmets are required by law.

6 Boating
With all the marinas up and down both coasts this mode of transport is a natural if you can afford it. But you'll need to be an experienced sailor to deal with the heavy currents that dominate the waters around the Strait of Gibraltar – for most, it's best to stick close to either coast. ✆ Royal Spanish Sailing Federation: 915 19 50 08; www.rfev.es

7 By Taxi
Taxis are an affordable way to get around towns – you can find plenty of them cruising the streets to be flagged down. Some have no meters, but the drivers are usually honest about how much the fare should be. It is customary to give the driver a small tip. ✆ Seville: 954 58 00 00 • Granada: 958 28 06 54 • Córdoba: 957 76 44 44 • Malaga: 952 33 33 33

8 By Bicycle
Cycling has taken on the dimensions of a major sport all over Spain – especially here, where the weather is so conducive. You'll see gaggles of Lycra-clad enthusiasts on many of the steepest mountain roads. ✆ Spanish Cycling Federation: 915 40 08 41, www.rfec.com

9 Hiking
This is the best way to explore mountainous areas, and there are many local organizations to help you with maps, suggestions and advice. Make sure you have adequate gear, including cold weather or sun protection. ✆ Federación Española de Deportes de Montaña, Granada: 958 29 13 40 • Nevadensis, C/Verónica, Pampaneira (Granada): 958 76 31 27

10 Walking
This is really the only practical way to take in Andalucía's cities and towns, mainly because every inch of their historic centres is worth a close look.

The heat in high summer can be crushing – always carry water, take a break during siesta time and wear a hat and sunscreen.

129

Left **Pavement peddlers** Right **Mountain road**

TOP 10 Things to Avoid

1 Tap Water
The region is subject to drought conditions with some regularity, and at such times the tap water can begin to taste fairly unpleasant. Although it is never dangerous, you might prefer to stick with bottled water. When hiking, never drink from streams – the days of pristine mountain springs are long gone.

2 Rancid Food
In the heat of the summer, it's wise to be attentive to the freshness of what you consume. *Tapas (see pp70–71)* that look as though they've been around a day too long, anything to do with mayonnaise that's been sitting out of the fridge and, of course, shellfish served in less than fastidiously hygienic establishments are probably best refused.

3 Religious Disrespect
Despite the casual dress code that predominates here, it is still a good idea to dress respectfully when you visit places of worship, and not to visit at all during mass or religious ceremonies.

4 Fakes & Forgeries
In the land of Picasso, it's wise to be wary of supposed "originals". Copies, prints, forgeries and outright fakes do brisk business. If you decide to buy any of these pieces, be very certain you're pledging your trust to a dealer whose credentials are beyond reproach – and get certificates of authentication and guarantees.

5 "Mystery" Tours
In the most heavily touristed zones you'll occasionally be offered a tour that, on the face of it, looks like something for nothing. It might be a daytrip to some interesting sight at a remarkably cut-rate price, or even an offer of cash or a lavish meal for just going to inspect a new condo or time-share project. These are not promotional bargains in the usual sense, but heavy-handed sales ploys and should be steered clear of.

6 Beach Snacks
Many of the snack bars you find along the beaches, especially the most popular beaches, are overpriced and sometimes the food is almost inedible, with a few exceptions. If you want to hang out in such a place for convenience and to enjoy the people-watching, then just get a drink. For meals, head away from the waterfront and into the towns.

7 Flower Girls
These women appear friendly enough when they flounce up to you and try to hand you a flower or a sprig of rosemary. But once you take the bait, they indignantly demand a lot of money for their cheery little "gift". Do your best to avoid them.

8 Peddlers
Most pavement peddlers will just call out to you a word or two about their merchandise, but once you evince an interest, you will be under pressure to buy something. Make it clear from the outset that you might want to look, but you'll decide what, if anything, you're going to buy. Check all merchandise thoroughly for defects, especially clothing, and then offer half the asking price.

9 Hair-Raising Roads
If Grand Prix-style driving is not your thing, it's best to avoid Andalucía's most challenging roads. The worst for sheer craziness remains the Costa del Sol's coastal highway. Some mountain roads are exceedingly narrow, winding and skirt yawning chasms.

10 Street Scams
An age-old gambling con in busy pedestrian areas is the shell game. The main man shuffles three cups, showing you how easy it is to follow the one that covers the pea, or whatever. Don't be taken in – you'll never win a game.

In peak seasons, traffic jams in towns and on the coastal highway may present the biggest challenge to visitors.

Left **Quiet off-season beach** Right **Picnic area sign**

🔟 Budget Tips

1 Package Deals
If you choose carefully, making sure that you end up in a fairly pleasant part of the coast or near the sights you want to see, all-inclusive packages can be excellent value. They are particularly appealing if all you mainly want is to be handily situated for the beach and have most of your meals covered into the bargain.

2 Picnicking
Given the wealth of natural beauty here, much of it now given over to parks and reserves, there are excellent picnicking opportunities everywhere. There are also plenty of grocers for all that you'll need to put together a memorable repast, with settings and views thrown in. Be sure to pick up your litter afterwards.

3 Self-Catering
You'll certainly need to book very much in advance to secure one of the less expensive self-catering apartments. But it's worth it, not only for the money you'll save but also for the freedom you'll enjoy in doing the region entirely your own way *(see p146)*.

4 Partying
Not all bars and clubs are pricey. Some of the most happening ones, in fact, are free to enter and require nothing of you but to have a good time and enjoy the ambience. No cover charges or minimum charges is a reality here – most of the bars are so busy that no one will notice that you're nursing your brew all night long.

5 Camping
There are some 130 authorized campsites in the region, mostly along the coast. Camping rough is legal, although not particularly encouraged. It's prohibited within 1 km (half a mile) of an official campsite, in urban areas, and in zones prohibited for military or ecological reasons. Get permission from the landowner first *(see p147)*.

6 IVA
If you buy anything that has a hefty sales tax tacked onto it and you are a non-EU citizen, keep the receipt, fill out the paperwork, then when you leave you can get a portion of it reimbursed at the airport. Another option for avoiding the 7 percent IVA tax is to have your purchases shipped directly home.

7 Menú del Día
The daily lunch menu in most restaurants can save you a great deal – as much as 75 per cent of the regular *à la carte* cost. Portions are generally generous, too, so you can make this your major meal of the day. It's also a great way to savour the cuisine of some of the top restaurants without forking out over-the-top prices.

8 Laundromats
A few *lavanderías automáticas* can be found in cities, but don't bother looking anywhere else. Regular laundries and *tintorerías* (dry-cleaners) are quite expensive, and hotel services are even more exorbitant. Bring a packet of travel washing detergent with you.

9 Reduced Admissions
Coupons for reduced group admissions to various attractions can help a lot when you've got a whole family to pay for. You'll find them in various magazines, weekly papers, flyers, brochures and handed out on the street in busy areas. Tourist offices also often have stacks of them lying around as promotional lures.

10 Off-Season Travel
This is by far the best way to make your money go further. Prices plummet as the throngs of July and August become a faint memory. Low-season prices for everything can delight the budget-minded traveller, plus you have the luxury of being one of only a few, rather than amid vast hordes.

Left **ATM machine** Centre **Logo of the Spanish telecom system** Right **Postbox**

🔟 Banking and Communications

1 Currency

Now that the euro is the currency of many European countries, life is much easier for visitors to the continent, although the changeover has resulted in some price inflation. Euro banknotes have the following denominations: 5, 10, 20, 50, 100, 200 and 500. Euro coins come in eight denominations: 1 euro, 2 euros, and 1, 2, 5, 10, 20 and 50 cents. Visitors from outside the euro zone should check the exchange rates at the time of travel.

2 Traveller's Cheques

If you're going to opt for this safety precaution, get your cheques directly in euros – you won't have to pay any commission to cash them and, in some places, you'll be able to use them as cash. Make sure you keep track of the serial numbers.

3 Cashpoints and ATMs

For ready cash, this is the best option. Bank machines are everywhere and very reliable. Spanish banks charge no transaction fee; you'll only have to pay your own bank's fee to pay for using a non-branch machine.

4 Credit Cards

Using your credit card is possible for almost everything in larger towns. Only the smallest places in the most off-the-beaten-track outposts will find it a problem. However, be aware that your own bank may charge you a 2 percent currency conversion fee for every card purchase you make, so it's cheaper to use your cash card option.

5 Wiring Money

This expensive, laborious process should be considered only as a last resort. You can have your bank send money to a bank in Spain, but you must organize things at the Spanish end first. Then expect it to take an indeterminate number of days and for there to be substantial charges at both ends of the process.

6 Post

Post offices (correos) are open 9am to 2pm and 5pm to 7:30pm, although larger offices do not close for siesta. For letters and postcards, you can also get stamps (sellos) at tobacco shops and newspaper stands. In general, Spanish post is reliable.

7 Telephones

Calling Spain from another country requires dialling 00 then the country code, 34. While you're in Andalucía you must always dial the regional area code, 95, even if calling locally. To call abroad from Spain, dial 00, then the country code, area code and number of your destination. For local and national information call 11850; for international enquiries call 11825.

8 Internet

Many hotels now allow you to use your laptop for accessing the Internet. Internet cafés are also common sights in every town and city, and even villages.

9 Newspapers and Magazines

In the larger towns, you'll find a good selection of international press: USA Today and the International Herald Tribune are available in the larger kiosks, as well as major British, German, French and Dutch papers. Costa del Sol English-language magazines include The Entertainers, Lookout and Marbella Life.

10 TV and Radio

The more expensive hotels all offer satellite TV, with many programmes in English, German, French and Italian – not to mention all the regular Spanish channels. Radio Gibraltar and US Armed Forces Radio from Rota provide English-language broadcasting, and there are others along the Costa del Sol. Spanish stations feature a mix of Spanish and international pop music. Canal Sur is the official Andalucían broadcasting system.

Mobile phones work well all over Andalucía but check with your network whether you are set up for international usage.

Left **Police car** Right **Pharmacy sign**

🔟 Security and Health

1 Precautions

There are no special inoculations required to visit Andalucía. The only protection you should be sure to use on a regular basis is sunscreen – sunburn and heat stroke are the main sources of discomfort. Some people also experience a slight upset stomach from the change in bacteria in the food and water, although tap water is safe to drink.

2 Prescriptions

If there are any prescription medicines you require, or may require, it's best to bring them along with you. Due to differing pharmaceutical regulations, different countries may or may not have the drugs you need, or they may be sold under a different name.

3 Emergencies

For any emergency, give precise information about what is needed and where exactly you are, in Spanish if you are able.

4 Pharmacies

Pharmacies *(farmacias)* are a good source of medical advice for minor complaints. The pharmacists are highly trained, often speak good English, and may be able to sell medicines that would normally only be available by prescription at home. In major towns you'll find at least one pharmacy open 24 hours.

5 Multilingual Doctors

If you are seriously ill and need a doctor who speaks your language, you can get details from your local consulate *(see p126)*, hotel, pharmacy or tourist office. If you need someone who works under the EU health plan, make sure that the doctor is part of the Spanish health care system; otherwise, be prepared to pay and be reimbursed later by your insurance company.

6 Disabled Travellers

Generally speaking, Andalucía is not very well set up for travellers with any sort of disability. The best bet for adequate facilities are the newer hotels, since the law requires that all new public buildings be fully accessible. Older structures will present problems for those in wheelchairs *(see p134)*.

7 Condoms

Condoms need no longer be smuggled into Spain, as they had to be during the Franco era.

Emergency Numbers

Any Emergency: *112*
Fire: *080*
Ambulance: *061*
National Police: *091*
Civil Guard: *062*
Local Police: *092*

They are available in pharmacies, bars and even vending machines on the street.

8 Accidents

In the case of an accident dial the emergency number or call the *Cruz Roja* (Red Cross), who will send an ambulance and paramedics. There are good international hospitals along the Costa del Sol, and in major cities.
⊗ *Red Cross: Hospital Victoria Eugenia; Avda de la Cruz Roja; Seville; 954 35 14 00 • Hospital Costa del Sol: Ctra Nacional 340 km 187; Marbella, 952 82 82 50 • Hospital Virgen de las Nieves: Avda de las Fuerzas Armadas, Granada; 958 02 00 00 • Hospital Reina Sofía: Avda Menéndez Pidal, Córdoba, 957 01 00 00*

9 Petty Crime

In any crowded area, there are bound to be pickpockets. The best solution is not to carry any valuables in easily accessible places. Wallets should be safely tucked into inside closed pockets or under your clothing in a money belt. Never leave bags unattended.

10 Serious Crime

Serious crime is virtually unheard of in this pleasure-loving land. Naturally, however, it's wise not to wander down a deserted, unlit alley at night, especially in the seedier quarters.

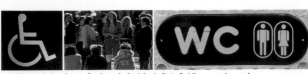

Left **Disabled sign** Centre **Students in Andalucía** Right **Public convenience sign**

TOP 10 Special Concerns

1 Disabled Travellers
Historically lagging behind in providing for people with mobility problems, Spain has begun to catch up in recent years. At least at the airport you should find adequate facilities – as long as you notify your travel agent and/or airline of your needs in advance and then reconfirm a week before departure.

2 Disabled Accommodation
The older buildings, often refurbished medieval structures, are usually entirely without facilities for the disabled – there are endless stairways and levels to contend with, sometimes even within a single room. Stay in the newest hotel you can find, where lifts and bathrooms will probably be large enough and will all comply with EU laws. But check details before booking.
◈ *Access-Able Travel Services: www.access-able.com • All Go Here: www.allgohere.com • Access Travel: 01942 888844; www.access-travel.co.uk • Mobility International USA, Eugene, OR; (541) 343-1284, www.miusa.org • Australian Council for Rehabilitation of the Disabled: 02 628 524 40, www.acrod.org.au • Organización Nacional de Ciegos de España (ONCE): C/Resolana 30, Seville; 954 90 16 16; www.once.es*

3 Senior Citizens
The area is very senior-friendly, given the large numbers of inter-national retirees who choose these sunny climes. Many apartment complexes are designed exclusively with seniors in mind, and hotels as well. Seniors also qualify for discounted fees to many sights, travel and even some hotels.

4 Resources for Seniors
There are several educational organizations that cater to seniors, with extensive residential cultural programmes of all types. In addition, the Junta de Andalucía has a helpline for those who can speak Spanish.
◈ *Senior Helpline: 900 22 22 23 • Elderhostel: www.elderhostel.org*

5 Women Travellers
Compared to Northern Europe, attitudes here towards women can be pretty macho. Still, women generally do not encounter harassment and can travel alone without a problem. Naturally, exercise normal care, especially after dark.

6 Helplines
The Junta de Andalucía runs several helplines, which are free calls from any phone, but they are Spanish-speaking only. ◈ *Women: 900 20 09 99 • Drug addiction: 900 16 15 15*

7 Student Travellers
Many students come to study in Seville, Granada and Córdoba. With a valid International Student ID Card, you're entitled to some price reductions on entrance fees and travel. There are student information centres in major cities.
◈ *Instituto Andaluz de la Juventud: C/O'Donnell 22, Seville; 955 03 57 00 • Centro Municipal de Información Juvenil: C/Varella 14 Bajo, Granada; 958 22 20 53 • La Casa de la Juventud: C/Campo Madre de Dios, Córdoba; 957 76 47 07*

8 Public Conveniences
Public toilets are scarce, but bars are everywhere and they are legally bound to let you use their facilities. A "S" on the door stands for *Señoras* (Ladies) and a "C" indicates *Caballeros* (Gents), although there are variations.

9 Gay Travellers
In more cosmopolitan areas, attitudes towards gays and lesbians are relaxed, but less so in rural areas. ◈ *Asociación Andaluza de Lesbianas y Gays: Granada, 958 20 06 02*

10 Gay Areas
Torremolinos is gay-central for nightlife *(see p104)*. Other cities with significant gay populations and venues are Seville, Granada and Cádiz.

Left **Andalucían theme park** Right **Family on the beach**

🔟 Tips for Families

1 Accommodation Breaks

Most accommodation options here – unless they specifically request "adults only" – truly welcome families. Hotels often allow you to include any children up to a certain age – sometimes as high as the teens – at no extra charge, except perhaps a nominal fee for the extra bed or two. The best option for most families is a self-catered apartment *(see p146)*.

2 Meals for Kids

Most restaurants have special kids' meals, and some even have separate menus with things that will please children's palates. Many will also prepare special foods for infants. There are also fast-food restaurants that cater to kids' tastes.

3 Shopping for Kids

There are shops galore that focus on what kids want, from toys to beach gear to clothes and gadgets. Most of the stuff is cheap – and cheaply made – so you can stock up on what they need without worrying about the budget.

4 Sights for Kids

Some of the theme parks and museums have exhibits and activities, as well as special playgrounds, that are designed entirely with children in mind. Andalucía's caves, too, are a big hit with young-sters, instilling them with a rich awareness of the wonders of nature.

5 Kids' Activities

Besides the sea, the region also has a number of commercial water-parks and amusement parks, replete with slides and other facilities for children to burn up a full-day's energy. It's healthy, outdoor fun that the whole family can participate in.

6 Teenagers

Teenagers of every nationality quickly fall in with each other soon after arrival in the most touristed areas, estab-lishing a routine of beaching it during the day and going out at night. There's plenty of high-energy action to get up to while the sun shines. When the sun goes down, it's time to prepare for the forth-coming social whirl.

7 Nightlife

In the very touristy resorts, which depend on families for much of their trade, many clubs will allow entrance for older teens, although the minimum legal age for drinking is 18. Depending on what curfew, if any, is imposed by parental authority, the dancing can go on till dawn. Spanish in general are very relaxed about the presence of children in bars and pubs.

8 Hotel Offerings

Many of the larger hotels and resorts have a full programme of activities for guests of every age. These may include water aerobics, water polo, or other exercise regimes – or anything from crafts classes for adults to organized games for pre-schoolers. Most such activities are scheduled on a weekly basis, with a monthly calendar posted in some conspicuous spot in the foyer.

9 Babysitting

Some hotels also offer babysitting services, especially those that cater primarily to pack-age tourists. The cost of this service may be included in the package, so confirm that it is, if such an option exists. Other hotels may have a play area, supervised by qualified personnel.

10 Transport Options

The best option when you have small children is not to move around much – the kids will be able to adjust and enjoy themselves more readily. Children under four travel free on trains; ages four to eleven pay 60 percent of the fare. Entry fees are either reduced or free to many sights and museums.

Left **Outside dining in Andalucía** Right **Seafood**

Eating and Drinking Tips

1 Eating Out
Both lunch and dinner hours tend to be late in Spain. Lunchtime is certainly no earlier than 1:30pm and even 3pm is perfectly normal. Dinner is usually no earlier than 9pm and sitting down at table as late as 11pm is not unheard of. A reservation is never a bad idea, and smart-casual dress is perfectly fine at most establishments.

2 Breakfast
As throughout most of the Mediterranean, breakfast here is little more than a coffee and *pasta* (pastry). Only foreign-run venues offer a full English or American breakfast. Many hotels cater to international taste with a buffet spread.

3 Tapas and Raciones
Tapas (see pp68–9) are a Spanish institution and nowhere more prevalent than here. Locals eat them as appetizers before heading off to dinner, but a few well-chosen *tapas* can easily make a full meal. *Raciones* are larger portions of the same dishes.

4 Menú del Día
Many places offer a *menú del día* (daily menu) at lunchtime, which usually means considerable savings compared to à la carte prices. You get a very

limited choice of a first course (typically soup or salad) and second course (fish or meat, with side orders) and dessert, with water and wine included. Coffee is usually extra, or in place of dessert.

5 Meats
Pork in all its guises is the central meat in the Andalucían diet, with Jabugo mountain-cured ham considered the crowning glory. Duck, rabbit, quail and other game are also quite common, with beef and veal present but not so important. Chicken is very common, and goat and lamb are also featured on many menus all over the region.

6 Seafood
Even along the crowded Costa del Sol, the few remaining fishermen still manage to haul in the full bounty that the Mediterranean has to offer. And the abundance from the Atlantic coast is even more impressive. A local speciality is *rape* (monkfish), and various types of crustacean and shellfish include lobster, crayfish, prawns and mussels *(see pp66–7)*.

7 Side Dishes and Dessert
Favourite side dishes include asparagus, both green and white, and mushrooms sautéed with garlic, as well as whatever vegetables may be

at their seasonal best. Fresh fruit is always an option for dessert, along with a range of baked treats and several types of custard.

8 Drinks
Wine and beer are the top choices, usually accompanied by a small bottle of mineral water, either still or sparkling. Sangría is prevalent, too, but the regional drink of choice is *vino de Jerez* (sherry), or one of the sweet wines from Málaga. Coffee can be with or without milk and you can also ask for it *descafeinado* (decaffeinated) *(see pp67)*.

9 Vegetarian and Vegan Options
Such choices are few and far between on most menus around the region. Meat is used in almost everything, and even the vegetable dishes are usually enhanced with a bit of pork. One good recourse would be to have the chef make a salad for you, leaving out any non-vegetarian ingredients. Or head for one of the few vegetarian restaurants.

10 Tipping
Tipping is not the absolute necessity here that it is in some countries. Nevertheless, it is customary to leave about 10 percent of the total bill, or at least to round the figure up.

Streetsmart

Left **Typical mountain hotel bedroom** Right **Hotel grading sign**

🔟 Accommodation Tips

1 Where to Stay
This extensive region offers a tremendous range of climes and terrains, from sophisticated city life, to mountains, to subtropical beaches, to wild, open plains. If you have the time, sample a bit of all of these, each of them beautiful and satisfying.

2 Accommodation Types
Determining your needs and desires before you book will ensure a happier stay. Andalucía has a vast range of accommodation options, from resorts (see p142), government-run paradors, often in historic buildings (see p140), converted farmhouses (see p145), to camping and hostels (see p147). If you want to see many of the region's sights but only want one base, consider renting a car.

3 Choosing the Best Base
Decide first how much of the region you want to see, and how much time you want to spend in differing terrains. Then choose whether to be based in a bustling area, in a smaller village, or in a more remote location. Options exist right on the sea, up in the mountains, or on private fincas (ranches), either working farms or those that have been transformed into pleasant resorts.

4 Price Considerations
The range of accommodation costs is very wide. You can get pretty much whatever you want in terms of location by spending very little. Andalucía tends to be less expensive than many other destinations of equal or greater quality.

5 Making Reservations
If you plan to visit in high season make reservations as far in advance as possible. The good-value accommodations fill up quickly and even high-end gems can be booked solid in the months of July and August. You will need a credit card number with expiry date to book, and you should confirm every detail – exact dates, type of accommodation, number of beds – with the hotel management by sending an e-mail and/or a fax.

6 Finding Something on the Spot
Unless you want to face hours of casting about for a room and possibly not finding anything in your price range, this practice is not recommended here, except in low season when you can, indeed, find plenty of options and good prices. Do be aware, however, that many establishments close for up to several months during the winter.

7 Tipping
Tipping in Spain, as in many countries in Europe, is not absolutely necessary. Workers are paid living wages and do not depend on your tips. However, a few coins for services rendered by the hotel staff are never amiss. You can tip porters and bellboys on the spot, and leave something for the maid in your room.

8 Hidden Extras
A tax of 7 percent may or may not be included in the quoted price of your accommodation. Parking, phone use and breakfast also may or may not be charged as extra, so determine what you are liable for in advance.

9 Travelling with Children
Andalucía is well set up for family travel. With very few exceptions, children are welcome at every hotel or resort, and those under certain ages may even stay free, with no extra charge for roll-away beds or cots. Many hotels have a schedule of events with kids in mind, often at no extra charge.

10 Language
With so many years of tourism, many Andalucíans are multi-lingual. However, it's a good idea to learn a little Spanish, at least for getting around the more rural areas.

There are no official tourist agencies that handle hotel reservations in Andalucía.

Left **Hotel Alfonso XIII** Right **Hotel Casa Imperial**

🔟 Seville Stays

1 Hotel Alfonso XIII
This historic palace, erected by the eponymous king to house royals and other dignitaries during the 1929 Exposition, is suitably sumptuous. Unfortunately, it's now part of a US chain, whose management just doesn't seem as *au fait* with the subtleties of European-style luxury. Still, it remains popular and is definitely worth a stroll-through to have a look. ❧ *C/San Fernando 2 • Map M4 • 954 91 70 00 • www.westin.com • €€€€€*

2 Hotel Casa Imperial
This luxurious choice in the Barrío de Santa Cruz provides a memorable stay. It's a converted 16th-century palace, set among a series of patios. Many rooms have sunken baths and all are uniquely decorated in the very finest taste, loaded with antiques. Included is the use of a nearby gym and pool. ❧ *C/Imperial 29 • Map N2 • 954 50 03 00 • www.casaimperial.com • €€€€€*

3 Hotel Taberna del Alabardero
Seven elegant rooms are gathered around a central patio filled with greenery and light. The restaurant boasts a Michelin star. ❧ *C/Zaragoza 20 • Map L3 • 954 50 27 21 • www. tabernadelalabardero.com • Closed Aug • €€€€*

4 Los Seises
Views of La Giralda are highlighted here from the rooftop pool. The building is the former archbishop's palace and the keynote is comfort and fine taste. It's an especially good choice for archaeological buffs – there are so many Roman and Moorish artifacts decorating the place that it's like a private museum. ❧ *C/Segovia 6 • Map M3 • 954 22 94 95 • www. hotellosseises.com • €€€€*

5 Doña María
Another great location, with a pool overlooked by the La Giralda tower. Furnishings include four-poster beds. ❧ *C/Don Remondo 19 • Map M3 • 954 22 49 90 • www.hdmaria.com • €€€€*

6 Hotel Murillo
Named after the artist who called this area home, this family-run place does, indeed, have a homey feel. Facilities are a bit cramped and the rooms basic, but it's comfortable. ❧ *C/Lope de Rueda 9 • Map M4 • 954 21 60 95 • www. hotelmurillo.com • €€*

7 Hotel Corregidor
Near the Alameda de Hercules, many of the rooms here face a patio and fountain. The decor is a mix of Moorish styles. ❧ *C/Morgado 17, cnr C/Amor de Dios 36 • Map M1 • 954 38 51 11 • www. sevillaonline.com • €€€*

8 Hotel Simón
This restored 18th-century mansion is beautiful and quite good value. You'll find all the signature Sevillian features, including a fern-filled patio, antiques, and a definite sense of style and class. It's right next to the cathedral, too. Not all rooms have en-suite facilities. ❧ *C/Garcia de Vinuesa 19 • Map L3 • 954 22 66 60 • www. hotelsimonsevilla.com • €€€*

9 Hostals Picasso, Van Gogh & Dali
These three cheery *pensions*, under the same management, are well located between the cathedral and the alcázar. Potted plants give the places an inviting feel and rooms are clean and comfortable. ❧ *Hostal Picasso: C/San Gregorio 1; Map M4; 954 21 08 64; €€ • Hostal Van Gogh: C/Miguel Mañara 4; Map M4; 954 56 37 27; €€ • Hostal Dali: C/ Puerta Jerez 3; 954 22 95 05; €€*

10 Instalación Juvenil Sevilla
Despite its location to the south of Parque María Luisa, this hostel gets very booked up very quickly. It's institutional, but a good budget option. ❧ *C/Isaac Perál 2 • Bus No. 34 • 955 05 65 00 • www.inturjoven. com • No credit cards • No en-suite facilities • No air conditioning • €*

 Note: *Unless otherwise stated, all hotels accept credit cards, have en-suite bathrooms and air conditioning*

Price Categories

For a standard, double room per night (with breakfast if included), taxes and extra charges.	€ under €50
	€€ €50–€100
	€€€ €100–€150
	€€€€ €150–€200
	€€€€€ over €200

Above **Alhambra Palace**

🔟 Granada Sojourns

1 Parador de San Francisco

You'll need to book about a year in advance to stay here, but it's the premier stay in town. Housed in a meticulously restored 15th-century monastery, it is utterly beautiful. For the maximum experience, get a room with a view out over the Albaicín on one side and the cloister on the other. ⊗ C/Real de la Alhambra • Map R2 • 958 22 14 40 • www.parador.es • €€€€€

2 Alhambra Palace

The style of this *belle époque* extravaganza is neo-Moorish. Located just steps away from the Nasrid area, it offers great views from every room, terrace and balcony. The public rooms are palatial. ⊗ C/Peña Partida 2–4 • Map R3 • 958 22 14 68 • www.h-alhambrapalace.es • €€€€

3 Hotel Casa Morisca

This 15th-century mansion makes a peaceful choice in a central location. The original features have been wonderfully preserved, such as the Mudéjar ceiling. Every room is decorated with period accents according to modern standards, with views of the Albaicín, the Alhambra or the courtyard. ⊗ Cuesta de la Victoria 9 • Map S2 • 958 22 11 00 • www.hotel casamorisca.com • €€€

4 Carmen de Santa Inés

This Moorish mansion has been remodelled over the centuries, in particular the wonderful big patio. The decor is elegant, although some rooms may be small, and you will find antiques everywhere. ⊗ Placeta Porras 7 • Map Q2 • 958 22 63 80 • €€€

5 Hotel Reina Cristina

Everything has been kept more or less the same as when the poet García Lorca was forced to hide out here – this is the last place the poet stayed, before his untimely end *(see p57)*. Each room has unique style and there are patios and fountains in the public areas. ⊗ C/Tablas 4 • Map F4 • 958 25 32 11 • www. hotelreinacristina.com • €€€

6 Casa del Aljarife

In this delightful 17th-century house you will find bathrooms, wooden floors, beamed ceilings, a charming patio and a sun-terrace. Ask for a room with a balcony and view over the rooftops. ⊗ Placita de la Cruz Verde 2 • Map R2 • 958 22 24 25 • www. granadainfo.com/most • €€

7 Cuevas El Abanico

In this "cave" hotel, the whitewashed interiors are immaculate and loaded with rustic charm. No need for air conditioning – you have an entire hill of earth overhead to keep out the heat. A picturesque and uniquely Andalucían choice. ⊗ Verea de Enmedio • Map F4 • www.el-abanico.com • €€

8 Hostal Suecia

In a leafy cul-de-sac, this is every inch a traditional Spanish house, with terracotta tiles, arched windows and a large patio. The rooftop terrace is perfect for admiring the nearby Alhambra. ⊗ C/Molinos (Huerta de los Angeles) 8 • Map R3 • 958 22 50 44 • No air conditioning • €

9 Posada Doña Lupe

For the price, this is unbeatable, if basic. There's a pool on the roof with great views of the Alhambra. Note that it closes at midnight. ⊗ Paseo del Generalife (C/Alhambra) • Map S3 • 958 22 14 73 • No en-suite bathrooms • No air conditioning • €

10 Instalación Juvenil Granada

This youth hostel is clean, although it is quite far away from the city centre. Its advantage, however, is that there are only two to a room and the bathrooms are all en-suite. ⊗ C/Ramón y Cajal 2 • Map F4 • 958 00 29 00 • www. inturjoven.com • Dis. access • No credit cards • No air conditioning • €

Note that hotel prices can double during local festivals. For dates of festivals See pp60–61

Left **Parador de Ronda** Right **Parador Arcos de la Frontera**

Paradors

1 Parador de Ayamonte
At the mouth of the River Guadiana, this modern facility features sunlit rooms and a perfect position for exploring the area where Huelva Province meets Portugal. Most rooms afford panoramic views of the Atlantic from the high point of town. Local cuisine emphasizes fish, such as ray and monkfish, as well as rural dishes. ◈ Avda de la Constitucíon s/n • Map A4 • 959 32 07 00 • Dis. access • €€€

2 Parador de Mazagón
Unspoiled beauty on the shores of the sea is what this modern property is all about. It's ideal for those who want to commune with nature, especially with the wonders of the Coto Doñana, nearby. Facilities include gardens, pools and a sauna – all facing on to Mazagón beach. Seafood and Iberian ham are culinary specialities. ◈ Playa de Mazagón • Map B4 • 959 53 63 00 • Dis. access • €€€

3 Parador Hotel Atlántico, Cádiz
This modern seaside complex has great views of the bay and is ideally located for getting to know the whole province, as well as the historic city. Facilities include a pool jutting out over the sea and most

rooms enjoy views of the water or of the old town. ◈ Avda Duque de Nájera 9 • Map B5 • 956 22 69 05 • Dis. access • €€€

4 Parador Arcos de la Frontera
Located on the banks of the Río Guadalete, this parador has an impressive view of the fertile plain of the river and of the old part of town. An ideal starting point for the *pueblos blancos* routes, as well as Jerez de la Frontera. The courtyard is graced with traditional lattice-work and ceramic tiles. ◈ Plaza del Cabildo • Map C5 • 956 70 05 00 • €€€

5 Parador Alcázar del Rey, Carmona
One of the most impressive of all the paradors, this is a 14th-century Moorish fortress-palace overlooking the Río Corbones. Rooms are large and decorated in classic Andalucían style, set off by antiques. Charming touches include a garden pool and expansive terrace. ◈ Alcázar • Map C3 • 954 14 10 10 • €€€

6 Parador de Ronda
One of the best sites in this evocative hill town. Set in the former town hall, views from the rooms are amazing, while the decor reflects the colours of the area. ◈ Plaza de España • Map D5 • 952 87 75 00 • €€€

7 Parador de Antequera
This quiet parador, surrounded by gardens and a swimming pool, is near the spectacular El Torcal (see p99). ◈ García del Olmo • Map D4 • 952 84 02 61 • Dis. access • €€€

8 Parador del Gibralfaro, Málaga
This parador stands surrounded by pine trees, facing the Alcázaba. It's handy for activities, notably golf and tennis, nearby. ◈ Castillo de Gibralfaro • Map S4 • 952 22 19 02 • Dis. access • €€€

9 Parador Castillo de Santa Catalina, Jaén
The superb location of this castle once made it the defensive bastion of Jaén. Inside, high crossed arches in the living and dining rooms show a marked Arabic character, and the comfortable bedrooms enjoy panoramic views. ◈ Map E3 • 953 23 00 00 • €€€

10 Parador Condestable Dávalos, Úbeda
Live like 16th-century nobility in this Renaissance palace, in the heart of one of Spain's most remarkably preserved historic centres. Rooms reflect the noble tone, with high ceilings and antique furnishings. ◈ Plaza de Vázquez Molina • Map F2 • 953 75 03 45 • €€€

For more information on paradors in Andalucía, visit the website www.parador.es

Price Categories

For a standard, double room per night (with breakfast if included), taxes and extra charges.

€	under €50
€€	€50–€100
€€€	€100–€150
€€€€	€150–€200
€€€€€	over €200

Above **San Roque Club Hotel**

🔟 Luxury Hotels

1 Hotel Jerez, Jerez

All rooms have been decorated in a warm and comfortable style, with views of the tropical gardens and a large pool. Room facilities include ADSL and ISDN lines, and many have Jacuzzis. 🕲 Avda Álvaro Domecq 35 • Map B5 • 956 30 06 00 • www.jerezhotel.com • Dis. access • €€€€

2 Reina Cristina, Algeciras

This marvellously grand, though somewhat faded, colonial hotel was the first on the Andalucían coast. In its heyday, among the famous who stayed here were García Lorca, Churchill, Roosevelt, De Gaulle, Cole Porter and Ava Gardner. 🕲 Paseo de la Conferencia • Map C6 • 956 60 26 22 • www.reinacristina.com • €€

3 San Roque Club Hotel, San Roque

This hotel, with a great 18-hole golf course (see p103), has more than 50 villas on site. The landscaping is beautiful, and the swimming pool is spectacular. 🕲 N340 km126.5 • Map C6 • 956 61 30 30 • Dis. access • €€€€€

4 Hotel Casa de Carmona

Welcome to 400 years of luxury. With unparalleled style and tranquillity, this 16th-century palace has been lovingly converted into a hotel, now joined to the exclusive Relais & Châteaux chain. Patios with lush plantings and the soothing sound of fountains, grand drawing rooms and exquisite decor create an opulent atmosphere. 🕲 Plaza de Lasso 1 • Map C3 • 954 19 10 00 • www.casa decarmona.com • Dis. access • €€€€

5 El Juncal, Ronda

An old Spanish farm has been brilliantly converted. The 11 rooms, most with private terrace, are spacious and refined. Other touches include a pool with a beach, Jacuzzi and sauna, set amid gardens. 🕲 Ctra Ronda El Burgo km1 • Map D5 • 952 16 11 70 • www.eljuncal.com • Dis. access • €€€

6 El Fuerte, Marbella

In the centre of Marbella, next to the sea and surrounded by subtropical gardens. Within easy walking distance of the historic quarter too, so that you can discover the "real" Marbella, as well as soak up the glamour. 🕲 Avda El Fuerte • Map D5 • 952 86 15 00 • www. fuertehoteles.com • Dis. access • €€€€€

7 Hotel-Casino Torrequebrada, Benalmádena

This deluxe, Vegas-style establishment also has a casino. All the rooms have a balcony with sea views. Recreation options include a pool, sauna, gym and tennis court. 🕲 Avda del Sol • Map D5 • 952 44 60 00 • www.torrequebrada.com • €€€€ • Dis. access

8 Hotel Meliá Córdoba

Right in the middle of the Jardines de la Victoria, this highrise is certainly convenient and luxurious, if a bit soulless. The big advantage is off-street parking for those travelling by car. 🕲 Avda Jardines de la Victoria • Map D3 • 957 29 80 66 • www.meliacordoba. solmelia.com • €€€

9 Palacio de la Rambla, Úbeda

This 16th-century palace offers eight wonderful rooms for guests to experience the refined atmosphere. The patio is said to have been designed by Vandelvira himself. 🕲 Plaza del Marqués 1 • Map F2 • 953 75 01 96 • €€€

10 Gran Hotel Almería, Almería

Although this is an undistinguished highrise to look at, its rooms enjoy a balcony with a view of the sea. Only steps from the beach, it has been recently refurbished with taste. 🕲 Avda Reina Regente 8 • Map G4 • 950 23 80 11 • www.granhotelalmeria. com • Dis. access • €€€

 Note: Unless otherwise stated, all hotels accept credit cards, have en-suite bathrooms and air conditioning

Left **Hotel Playa Victoria** Right **Hotel La Fuente de la Higuera**

TOP 10 Resorts

1 Hotel Riu Canela, Isla Canela

A vast resort offering every facility you can think of amid its gardens and neo-Moorish splendours, including several swimming pools, one for children, and a playground. ✪ *Paseo de los Gavilanes • Map A4 • 959 47 71 24 • www.riu.com • Closed Nov–Jan • Dis. access • €€€€*

2 Monte Castillo, Jerez

This hotel towers like a castle of pink stucco beside one of Europe's top golf courses. Expect top service and lots of activity options. There are several restaurants and snack bars to choose from. ✪ *Ctra Jerez-Arcos km 9.6 • Map B5 • 956 15 12 00 • www.montecastillo. com • Dis. access • €€€€*

3 Hotel Playa Victoria, Cádiz

A highrise hotel with a swimming pool over the beach. It's in the new city, but it's a pleasant walk to the old town. ✪ *Glorieta Ingeniero de la Cierva 4 • Map B5 • 956 20 51 00 • www. palafoxhoteles.com • Dis. access • €€€€*

4 Hotel Fuerte Conil, Conil de la Frontera

This resort is an award-winner, in recognition of its environmentally friendly practices. Located right on the beach, it's done up in Neo-Moorish style and not far from the fishing village of Conil. Most rooms have balconies and sea views. There's a choice of restaurants, a pool, spa treatments and sports facilities. ✪ *Playa de la Fontanilla • Map B5 • 956 44 33 44 • www. fuertehoteles.com • Closed Nov–Feb • Dis. access • €€€*

5 Kempinski Resort Hotel, Estepona

One of the "Leading Hotels of the World", this place is nothing short of magnificent. The style is a whimsical take on Moorish and regional architecture that suits the seaside setting perfectly. ✪ *Ctra de Cádiz km 159 • Map D5 • 952 80 95 00 • www.kempinski-spain.com • €€€€€*

6 Marbella Club Hotel, Marbella

Another of the "Leading Hotels of the World", the beachfront rooms and suites harmonize with Andalucían-style villas enjoying private gardens and some with private pools. ✪ *Bulevar Príncipe Alfonso von Hoenlome • Map D5 • 952 82 22 11 • www.marbellaclub.com • €€€€€*

7 Hotel La Fuente de la Higuera, Ronda

In a renovated olive oil mill, traditional Spanish architecture has met post modern design. Individually designed interiors are detailed down to the last bathroom fitting. All rooms have a garden or terrace. ✪ *Partido de los Frontones • Map D5 • 952 11 43 55 • www. hotellafuente.com • Closed Jan–Feb • Dis. access • €€€*

8 Hotel Vincci Rumaykiyya, Sierra Nevada, Monachil, Granada

With beautiful alpine decor and wonderful interior design this hotel is both spacious and luxurious. At the heart of this ski resort, the hotel has a chair lift service at its door. ✪ *Map F4 • 958 48 25 08 • www.vinccisierra nevada.com • Closed May–Nov • €€€€€*

9 Hotel Paraíso del Mar, Nerja

This hotel enjoys a view of the coast. Rooms facing the mountains are generally larger or with a Jacuzzi to compensate. ✪ *C/Prolongación de Carabeo 22 • Map E5 • 952 52 16 21 • www. hotelparaisodelmar.com • €€€*

10 Finca La Bobadilla, Granada Province

A fabulous resort, reminiscent of a tiny Moorish village with its own chapel. It is interlaced with gardens and patios. ✪ *exit 175 from A92 • Map E4 • 958 32 18 61 • www. la-bobadilla.com • €€€€€*

 Note: *Unless otherwise stated, all hotels accept credit cards, have en-suite bathrooms and air conditioning*

Price Categories

For a standard, double room per night (with breakfast if included), taxes and extra charges.

€	under €50
€€	€50–€100
€€€	€100–€150
€€€€	€150–€200
€€€€€	over €200

Above **María de Molina**

🔟 Historic Finds

1 El Cortijo de los Mimbrales, El Rocío

Grouped around flower-decked patios, this con-verted farm is a series of comfortable cottages that retain an authentic flavour. Private balconies and gardens grace many of the accommodations, and all around there are orange trees, bougain-villea, wisteria and jasmine perfuming the air. ✆ Ctra Rocío-Matalascañas A483 km 30 • Map B4 • 959 44 22 37 • www.cortijomimbrales. com • Dis. access • €€€

2 Monasterio San Miguel, El Puerto de Santa María

This former monastery with Baroque architec-ture and art is neverthe-less up-to-date with the luxuries it offers. Facilities include an excellent restaurant, pool, gardens and a solarium. ✆ C/Larga 27 • Map B5 • 956 54 04 40 • www.jale.com/ monasterio • Dis. access • €€€€

3 Cortijo Faín, Arcos de la Frontera

A converted 17th-century farmhouse 3 km (2 miles) southeast of town. Sur-rounded by olive groves and walls covered in bougainvillea, the atmos-phere is intimate. Facilities include a restaurant, pool, horse-riding and a library. ✆ Ctra del Algar km 3 • Map C5 • 956 23 13 96 • www. cortijofain.en.eresmas • €€

4 La Casa Grande, Arcos de la Frontera

In 1729 the Nuñez de Prado family erected this mansion, which has preserved its original structure. Perched over the cliff of La Peña, terra-cotta floors, wood beams, stone columns, ceramic tiles, hand-woven bed-spreads and antiques are among the many details. ✆ C/Maldonado 10 • Map C5 • 956 70 39 30 • www. lacasagrande.net • Closed 6 Jan–6 Feb • €€

5 Amanhavis Hotel, Benahavis

In the hills just outside Marbella, this place is like an Andalucían theme park, albeit very tasteful. Gardens and pools set off the nine rooms with names like "The Christopher Columbus Berth" and "The Spice Trader's Caravan" – all decorated accordingly. ✆ C/del Pilar 3 • Map D5 • 952 85 60 26/61 51 • www.aman havis.com • Closed mid-Jan–mid-Feb • €€€

6 Hotel González, Córdoba

This charming hotel typi-fies the old houses of the Jewish Quarter, with a central patio and an elegant marble entrance replete with antiques and high ceilings. The building was a 16th-century palace, recently converted. Many rooms look onto the patio. ✆ C/Manriquez 3 • Map D3 • 957 47 98 19 • €€

7 NH Amistad Córdoba

Five minutes' walk from La Mezquita and built into the large old city walls. The large patio-cloisters are lovely, and there's also a plunge pool and sun terrace. ✆ Plaza de Maimónides 3 • Map D3 • 957 42 03 35 • www.nh-hotels.com • Dis. access • €€€

8 El Castillo, Castillo de Monda

If you're in the mood for Moorish opulence, this castle high above the town fits the bill. Elegant and rich furnishings, and a gourmet restaurant too. ✆ Avda de Castillo • Map D5 • 952 45 71 42 • www. costadelsol.spa.es/hotel/ monda • €€€

9 Hotel Palacete Santa Ana, Baeza

This hotel occupies a 16th-century palace, beautifully restored and set off with priceless antiques and paintings. ✆ C/Santa Ana Vieja 9 • Map F2 • 953 74 16 57 • www.palacetesantana. com • €€

10 María de Molina, Úbeda

The central courtyard, with its antique marble columns is exquisite, and the location is ideal. A gorgeous staircase leads to the upper floors. ✆ Plaza del Ayuntamiento • Map F2 • 953 79 53 56 • www.hotel-maria-de-molina.com • €€

Left **Hotel Francia y Paris** Right **Hotel Posada de Vallina**

Budget Charmers

1 Hotel Francia y Paris, Cádiz

The best choice in this old city. Situated on an inviting plaza, with a handsome exterior and a vast foyer, it's convenient to all the major sights. Comfortable rooms, some with balconies. ✆ *Plaza San Francisco 6 • Map B5 • 956 21 23 19 • www. hotelfrancia.com • €€*

2 Doña Blanca, Jerez de la Frontera

For the price, this place is really rather grand, providing all the services you'd expect of more high-end properties and it's well located right in the centre of the city. The common areas and rooms are a little spare, but perfectly maintained, and the building has its own garage. ✆ *C/Bodegas 11 • Map B5 • 956 34 87 61 • www.hoteldonablanca. com • €€*

3 Hotel El Convento, Arcos de la Frontera

This wonderful period building has preserved its atmospheric cloisters and charm, right in the heart of this captivating town. Most of the rooms have views of the castle, plus there's a great roof terrace. Don't overlook the excellent restaurant, specializing in local cuisine. ✆ *C/Maldonado 2 • Map C5 • 956 70 23 33 • www.webdearcos.com/ elconvento • €€*

4 Hotel Marqués de Torresoto, Arcos de la Frontera

This 17th-century mansion has been exquisitely converted into an extremely comfortable hotel. Sit in the porticoed inner courtyard or linger in the Baroque family chapel and soak up the age-old ambience. ✆ *C/Marqués de Torresoto 4 • Map C5 • 956 70 07 17 • www.hmde torresoto.com • €€*

5 Hotel Los Patios, Córdoba

Situated directly across from La Mezquita, this picturesque place offers tremendous value for money. The main patio is a perfect spot to enjoy breakfast each morning. Rooms are clean and serviceable, with nice bathrooms, and all of them overlook the inner courtyard. ✆ *C/Cardenal Herrero 14 • Map D3 • 957 47 83 40 • www.lospatios. net • €€*

6 Hotel Posada de Vallina, Córdoba

The hotel is located facing the southern wall of La Mezquita, in an old converted mansion. According to archaeologists, the site dates back to Roman times. The rooms are all relatively spacious, if simple, and there's an excellent restaurant featuring local dishes. ✆ *C/Corregidor Luis de la Cerda 83 • Map D3 • 957 49 87 50 • www. hotelvallina.com • €€*

7 Hostal Lineros, Córdoba

With its striking Mudéjar-style architecture, this building epitomizes the city's cross-cultural charm. It's a great choice in the old quarter. ✆ *C/Lineros 38 • Map D3 • 957 48 25 17 • www. hostallineros38.com • €€*

8 Hotel San Gabriel, Ronda

In the historic Ciudad and built in 1736 this converted mansion, with its original coat of arms and handsome façade, offers remarkably sumptuous rooms for the price. ✆ *C/Marqués de Moctezuma 19 • Map D5 • 952 19 03 92 • www. hotelsangabriel.com • €€*

9 Cortijo Torrera, Near Motril

Set in mountainous scenery but facing the sea (and with a pool too!), the structure maintains its rustic charm whilst providing many modern comforts. ✆ *Rambla de Lújar • Map F5 • 958 34 91 39 • www. torrera.com • No air-conditioning • €*

10 Hotel TRH, Baeza

Right in the heart of this Renaissance town, is this oasis of quiet beauty. It's part of a chain, with all the conveniences, yet evokes timeless style. ✆ *C/Concepción 3 • Map F2 • 953 74 81 30 • www. trhhoteles.com • €€*

For budget hotels in Seville and Granada See pp138–9

Price Categories

For a standard, double room per night (with breakfast if included), taxes and extra charges.

€ under €50
€€ €50–€100
€€€ €100–€150
€€€€ €150–€200
€€€€€ over €200

Above **Alquería de Morayma**

🔟 Rural Retreats

1 Finca Buen Vino, Sierra de Aracena

Set amid green hills, this converted ranch is filled with an eclectic mix of furniture, paintings, pottery and books. Rooms are all distinctive, whether due to hand-painted walls, Oriental hangings, a bathtub with a view, or a fireplace. In spring, the valley below the house is filled with white heather, primroses and the sound of nightingales; summer days can be spent beside the spectacular pool. 🚫 *Nr Los Marines, N433 km95 • Map A2 • 959 12 40 34 • www.fincabuenvino. com • €€€*

2 Antonio, Zahara de los Atunes

This seaside retreat is decorated in a traditional style, with whitewashed walls, and there's a nice pool. Most rooms have terraces overlooking the sea. 🚫 *Atlanterra km1 • Map C6 • 956 43 91 41 • www.antoniohoteles.com • Dis. access • €€*

3 Alcázar de la Reina, Carmona

In the historic centre of this small town the façade of this hotel stands out, while the interior reflects the style of Mudéjar craftsmanship. No two rooms are alike, but they all have marble bathrooms and several enjoy spectacular views. 🚫 *Plaza de Lasso 2 • Map C3 • 954 19 62 00 • www.alcazar-reina.es • €€€*

4 Hotel Humaina, Montes de Málaga

This is a small, family-run hotel, set in the mountains, and the emphasis is on relaxation, whether that is reading a book in the library, swimming in the pool or enjoying a glass of Málaga wine. Cycling, horse riding and rambling are also on offer. 🚫 *Ctra Colmenar • Map E5 • 952 64 10 25 • www.hotelhumaina.es • €€*

5 Finca Buytrón, outside Montilla

This charming 16th-century farmhouse sits amid olive groves. The interior is welcoming and comfortable, with original stone floors. Outside, the grounds are spacious, with a wide terrace, a barbecue and a pool. 🚫 *C/Gran Capitán 24 • Map D3 • 957 65 01 52 • No air-conditioning • €*

6 Posada La Niña Margarita, Los Villares

This leafy rural house is two storeys of history and rustic charm. Set in parkland, it's perfect for cycling, hiking and other outdoor activities. It has a pool and restaurant and full board is an option. The common room has a lovely fireplace. 🚫 *5km from Carcabuey • Map E3 • 957 70 40 54 • www. casasdelasubbetica.com • No en-suite bathrooms • No air-conditioning • €*

7 Cuevas La Granja, near Benalúa

A complex of restored cave dwellings, each of which preserves their original style. The location provides the perfect setting for rest and relaxation. 🚫 *Camino de la Granja • Map F3 • 958 67 60 00 • www. cuevas.org • No air-conditioning • €€*

8 Cuevas Pedro Antonio de Alarcón, Guadix

Another charming cave dwelling, yet with modern comforts. Beautiful views over the city of Guadix and the Sierra Nevada. There's a pool too. 🚫 *Bda San Torcuato • Map F4 • 958 66 49 86 • www.andalucia. com/cavehotel • Dis. access • No air-conditioning • €€*

9 Cuevas de Orce, Ctra de María, Orce

A luxury complex of cave dwellings with a large pool. 🚫 *Ctra de María • Map G3 • 958 74 62 81 • www.cuevasdeorce.com • Dis. access • No air-conditioning • €€*

10 Alquería de Morayma, East Alpujarras

A lovely retreat, nestled in farmland, with vines, almonds and olives. Two restaurants. 🚫 *A348 Ctra Trovizcón-Cádiar • Map G4 • 958 34 32 21 • www. alqueriamorayma.com • No air-conditioning • €€*

Left & Right **Cantueso, Periana**

Self-Catering Options

1 Casas Rurales Los Gallos, Almonaster la Real
Whitewashed cottages are set amid woods, patios, arcades, pools and flowers. Each one has a different feel and colour scheme, and all are loaded with rustic charm and antiques as well as modern conveniences. ⌖ *Finca Los Gallos, Estación de Almonaster • Map B3 • 959 50 11 67 • www.usuarios.lycos.es/losgallos • No credit cards • No air-conditioning • Dis. access • €€*

2 Villa Turística Grazalema
Despite the price, this is a fairly luxurious choice for those who want their own apartment. The property includes a hotel, the homes, a pool, parking and a bar-café. The terrace, offering views of the mountains, is surrounded by gardens. ⌖ *Ctra Olivar • Map C5 • 956 13 21 36 • No air-conditioning • www.tugasa.com • €€*

3 Casas Karen, Costa de la Luz
Typical Andalucían houses and apartments, and native-style straw roof bungalows, nestle between pinewoods and the beach. Follow signs to Faro de Trafalgar. ⌖ *Fuente del Madroño 6, nr Cabo Trafalgar • Map C6 • 956 43 70 67 • www.casaskaren.com • No air-conditioning • €€*

4 Apartamentos Murillo, Seville
These lovely apartments are named after the Baroque painter who hailed from the Barrio de Santa Cruz, right in the middle of this flower-decked old quarter. ⌖ *C/Reinosa 6 • Map M4 • 954 21 60 95 • www.hotelmurillo.com • €€*

5 Villa Turística de Cazalla
For easy access to, and views of, the Sierra Norte de Sevilla, this is the spot. Facilities include a tennis court, a pool and a restaurant. The management organizes nature hikes, horse-riding and tours. ⌖ *Ctra Cazalla-Constantina, km3 • Map C3 • 954 88 33 10 (954 88 39 08 Fax) • €€*

6 Hostal La Posada, Mijas
A great opportunity to rent a fully equipped apartment in this attractive town and to sample a bit of the real Andalucía. ⌖ *C/Coin 47 & 49 • Map D5 • 952 48 53 10 • No credit cards • No air-conditioning • €*

7 Hacienda La Colorá, Montoro
You can go for a studio, an apartment or a grand suite in this 18th-century country mansion. It's a garden of loveliness, cultivating olives and honey, and there's a beautiful pool. If you like, you can take painting classes. ⌖ *9 km (6 miles) NW of Montoro along the CO414 • Map E2 • 957 33 60 77 • www.lacolora.com • No air-conditioning • €€*

8 Cantueso, Periana
Wood-beam ceilings and rustic comfort in a gorgeous setting. Outdoor barbecues and a pool will complement your bungalow. ⌖ *The Axarquía • Map E4 • 699 94 62 13 • www.cantueso.net • No credit cards • No air-conditioning • €€*

9 Casa La Piedra, Cómpeta
This romantic house is a good choice for tranquillity combined with easy access to the coast. The rooms are inviting, most with terracotta floors and wood-beam ceilings. One week minimum stay. ⌖ *Plazoleta 17, the Axarquía • Map E4 • 952 51 63 29 • www.2sandra.com • No credit cards • No air-conditioning • €€*

10 Santa Ana Apartamentos Turísticos, Granada
Situated just above the river, these apartments come with views of the Albaicín quarter. Each apartment has large, comfortable rooms, which are decorated with style. Minimum two nights stay. ⌖ *Puente Cabrera 9 • Map F4 • 958 22 81 30 • www.apartamentos-santaana.com • €€*

Price Categories

For a double room per night, including taxes and extra charges, a night's camping fee or a night in self-catering.

€	under €50
€€	€50–€100
€€€	€100–€150
€€€€	€150–€200
€€€€€	over €200

Above **Hostal Séneca**

🔟 Hostals and Camping

1 Hostal La Malagueña, Estepona

Although it isn't an official hostel or even aimed at backpackers, the price doesn't get any better than this. The airy rooms have balconies facing the square. You can stroll along the sandy beaches or wander around the shops of this old and still authentic fishing village. ✪ *C/Castillo 1 • Map D5 • 952 80 00 11 • No air-conditioning • €*

2 Pensión La Purísma, Ronda

Bright, clean, family-run and friendly, this old-fashioned place offers basic comfort. As with all of the cheaper accommodations in Ronda, it's in the newer part of town, but it's a rewarding walk over the Puente Nuevo to get to the historic old part. ✪ *C/Sevilla 10 • Map D5 • 952 87 10 50 • No credit cards • No air-conditioning • €*

3 Hostel, Marbella

Double rooms, some with adjoining bath, a pool, and lots of recreational options make this an excellent find. It's just north of the lovely old quarter, where you can see the real Marbella and not just the glitz. Walk through it to get to the beach and the port. ✪ *C/Trapiche 2 • Map D5 • 952 77 14 91 • www.inturjoven.com • Dis. access • No credit cards • No air-conditioning • €*

4 Hostal Séneca, Córdoba

Friendly and delightful, as well as excellent value. Stained-glass windows on the first floor and a patio with Moorish touches add to the grace. Book ahead. ✪ *C/Conde y Luque • Map D3 • 957 47 32 34 • No credit cards • No en-suite bathrooms • No air-conditioning • €*

5 Hostel, Málaga

Modern double rooms and a sun-terrace make this an acceptable option. Although it is not particularly near to the centre, it's well connected by public transport. ✪ *Plaza Pío XII 6 • Map E5 • 952 30 85 00 • www.inturjoven.com • Dis. access • No credit cards • No en-suite bathrooms • No air-conditioning • €*

6 Instalación Juvenil, Solynieve, Sierra Nevada

Located near the top of the ski station, with rooms holding two to six, ideal for skiers in the winter or trekkers in the summer. They will also rent skis and other equipment. ✪ *C/Peñones 22 • Map F4 • 958 48 03 05 • www.inturjoven.com • Dis. access • No credit cards • No air-conditioning • €*

7 Instalación Campamento Juvenil Mazagón

Here you'll find four-person cabins with private bathroom, as well as a campsite. It's handy for the beach, there's a TV room, dining room and various sports facilities. ✪ *Ctra A-494 km 27.5 • Map B4 • 959 53 62 62 • www.inturjoven.com • Closed Sep–Mar, May–Jun • No credit cards • No air-conditioning • €*

8 Camping El Sur, Ronda

Camping and bungalows are available here. It's a chance to take beautiful walks or horse-ride in the countryside around Ronda. ✪ *Ctra Ronda-Algeciras km1.5 • Map D5 • 952 87 59 39 • www.campingelsur.com • No credit cards • No en-suite facilities • Dis. access • No air-conditioning • €*

9 Camping Embalse Conde de Guadalhorce, Ardales

This campsite offers a shady area for tents, trailers and RV hookups, as well as apartments. The area is known for its Cuevas de Ardales, containing Paleolithic paintings and carvings. ✪ *Map D4 • 952 11 24 01 • No credit cards • €*

10 Camping Sierra Nevada, Granada

One of the most convenient camping choices in the region. There are big, clean bathrooms, a pool and a laundry. ✪ *Avda de Madrid 107 • Map F4 • 958 15 00 62 • Closed Nov–Feb • No credit cards • Dis. access • €*

General Index

A

Abd el Rahman I, Caliph 20
Abd el Rahman III, Caliph 16, 35, 119
Las Acacias (Málaga) 105
accidents 133
admission prices 131
agriculture 36, 110
Agroalimentaria Virgin Del Rocio 67
air travel 128
Aires de Doñana (El Rocío) 93
La Alacena (Granada) 114
Alájar 42, 90
  hiking 52
  restaurants 93
Alameda de Hércules (Seville) 79
La Albahaca (Seville) 85
Albaicín (Granada) **12–13**, 111, 114
La Alcaicería (Granada) 111, 114
Alcaidesa Links 103
Alcalá La Real 121
  Fortaleza de la Mota 38
Alcazaba (Almería) 37
Alcazaba (Granada) 8
Alcazaba (Málaga) 37
alcázares 38
  Alcázar de Jerez 99
  Alcázar de la Reina (Carmona) 145
  Alcázar de los Reyes Cristianos (Córdoba) 18, 47
Alfonso X the Wise 17
Alfonso XI of Castile 16
Alfonso XIII, King 138
Algeciras 99
  hotels 141
Alhama de Granada 110
  restaurants 117
Alhambra (Granada) **8–9**, 11
Alhambra Palace (hotel, Granada) 139
La Alicantina (Seville) 84
Almería 111
  Alcazaba 37
  drive from Nerja 52
  flamenco 59
  hotels 141
  Mini Hollywood 63
  nightlife 115

Almería (cont.)
  restaurants 117
  tearooms and tapas bars 116
Almería Province see Granada and Almería Provinces
Almohad dynasty 36
Almonaster La Real 37, 40, 42, 90
  self-catering accommodation 146
Almudaina (Córdoba) 123
Almuñécar 110
  Aquatropic 63
  beaches 49
  Museo Arqueológico Cueva de Siete Palacios 55
  restaurants 117
  tearooms and tapas bars 116
Las Alpujarras 33, 37
  crafts 114
  drives 53
  hotels 145
Alquería de Morayma (East Alpujarras) 145
Amanhavis Hotel (Benahavis) 143
ambulances 133
El Ancladero (Nerja) 105
El Ángel Azul (Granada) 115
Angeles Méndez (Seville) 82
Antequera 96
  Museo Municipal 55
  walks 53
Antigua Casa de Guardia (Málaga) 107
Antonio (Zahara de los Atunes) 145
Antonio Martín (Málaga) 107
Apartamentos Murillo (Seville) 146
Aqua Discoteca (Benalmadena) 104
Aquatropic (Almuñécar) 63
Aracena 90
  cafés and tapas bars 92
architecture
  Caliphal style 20
  Moorish 36
  Renaissance 29
Archivo de Indias La Lonja (Seville) 54
Arcos (Granada) 114

Arcos de la Frontera 42, 98
  hotels 143, 144
Ardales
  camping 147
El Arenal (Seville) 81
Arfe, Juan de 15
La Argentina 58
Aristotle 36
Aroche 90
  cafés and tapas bars 92
  markets 91
  restaurants 93
Los Arqueros 103
Arrayanes (Granada) 117
art and culture 56–7
  Moorish 36
Arte Cordobés (Córdoba) 122
Artesania El Suspiro (Granada) 114
Ascension of the Virgin 61
ATMs 132
Averroës 36
Axarquía
  hotels 142
Ayamonte
  beaches 48
  cafés and tapas bars 92
  restaurants 93
Ayuntamiento (Seville) 38, 76

B

Babylon (Granada) 115
babysitting 135
Baena
  olive oil 120
  shops and markets 122
Baeza 7, **28–9**, 119
  hotels 143, 144
  Palacio de Jabalquinto 39
  Paseo de la Constitución 47
  restaurants 123
  walks 53, 121
banking 132
Baños Arabes (Moorish baths)
  Granada 12
  Ronda 25, 37
Baños de la Encina 39
Bar Altamirano (Marbella) 105
Bar Bistec (Seville) 84
Bar Chimbito (Punta Umbria) 92

Bar España (Seville) 85
Bar Juanito (Jerez) 107
Bar La Farola (Ronda) 107
Bar La Reja (Écija) 92
Bar Lalo (Aroche) 92
Bar Plaza (Carmona) 92
Bar San Lorenzo (Seville) 84
Baraka (Córdoba) 122
Barbacoa Colóniales (Seville) 84
Barranco de Poqueira 33
Barrio del Pópulo (Cádiz) 22
Barrio de Triana (Seville) 78
bars see tapas bars
beaches 48–9
    Almuñécar 49
    Ayamonte 48
    Cabo de Gata 49
    Chipiona 48
    Marbella 49
    Mazagón 48
    Nerja 49
    snacks 130
    Tarifa 48
    Torre del Mar 49
    Torremolinos 49
beer 69
Benahavis
    hotels 143
Benalmádena 27
    hotels 141
    nightlife 104
    SeaLife 63
    Tívoli World 62
Benalmádena Costa
    nightlife 104
    restaurants 105
Benalúa
    hotels 145
Biblioteca Colombina (Seville) 15
bicycles 129
Bizet, Georges 75
Boabdil 11, 33, 35
boating 51, 129
bodegas 66–7
    Bodega El Pimpi (Málaga) 67
    Bodega Francisco (Almuñécar) 116
    Bodegas Alvear (Montilla) 66
    Bodegas Andrade 67
    El Bodegas Castañeda (Granada) 116
    Bodegas Gomara 67
    Bodegas Mezquita (Córdoba) 122

bodegas (cont.)
    Bodegas Quitapeñas (Torremolinos) 105
    Bodegas Robles (Montilla) 66
    Cooperativa Nuestra Señora del Rocío 67
    González-Byass 66
    Osborne Bodega 66
    Pedro Domecq 66
    Sandeman 66
    tours 127
El Bosque (Jerez) 107
Botticelli, Sandro 109
brandy 69, 98
breakfast 136
Brenan, Gerald 33
budget travel 131, 144
La Bulería (Jerez) 59
bullfighting 25, 51
    La Maestranza (Seville) 78
    Museo de la Maestranza (Seville) 54
    Museo Taurino (Córdoba) 19
    Plaza de Toros (Ronda) 25
Buñuel, Luis 57
buses 128, 129
Byron, Lord 22, 57

C
Cabo de Gata 45, 49
Cádiz 6, 22–3, 95
    drive from Tarifa 53
    flamenco 59
    hotels 142, 144
    Museo de Cádiz 54
    nightlife 106
    Oratorio de San Felipe Neri 40
    paradors 140
    Parque Genovés 46
    Plaza San Juan de Dios 46
    restaurants 107
    shopping 102
    walks 53
Cádiz Province see Málaga and Cádiz Provinces
Café Bar Manzano (Aracena) 92
Café Carabeo (Nerja) 105
Cafetería Acapulco (Guadix) 116
cafés
    Sevilla and Huelva Provinces 92
    Seville 84
Calderón de la Barca, Pedro 57

Caliphal style, architecture 20
Calle Sierpes (Seville) 79
Las Camachas (Montilla) 123
Cambio de Tercio (Cazalla) 93
El Camborio (Granada) 115
Camino Verde (Granada) 50
La Campiña 88
camping 131, 147
Camping El Sur (Ronda) 147
Camping Embalse Conde de Guadalhorce (Ardales) 147
Camping Sierra Nevada (Granada) 147
La Cañada 103
Cano, Alonso 54, 56, 75, 109
Cantueso (Periana) 146
El Cañuelo Periana
    hotels 142
Capilla Mayor (Seville) 15
Capilla Real (Córdoba) 21
Capilla Real (Granada) 41, 109, 111
Capilla del Salvador (Úbeda) 41
Capilla de Villavisiosa (Córdoba) 21
Caravaggio 56
La Carbonería (Seville) 81
Carlos V, King 16, 35
Carmen Amaya 58
Carmen de Santa Inés (Granada) 139
Carmona 88–9
    cafés and tapas bars 92
    hotels 145
    paradors 140
    restaurants 93
Carnaval 60
    Cádiz 23
Carromato de Max (Mijas) 62
cars 128, 129
    rentals 128
    safety 130
    see also drives
Cartuja de Santa María de las Cuevas (Seville) 77
Casa del Aljarife (Granada) 139
Casa de Castril (Granada) 12
Casa de la Condesa de Lebrija (Seville) 78
Casa de la Contratación (Seville) 17
Casa Curro (Osuna) 92
Casa El Padrino (Alajar) 93
Casa Enrique (Granada) 116
Casa Flores (El Puerto de Santa María) 107

Index

La Casa Grande (Arcos de la Frontera) 143
Casa Luciano (Ayamonte) 93
Casa de la Memoria de al-Andalus (Seville) 59, 81
Casa Morales (Seville) 85
Casa La Piedra (Cómpeta) 146
Casa de Pilatos (Seville) 38, 75
Casa Placido (Seville) 85
Casa Puga (Almería) 116
Casa del Rey Moro (Ronda) 24
Casa Rubio (Córdoba) 123
Casas Karen (Costa de la Luz) 146
Casas Rurales Los Gallos (Almonaster la Real) 146
cashpoints 132
Casino Torrequebrada (Benalmádena Costa) 104
El Castillo (Castillo de Monda) 143
Castillo de Monda
 hotels 143
castillos 38–9
 Castillo de Almodóvar del Río 120
 Castillo de Burgalimar (Baños de la Encina) 39
 Castillo de Lacalahorra 39
 Castillo de Santa Catalina (Jaén City) 39
 Castillo de Vélez Blanco 39
 Fortaleza de la Mota (Alcalá la Real) 38
Castril 43
 tearooms and tapas bars 116
Catedrals
 Baeza 28
 Cádiz 22
 Córdoba 21
 Granada 41, 109, 111
 Jaén 41
 Seville 6, **14–15**, 40, 75, 77
caves
 Cuevas de Nerja 63
 Gruta de las Maravillas 87
 gypsy dwellings 59
 Sacromonte Gypsy Caves 12
 spelunking 50
Cazalla de la Sierra 88
 cafés and tapas bars 92
 restaurants 93

Cazorla 43
Cerámica Santa Ana (Seville) 80
ceramics 29, 64, 65, 91, 122
Cervecería Giralda (Seville) 77, 84
charter flights 128
Chateaubriand, François René, Vicomte de 57
Chez Jacquy (Playa Cotobro) 117
children 62–3, 135
 in hotels 135, 137
Chipiona 99
 beach 48
El Chorro 99
churches 40–41
 etiquette 130
Churchill, Winston 62
El Churrasco (Córdoba) 123
climate 126
clothes
 in churches 130
 what to take 126
clubs, budget travel 131
coffee 69
La Colegiata de Santa María de la Asunción (Osuna) 40
Columbus, Christopher 15, 35, 77, 79, 87, 89
La Comedia (Marbella) 104
communications 132
Compas Sur (Seville) 80
Cómpeta
 self-catering accommodation 146
El Condado Wine District 91
Conil de la Frontera
 hotels 142
consulates 126
Convento de Santa Clara (Moguer) 89
Convento de Santa Paula (Seville) 78
Córdoba 6, **18–21**, 119
 Alcázar de los Reyes Cristianos 47
 flamenco 59
 hostals 147
 hotels 141, 143, 144
 map 19
 La Mezquita 6, 18, **20–21**, 37, 40
 Museo Arqueológico 55
 Plaza de la Corredera 47
 restaurants 123
 shops and markets 122

walks 53
Córdoba and Jaén Provinces 118–23
 drives 53
 map 118
 restaurants 123
 shops and markets 122
Corpus Christi 60
El Corte Inglés (Seville) 80
Cortegana 90
Cortijo Fain (Arcos de la Frontera) 143
El Cortijo de los Mimbrales (El Rocío) 143
Cortijo Torrera (Costa Tropical) 144
Costa de la Luz 98
 self-catering accommodation 146
Costa del Sol 7, **26–7**, 95
 golf courses 103
 map 27
 nightlife 104
 restaurants 105
Costa Tropical, hotels 144
Coto Doñana, Parque Nacional del 7, **30–31**, 44, 87
crafts
 Granada and Almería Provinces 114
 Moorish 37
 Sevilla and Huelva Provinces 91
 souvenirs 64
Crafts Market (Seville) 80
credit cards 132
crime 133
Cuevas El Abanico (Granada) 139
Cuevas La Granja (Benalúa) 145
Cuevas de Nerja 63
Cuevas de Orce 145
Cuevas Pedro Antonio de Alarcón (Guadix) 145
cultural study holidays 127
Cunini (Granada) 117
currency 132
cycling 129

D
Dalí, Salvador 57
dance
 festivals 61
 gypsy 58–9
 specialist holidays 127
Darro River 10

dialling codes 132
disabled travellers 133, 134
diving 50
doctors 133
Doña Blanca (Jerez de la Frontera) 144
Doña María (Seville) 138
Dreamers (Marbella) 104
drinks 69, 136
    see also wine
drives 52–3
    Las Alpujarras 53
    Guadalquivir Valley 53
    Nerja to Almería 52
    Ronda to Jerez 52
    Tarifa to Cádiz 53
La Duquesa 103
Los Duros Antiguos (Cádiz) 102

E
Easter 15, 60
Écija 88
    cafés and tapas bars 92
    restaurants 93
Eiffel, Gustave 97
electricity 126
embassies 126
emergencies 133
Escalera del Agua (Granada) 11
Eshavira (Granada) 115
Eslava (Seville) 85
Espuma del Mar (Isla Canela) 92
La Esquinita (Granada) 116
Estepona 26
    hostals 147
    hotels 142
    restaurants 105
El Estrecho (Marbella) 105
etiquette, in churches 130
extreme sports holidays 127

F
Fábrica Real de Tabacos (Seville) 75
fakes 130
Falla, Manuel de 57
families 135
El Faro (Cádiz) 107
Felipe V 35
ferias 61
    Feria de Abril 61, 76
    Feria del Caballo 61
    Feria de Jamón 61
Fernando, King 11, 17, 41
Fernando the Saint, King 79

ferries 128
festivals 61
    religious 60–61
Fiesta de la Aceituna 61
Fiesta de las Cruces 60
Fiesta de los Reyes Magos 60
Fiesta de San Miguel 61
Fiesta de los Verdiales 61
Figueroa, Leonardo de 57, 78
filigree 64
El Fillo 58
Finca La Bobadilla (Granada Province) 142
Finca Buen Vino (Sierra de Aracena) 145
Finca Butyrón (Montilla) 145
fire services 133
fishing 51
flamenco 58–9, 61
    Cádiz 106
    costumes 102
    Jerez 106
    Seville 83
    souvenirs 64
    tours 127
Flea Market (Jaén City) 122
flora and fauna 45
flower girls 130
food and drink 65, 68–9, 136
    Moorish 37
    picnics 131
    safety 130
    shopping 91
    see also restaurants; tapas bars
football 51
Forestier, Jean-Claude Nicolas 46
forgeries 130
Fortaleza de la Mota (Alcalá la Real) 38
Franco, General 27, 90, 97
Fuengirola 26
El Fuerte (Marbella) 141
fútbol (football) 51

G
Galería de Vinos Caldos (Jaén City) 122
galleries see museums and galleries
Los Gallos (Seville) 81
gambling, Gibraltar 106
gardens see parks and gardens
Gautier, Théophile 57
gay travellers 134

Torremolinos 104
Generalife (Granada) 10–11
Ghadamés (Córdoba) 122
Gibraltar 97
    nightlife 106
    shopping 102
La Giralda (Seville) 6, 15, 75
gold filigree 64
La Goleta (San Miguel del Cabo de Gata) 117
golf 51
    Costa del Sol 103
    specialist holidays 127
Golf El Paraíso 103
González, Felipe 35
González-Byass 66, 97
Goya y Lucientes, Francisco José de 15, 19, 23
Gran Hotel Almería (Almería) 141
Gran Tino (Seville) 84
Granada
    Albaicín **12–13**
    Alhambra **8–9**, 11
    camping 147
    Capilla Real 41, 109, 111
    Catedral 41, 109, 111
    flamenco 59
    Generalife **10–11**
    hotels 139
    Monasterio de San Jerónimo 41
    Moorish Granada 6, **8–13**, 37, 109
    nightlife 114, 115
    Plaza Nueva 47
    restaurants 117
    self-catering accommodation 146
    souvenirs 64
    tearooms and tapas bars 116
    walks 53, 111
Granada and Almería Provinces 108–17
    hotels 142
    map 108
    nightlife 115
    restaurants 117
    tearooms and tapas bars 116
    traditional handicrafts 114
Granada 10 (Granada) 115
El Greco 23, 54, 75
Gruta de las Maravillas 87
Guadalquivir, Río 30, 53, 74
Guadiamar River 31
Guadix 110

Index

hotels 145
gypsies 58–9
  Sacromonte Gypsy Caves 12

H

Hacienda La Colorá 146
Hadrian, Emperor 35, 89
Hannibal 121
health 133
Hecho en Cádiz (Cádiz) 102
helplines 134
Hemingway, Ernest 57
La Herradura
  restaurants 117
hiking 50, 52–3, 129
  Alájar to Linares de la Sierra 52
  Río Borosa 52
  Rute to Iznájar 52
  Serranía de Ronda 52
  Sierra Nevada 32
  Southern Tahá 52
  specialist holidays 127
  see also walks
Hill of the Sun (Granada) 10
history 34–5
horse-riding 50
  equipment shops 102
  gypsies 59
  specialist holidays 127
Hospital de la Caridad (Seville) 78
Hospital de Mujeres (Cádiz) 23
Hospital de los Venerables (Seville) 77, 78
hospitals 133
Hostal Dali 138
Hostal Lineros (Córdoba) 144
Hostal La Malagueña (Estepona) 147
Hostal Picasso (Seville) 138
Hostal La Posada (Mijas) 146
Hostal Séneca (Córdoba) 147
Hostal Suecia (Granada) 139
Hostal Van Gogh (Seville) 138
hostals 147
Hostería del Laurel (Seville) 85
Hotel Alfonso XIII (Seville) 138
Hotel Casa de Carmona 141
Hotel Casa Imperial (Seville) 138
Hotel Casa Morisca (Granada) 139
Hotel El Convento (Arcos de la Frontera) 144
Hotel Corregidor (Seville) 138

Hotel Francia y París (Cádiz) 144
Hotel La Fuente de la Higuera (Ronda) 142
Hotel Fuerte Conil (Conil de la Frontera) 142
Hotel González (Córdoba) 143
Hotel Humaina (Montes de Málaga) 145
Hotel Jerez (Jerez) 141
Hotel Marqués de Torresoto (Arcos de la Frontera) 144
Hotel Meliá (Córdoba) 141
Hotel Murillo (Seville) 138
Hotel Palacete Santa Ana (Baeza) 143
Hotel Paraíso del Mar (Nerja) 142
Hotel Los Patios (Córdoba) 144
Hotel Playa Victoria (Cádiz) 142
Hotel Posada de Vallina (Córdoba) 144
Hotel Reina Cristina (Granada) 139
Hotel Riu Canela (Isla Canela) 142
Hotel San Gabriel (Ronda) 144
Hotel Simón (Seville) 138
Hotel Taberna del Alabardero (Seville) 138
Hotel Torrequebrada (Benalmádena) 141
Hotel TRH (Baeza) 144
Hotel Vincci Rumaykiyya (Sierra Nevada) 142
hotels 137–45
  children in 135, 137
  disabled travellers 134
Huelva City 87, 89
  restaurants 93
  shopping 91
Huelva Province see Sevilla and Huelva Provinces

I

Iglesia de San Luis (Seville) 78
Iglesia de San Mateo (Lucena) 40
Iglesia de San Pedro y San Pablo (Granada) 12
Iglesia de Santa Ana (Granada) 12
Iglesia de Santa Cruz (Cádiz) 22
Iglesia de Santa María la Mayor (Ronda) 25

La Illustre Víctima (Seville) 84
Instalación-Campamento Juvenil Mazagón 147
Instalación Juvenil (Solynieve) 147
Instalación Juvenil Granada (Granada) 139
Instalación Juvenil Sevilla (Seville) 138
insurance 126
Internet 126, 132
Irving, Washington 11, 57, 77
Isabel, Queen 11, 17, 35, 41, 89, 110
Isla Canela
  cafés and tapas bars 92
  hotels 142
Isla Mágica (Seville) 62
Itálica 89
IVA tax 131
Iznájar
  hiking 52
Iznatoraf 43

J

Jabugo 90
Jaén, Bartolomé de 109, 121
Jaén City 121
  Castillo de Santa Catalina 39
  Catedral 41
  Museo Provincial y de Bellas Artes 55
  restaurants 123
  shops and markets 122
Jaén Province see Córdoba and Jaén Provinces
Jardín Botánico La Concepción (Málaga) 47
Jardines Altos (Granada) 11
Jardines de Murillo (Seville) 77, 79
Jardines Neptuno (Granada) 115
Jardines Nuevos (Granada) 10–11
Jardines de San Telmo (Seville) 79
Jerez de la Frontera 98
  drive from Ronda 52
  flamenco 59
  hotels 141, 142, 144
  nightlife 106
  Parque Zoológico 46, 62
  restaurants 107
  walks 53, 97
jewellery 64
Jews, Judería (Córdoba) 18

Jordaens, Jakob 15
Juan Villar (Cádiz) 59
Judería (Córdoba) 18
El Juncal (Ronda) 141

K
Kasbah (Granada) 116
Kempinski Resort Hotel
  (Estepona) 142
Kennedy, John F 90
King, Martin Luther 97
Kiu (Benalmádena) 104

L
La Rábida
  cafés and tapas bars 92
  Muelle de las Carabelas 62
language 137
  Moorish 37
  specialist holidays 127
Lanjarón 33
Latimore 80
laundromats 131
leather 65, 91, 102
Leonardo da Vinci 62
Linares de la Sierra
  hiking 52
liqueurs 69
literature 57
Livermore, Amalia 47
La Lonja (Seville) 78
Lorca, Federico García 57,
  96, 139
  Museo-Casa Natal
  Federico García Lorca 110
Lucena
  Iglesia de San Mateo 40
Lucía, Paco de 58
luxury hotels 141
luxury tours 127

M
La Macarena (Seville) 78
Machado, Manuel 57
Machuca, Pedro 9
La Maestranza (Seville)
  78
magazines 132
mail services 132
Maimonides 36
Málaga 27, 96
  Alcazaba 37
  Bodega El Pimpi 67
  flamenco 59
  hostals 147
  Jardín Botánico La
  Concepción 47
  Museo Picasso 55

Málaga (cont.)
  nightlife 106
  restaurants 105, 107
  walks 53
  wines 102
Málaga and Cádiz Provinces
  94–107
  Costa del Sol golf courses
  103
  map 94
  nightlife 104, 106
  restaurants 105, 107
  shopping 102
Mañara, Miguel de 78
Mango (Seville) 80
Manolete 19
Manuel Morillo Castillo
  (Granada) 114
Marbella 26
  beach 49
  hostals 147
  hotels 141, 142
  nightlife 104
  restaurants 105
Marbella Club Hotel
  (Marbella) 142
María de Molina (Ubeda) 143
Marinaleda 88
markets, Córdoba and Jaén
  Provinces 122
El Martinete (Cazalla) 92
Mazagón
  beach 48
medicines 133
Medina Azahara (Córdoba)
  37, 119
Medina Sidonia 99
Mediterráneo (Cádiz) 102
Melkarth 35
Mena, Alonso de 41, 111
Mena, Pedro de 55
menú del día 131, 136
El Mercadillo (Seville) 80
Mesa, Juan de 40
Mesón Las Candelas
  (Aljaraque) 93
Mesón Navarro (Ubeda) 123
metalwork 65
Metro Subway System
  (Seville) 129
La Mezquita (Córdoba) 6, 18,
  20–21, 37, 40
Michelangelo 41
Mijas 26
  Carromato de Max 62
  self-catering
  accommodation 146
Minarete de San Sebastián

(Ronda) 25
Mini Hollywood (Almería) 63
mint tea 69
Mirador de Aixa (Granada) 117
El Mirador de San Nicolás
  (Granada) 13
Miraflores 103
Moguer 89
Monasterio de la Cartuja
  (Granada) 109
Monasterio de San Jerónimo
  (Granada) 41
Monasterio San Miguel (El
  Puerto de Santa María) 143
money 132
Monte Castillo (Jerez) 142
Montes de Málaga
  hotels 145
Montilla 120
  Bodegas Alvear 66
  Bodegas Robles 66
  hotels 145
  restaurants 123
Montoro 120
Moorish baths (Baños
  Arabes)
  Granada 12
  Ronda 25, 37
Moors
  aspects of Moorish
  heritage 36–7
  Moorish Granada 6, **8–13**,
  37, 109
  Moroccan shops, Granada
  13
Moros y Cristianos 61
mosques
  Almonaster la Real 40
  La Mezquita (Córdoba) 6,
  18, **20–21**, 37, 40
motorcycles 128, 129
Muelle de las Carabelas
  (Huelva City) 89
Muelle de las Carabelas (La
  Rábida) 62
Murillo, Bartolomé Esteban
  15, 19, 23, 54, 56, 75, 138
  home of 77
  Jardines de Murillo
  (Seville) 79
museums and galleries 54–5
  Archivo de Indias La Lonja
  (Seville) 54
  Casa de Castril (Granada) 12
  Museo Arqueológico
  (Córdoba) 19, 55
  Museo Arqueológico
  (Seville) 76

Museo Arqueológico Cueva de Siete Palacios (Almuñécar) 55
Museo de Artes y Costumbres Populares (Seville) 78
Museo del Bandolero (Ronda) 25, 54–5
Museo de Bellas Artes (Córdoba) 19
Museo de Bellas Artes (Seville) 54, 75
Museo de Cádiz 23, 54
Museo-Casa Natal Federico García Lorca 110
Museo de las Cortes de Cádiz 23
Museo de la Maestranza (Seville) 54
Museo Municipal (Antequera) 55
Museo Picasso (Málaga) 55
Museo Provincial y de Bellas Artes (Jaén) 55
Museo Taurino (Córdoba) 19
music
festivals 61
gypsy 58
Moorish 36
"mystery" tours 130

N
Napoleon I, Emperor 79
Nasrid dynasty 8
nature reserves 44–5
Cabo de Gatar-Níjar 45
Parque Nacional del Coto Doñana 7, **30–31**, 44, 87
Parque Natural de los Montes de Málaga 45
Parque Natural de la Sierra de Cardeña y Montoro 44
Sierra de Aracena y Picos de Aroche Park 44
Sierra de Cazorla 44
Sierra de Grazalema 45
Sierra Nevada 44
Sierra Norte 44
El Torcal 45
nature tours 127
Nerja 27
beach 49
drive to Almería 52
hotels 142
nightlife 106
restaurants 105
newspapers 132
NH Amistad (Córdoba) 143

Nicephorus III, Emperor 21
Niebla 90
nightlife
Costa del Sol 104
for families 135
Granada and Almería Provinces 115
Málaga and Cádiz Provinces 104, 106
Níjar 114
La Niña de los Peines 58
Nucra (Córdoba) 122
Nuñez de Prado (Baena) 122

O
Old Train Station Shopping Centre (Seville) 80
olive oil 120
Olivia Valere (Marbella) 104
opera 57
Oratorio de San Felipe Neri (Cádiz) 40
Oratorio de la Santa Cueva (Cádiz) 23
Orce 145
Órgiva 33
Osborne Bodega 66
Osuna 88
cafés and tapas bars 92
La Colegiata de Santa María de la Asunción 40
Palacio del Marqués de la Gomera 38
restaurants 93
Osuna, Dukes of 88
outdoor activities 50–51
Oyarzábal, Jorge Loring 47

P
package holidays 128, 131
Padilla, María de 17, 75
palacios 38–9
Alcázar de los Reyes Cristianos (Córdoba) 18
La Casa de Pilatos (Seville) 38
Medina Azahara (Córdoba) 37
El Palacio de Acebrán 31
Palacio de Carlos V (Granada) 9
Palacio Gotico (Seville) 17
Palacio de Comares (Granada) 9
Palacio Episcopal (Córdoba) 18
Palacio de Jabalquinto (Baeza) 29, 121

palacios (cont.)
Palacio de los Leones (Granada) 9
Palacio del Marqués de la Gomera (Osuna) 38
Palacio del Marqués de Salvatierra (Ronda) 24
Palacio de los Marquesas de Viana (Córdoba) 19
Palacio de Mexuar (Granada) 9
Palacio de Mondragón (Ronda) 25
Palacio de la Rambla (Úbeda) 141
Real Chancillería (Granada) 12
Reales Alcázares (Seville) 6, **16–17**, 37, 38, 75, 77, 79
El Palenque (Seville) 81
The Palladium (Torremolinos) 104
Parador Alcázar del Rey (Carmona) 140
Parador de Antequera 140
Parador Arcos de la Frontera 140
Parador de Ayamonte 140
Parador Castillo de Santa Catalina (Jaén) 140
Parador Condestable Dávalos (Úbeda) 140
Parador del Gilbralfaro (Málaga) 140
Parador Hotel Atlántico (Cádiz) 140
Parador de Mazagón 140
Parador de Ronda 140
Parador de San Francisco (Granada) 139
paradors 140
parks and gardens 46–7
Alcázar de los Reyes Cristianos (Córdoba) 47
Generalife (Granada) **10–11**
Granada 9
Jardín Botánico La Concepción (Málaga) 47
Jardines de Murillo (Seville) 77, 79
Jardines de San Telmo (Seville) 79
Moorish 36
Parque Genovés (Cádiz) 46
Parque de María Luísa (Seville) 46, 79
Plaza Nueva (Seville) 79

parks and gardens (cont.)
Reales Alcázares (Seville) 79
Seville 17
Parque Acuático Aquavera (Vera) 63
El Parque Minero de Río Tinto 87
Parque Nacional del Coto Doñana 7, **30–31**, 44, 87
Parque Natural de los Montes de Málaga 45
Parque Natural de la Sierra de Cardeña y Montoro 44
Parque de la Sierra de Aracena y Picos de Aroche 90
Parque Zoológico (Jerez) 46, 62
La Parrala (Moguer) 89
Partal (Granada) 9
partying 131
Paseo de la Constitución (Baeza) 29
Paseo de los Tristes (Granada) 12
paseos 46–7
Paseo Alcalde Marqués de Contadero (Seville) 79
Paseo de la Constitución (Baeza) 47, 121
Paseo Marqués de Contadero (Seville) 46
passports 126
Patio de la Acequia (Granada) 11
Patio de los Cipreses (Granada) 11
Patio de las Doncellas (Seville) 17
Patio de la Montería (Seville) 17
Patio de las Muñecas (Seville) 17
Patio de los Naranjos (Córdoba) 20
Patio de los Naranjos (Seville) 14
Patio San Eloy (Seville) 84
El Patio Sevillano (Seville) 81
Patio del Yeso (Seville) 16
peddlers 130
Pedro I the Cruel 16, 17, 75
Pedro Domecq 66, 97
La Peña Platería (Granada) 59
Peña El Taranto (Almería) 59, 115
Las Peñas (Aroche) 93

Pensión La Purísima (Ronda) 147
Periana
self-catering accommodation 146
Pervane (Granada) 116
pharmacies 133
philosophy, Moorish 36
Picasso, Pablo 57, 96
Museo Picasso (Málaga) 55
picnics 131
Pie de la Vela (Granada) 115
Pilate, Pontius 75
pilgrimages 127
Pisano, Nicola 78
places of worship 40–41
planning 126
Planta Baja (Granada) 115
plasticultura 110
Plata (Seville) 84
Playa Cotobro 117
plazas 46–7
Plaza de la Alfalfa (Seville) 79
Plaza de los Aljibes (Granada) 8
Plaza de la Corredera (Córdoba) 47
Plaza de España (Seville) 76
Plaza de las Flores (Cádiz) 23
Plaza Larga (Granada) 13
Plaza Nueva (Granada) 47, 111
Plaza del Pópulo (Baeza) 28, 121
Plaza del Potro (Córdoba) 19
Plaza del Primero de Mayo (Úbeda) 29
Plaza de San Francisco (Seville) 79
Plaza San Juan de Dios (Cádiz) 22, 46
Plaza San Lorenzo (Úbeda) 29
Plaza San Pedro (Úbeda) 29
Plaza de Santa Cruz (Seville) 77, 79
Plaza Santa María (Baeza) 28, 121
Plaza de Toros (Ronda) 25
Plaza de Vázquez de Molina (Úbeda) 29
police 133
Porter, Cole 97
La Posá Dos (Estepona) 105
Posada Doña Lupe (Granada) 139

Posada La Niña Margarita (Los Villares) 145
postal services 132
pottery 29, 64, 65, 91, 122
prescription medicines 133
public toilets 134
pueblos blancos (white villages) 24, 96–7
Puente Nuevo (Ronda) 24
Puente Romano (Córdoba) 19
Puente de San Miguel (Ronda) 24
Puente Viejo (Ronda) 24
La Puerta Ancha (Ayamonte) 92
Puerta de Jaén (Baeza) 28, 121
Puerta de la Justicia (Granada) 8
Puerta del León (Seville) 16
Puerta del Perdón (Córdoba) 20
Puerta del Perdón (Seville) 14
Puerta del Vino (Granada) 8
El Puerto de Santa María 99
hotels 143
restaurants 107
Puerto del Suspiro del Moro 33
Punta Umbria
cafés and tapas bars 92

Q
El Quinto Toro (Almería) 116

R
raciones 136
radio 132
railways 128, 129
Real Alcázar (Seville) 6, **16–17**, 37, 38, 75, 77, 79
Real Chancillería (Granada) 12
Real Club de Golf Sotogrande 103
Real Club Las Brisas 103
Reina Cristina (Algeciras) 141
religion
festivals 60–61
pilgrimages 127
Renaissance architecture 29
resort hotels 142
Restaurante Andrés de Vandelvira (Baeza) 123
Restaurante Doña Guadalupe (Osuna) 93
Restaurante El Faro (Seville) 85
Restaurante La Escalera

(Torremolinos) 105
Restaurante Gaitán (Jerez de la Frontera) 97
Restaurante González (Trevélez) 117
Restaurante La Sirena (Benalmadena Costa) 105
Restaurante Las Ninfas (Écija) 93
Restaurante Pesetas (Salobreña) 117
Restaurante Sali (Baeza) 121
Restaurante San Fernando (Carmona) 93
Restaurante Tene2Ores (Cazorla) 123
Restaurante Valentín (Almería) 117
Restaurante El Ventorro (Alhama de Granada) 117
restaurants 136
  budget travel 131
  children in 135
  Córdoba and Jaén Provinces 123
  Costa del Sol 105
  Granada and Almería Provinces 117
  Málaga and Cádiz Provinces 105, 107
  Sevilla and Huelva Provinces 93
  Seville 85
  see also food and drink
Riaño, Diego de 38
Ribera, José de 19, 40, 54, 56, 88
El Rinconcillo (Seville) 85
El Rinconcito (Huelva City) 93
Río Borosa
  hiking 52
Río Tinto 31, 87
road safety 130
El Rocío 42, 87, 114
  hotels 143
  restaurants 93
  Romería 31
Roldán, Pedro 41, 56
Romerías 31, 60
Romero, Pedro 25
Ronda 7, **24–5**, 95
  drive to Jerez 52
  hostals and camping 147
  hotels 141, 142, 144
  map 25
  Museo del Bandolero 54–5
  nightlife 106
  restaurants 107

Ronda (cont.)
  shopping 102
  walks 53
Rubens, Peter Paul 54
Ruiz-Picasso, Bernard 55
Ruiz-Picasso, Christine 55
rural hotels 145
Rushdie, Salman 57
Rute 52

S
Sabiote 43
La Sacristía (Seville) 85
Sacristía de los Cálices (Seville) 15
Sacristía Mayor (Seville) 15
Sacromonte Gypsy Caves 12
safety 130
sailing 51, 129
Sala Capitular (Seville) 15
Sala de Justicia (Seville) 16
Sala Príncipe (Granada) 115
Salobreña 117
Salón de Embajadores (Seville) 17
salsa holidays 127
San Juan 61
San Miguel del Cabo de Gata 117
San Roque 103
  hotels 141
Sandeman 66
sangría 69
Sanlúcar de Barrameda 59
Santa Ana Apartamentos Turísticos (Granada) 146
Santa Olalla del Cala 90
Sargadelos (Seville) 80
scams 130
science, Moorish 37
sea travel 128
SeaLife (Benalmádena) 63
security 133
Los Seises (Seville) 138
self-catering accommodation 131, 146
Semana Santa 15, 60
senior citizens 134
Serranía de Ronda
  hiking 52
Sevilla and Huelva Provinces 86–93
  cafés and tapas bars 92
  map 86
  restaurants 93
  shopping 91
  walks 89

Seville 74–85
  accommodation 146
  Archivo de Indias La Lonja 54
  Ayuntamiento 38
  cafés and tapas bars 84
  La Casa de Pilatos 38
  Cathedral 6, **14–15**, 40, 75, 77
  flamenco and theatre venues 59, 83
  La Giralda 6, **14–15**, 75
  hotels 138
  Isla Mágica 62
  map 74
  Museo de Bellas Artes 54, 75
  Museo de la Maestranza 54
  parks, paseos and plazas 79
  Parque de María Luisa 46
  Reales Alcázares 6, **16–17**, 37, 38, 75, 77, 79
  restaurants 85
  shopping 80
  walks 53, 77
sherry 69, 98, 102
  bodegas and wineries 66–7, 127
  festivals 61
shopping
  for children 135
  Córdoba and Jaén Provinces 122
  Granada 13
  Málaga and Cádiz Provinces 102
  Sevilla and Huelva Provinces 91
  Seville 80
Sierra de Aracena y Picos de Aroche Park 44
  hotels 145
Sierra de Cazorla 44
Sierra de Grazalema 45
Sierra Nevada 7, **32–3**, 44, 109
  hostals 147
Sierra Norte 44
Siloé, Diego de 12, 41
silver filigree 64
skiing 32, 50
Solynieve 32
Southern Tahá
  hiking 52
souvenirs 64–5
  Sevilla and Huelva Provinces 91
specialist holidays 127
spelunking 50

sports 50–51
student travellers 134
surfing 50

T
Taberna de Alabardero
  (Seville) 85
La Taberna Flamenca (Jerez)
  59
Taberna La Manchega (Jaén
  City) 123
Taberna Salinas (Córdoba) 123
Taberna Sociedad de
  Plateros (Córdoba) 123
Tablao Flamenco Cardenal
  (Córdoba) 59
El Tajo (Ronda) 24
tapas bars
  budget travel 131
  Granada and Almería
    Provinces 116
  Sevilla and Huelva
    Provinces 92
  Seville 84
  tapas dishes 70–71, 136
Tarifa 99
  beach 48
  drive to Cádiz 53
  nightlife 106
taxes 131, 137
taxis 129
tea, mint 69
tearooms
  Granada 13
  Granada and Almería
    Provinces 116
Teatro (Granada) 10
Teatro Alameda (Seville) 81
Teatro Central (Seville) 81
Teatro Lope de Vega (Seville)
  81
Teatro de la Maestranza
  (Seville) 81
Teatro Romano (Cádiz) 22
teenagers 135
El Tejar (Seville) 84
telephones 132
television 132
Tetería Al-Zahra (Ronda) 107
La Tetería del Bañuelo
  (Granada) 111, 116
La Tienda del Olivo
  (Córdoba) 122
time zone 126
El Tinao del Mar (La
  Herradura) 117
El Tintero II (Málaga) 105
tipping 136, 137

Tívoli World (Benalmádena) 62
toilets, public 134
El Torcal 45, 99
Torre del Alminar (Córdoba) 21
Torre del Mar 27, 49
Torre del Oro (Seville) 76–7
Torre de Plata (Seville) 76–7
Torre Tavira (Cádiz) 23
Torregiano, Pietro 75
Torremolinos 27
  beach 49
  nightlife 104
  restaurants 105
tourist offices 126
Towers (Granada) 10
Tragabuches (Ronda) 107
trains 128, 129
Trajan, Emperor 35, 89
travel 128–9, 135
traveller's cheques 132
Trevélez 117

U
Úbeda 7, **28–9**, 119
  Capilla del Salvador 41
  hotels 141, 143
  restaurants 123
  shops and markets 122
  walks 53
UNESCO Biosphere
  Reserves 44, 45

V
Valderrama 103
Valdés Leal, Juan de 19, 54,
  75, 78
Valle de Lecrín 33
Valle de los Pedroches 120
Vandelvira, Andrés de 56
  Capilla del Salvador
    (Úbeda) 29, 41
  Catedral (Baeza) 28
  Catedral (Jaén) 41, 121
  Sabiote 43
Varsovia (Málaga) 106
Vásquez 54
Vega, Lope de 81
vegetarian food 136
Vejer de la Frontera 37, 42, 99
Velázquez, Diego Rodríguez
  de Silva y 38, 54, 56
Vélez-Málaga 27
Venta El Gallo (Granada) 59
Ventorrillo del Chato (Cádiz)
  107
Vera, Parque Acuático
  Aquavera 63
Verámica Fabre (Granada) 114

Veronica, St 41
Villa Turística de Cazalla 146
Villa Turística Grazalema 146
villages 42–3
Villares, Los 145
Virgen del Carmen 61
visas 126
Visigoths 21

W
walks 53, 129
  Baeza 121
  Granada 111
  Jerez de la Frontera 97
  Sevilla and Huelva
    Provinces 89
  Seville 77
  walking tours 127
  see also hiking
water, drinking 69, 130
weather 126
weavings 65
Weyden, Roger van der 109
"Wild West" towns 111
wildlife
  specialist holidays 127
  see also nature reserves
windsurfing 50
wine 69, 98
  bodega tours 127
  festivals 61
  Málaga 102
  wineries 66–7
women travellers 134
writers 57

X, Y, Z
Yegen 33
Zahara de la Sierra 43
Zahara de los Atunes 145
Az-Zahra 119
Zara (Seville) 80
zoos
  Parque Zoológico (Jerez)
    46, 62
  SeaLife (Benalmádena) 63
Zoraya 11
Zufre 90
Zurbarán, Francisco de 15,
  19, 23, 38, 54, 56, 75, 97
  St Luke before Christ 56
ZZ Pub (Málaga) 106

Acknowledgements

Main Contributor
American-born Jeffrey Kennedy now lives mainly in Italy and Spain. A graduate of Stanford University, he divides his time between producing, acting and writing. He is the co-author of *Top 10 Rome* and the author of the Top 10 guides to *Mallorca, Miami and the Keys* and *San Francisco.*

Produced by Sargasso Media Ltd, London

Editorial Director Zoë Ross
Art Editor Janis Utton
Picture Research Monica Allende
Proofreader Stewart J Wild
Indexer Hilary Bird
Editorial Assistance Cristina Barrallo

Main Photographer
Peter Wilson
Additional Photographers
Neil Lukas, John Miller, Linda Whitwam

Illustrator
chrisorr.com

FOR DORLING KINDERSLEY
Publisher Douglas Amrine
Publishing Manager Anna Streiffert
Managing Art Editor Jane Ewart
Senior Cartographic Editor Casper Morris
DTP Jason Little
Production Melanie Dowland

Maps James Macdonald, Mapping Ideas Ltd

Picture Credits
t-top; tc-top centre; tr-top right; cla-centre left above; ca-centre above; cra-centre right above; cl-centre left; c-centre; cr-centre right; clb-centre left below; cb-centre below; crb-centre right below; bl-below left; bc-below centre; br-below right.
Every effort has been made to trace the copyright holders, and we apologize in advance for any unintentional omissions. We would be pleased to insert the appropriate acknowledgements in any subsequent edition of this publication.

The publishers would like to thank the following individuals, companies, and picture libraries for permission to reproduce their photographs:

AISA, Barcelona: 7b, 13t, 23cr, 29t, 30b, 30–31, 31cra, 31crb, 31b, 32–3, 34t, 35r, 44tr, 44tl, 50b, 50tr, 52tr, 56tl, 56tr, 56b, 57b, 57r, 58tl, 60b, 61r, 66tr, 66b, 67cl, 87t, 87b, 90 tr, 97t. 134tc

CORBIS: 103tl, 103tr; COVER, Madrid: 13b, 34b

www.dreamers-disco.com, Marbella: 104tl

GETTY IMAGES: 1

www.leonardo.com:141; MARCO POLO, Madrid : 30t, 31t, 33crb

TOURIST OFFICE, Andalucia: 59c, 59r, 60tl, 60tr, 61t, 62tr, 93t, 135tr

All other images are © Dorling Kindersley. For further information see:
www.dkimages.com.